Vergil

Aeneid Book 6

The Focus Vergil Aeneid Commentaries

For intermediate students

Aeneid 1 • *Randall Ganiban, editor* • *Available now*
Aeneid 2 • *Randall Ganiban, editor* • *Available now*
Aeneid 3 • *Christine Perkell, editor* • *Available now*
Aeneid 4 • *James O'Hara, editor* • *Available now*
Aeneid 5 • *Joseph Farrell, editor* • *Available 2012*
Aeneid 6 • *Patricia Johnston, editor* • *Available now*

For advanced students

Aeneid 1–6 • *Available 2012 (Single volume. Contributers as listed above)*
Aeneid 7–12 • *Available 2013 (Available only as a single volume)*
    Contributors:
    Randall Ganiban, editor • *Aeneid 7*
    James O'Hara, editor • *Aeneid 8*
    Joseph Farrell, editor • *Aeneid 9*
    Andreola Rossi, editor • *Aeneid 10*
    Charles McNelis, editor • *Aeneid 11*
    Christine Perkell, editor • *Aeneid 12*

VERGIL

Aeneid Book 6

Patricia A. Johnston
Brandeis University

Focus Publishing

Vergil Aeneid Book 6

© 2012 Patricia A. Johnston

Focus Publishing/R. Pullins Company
PO Box 369
Newburyport, MA 01950
www.pullins.com

Interior illustration by Sam Kimball.

ISBN 13: 978-1-58510-230-3

To see available ebook versions, visit www.pullins.com

Library of Congress Cataloging-in-Publication Data

Johnston, Patricia A.
  Vergil Aeneid book 6 / Patricia A. Johnston.
    pages cm. -- (The Focus Vergil Aeneid commentaries for intermediate students)
  ISBN 978-1-58510-230-3
  1. Virgil. Aeneis--Commentaries. I. Virgil. Aeneis. Liber 6. Latin. 2012.
II. Virgil. Aeneis. Liber 6. English. 2012. III. Title. IV. Series: Focus
Vergil Aeneid commentaries for intermediate students.
  PA6825.J65 2012
  873'.01--dc23
                          2012007612

Printed in the United States of America.

10 9 8 7 6 5 4 3 2 1

0312W

Table of Contents

Preface

This volume contains an introductory commentary on the sixth book of Vergil's *Aeneid* for use at the intermediate level or higher. It provides a generous amount of basic information about grammar and syntax so that students of varying experience will have what they need to translate and interpret the Latin, and thereby have a richer experience in reading the poem. Extensive bibliographic notes have also been added to help readers pursue areas of special interest.

This commentary is part of a series of commentaries on the *Aeneid*, with individual volumes for each book, and also as part of a more trimmed-down, single-volume collection of the first six books, also published by Focus Publishing. Our starting-point for these volumes were the 1892 commentaries by T.E. Page, later reprinted without vocabulary in his *Virgil: Aeneid 1-6* (1894). His vocabulary list is the basis for the one here, which I have updated and revised. Here his notes have been updated, modified, and expanded throughout. In addition, new materials have been added, including appendices on meter and style, and a general index. A wide range of other commentaries have been consulted and in some cases incorporated here, particularly (for book 6) those of Austin and Williams. The Latin text used here is that of F.A. Hirtzel (Oxford 1900), with the following differences in readings 249: the archaic *succipiunt* for *suscipiunt*; 255: *limina* for *lumina*; 586: *flammas* for *flammam*; 602: *quos* for *quo*; and 852 *pacique* for *pacisque*.

The Stylistic Terms (Appendix B) are based upon a similar list of terms by Randall Ganiban, whose *Introduction to Vergil's Aeneid* is also included here. His editing of this volume has been a great help to me, for which I thank him.

This commentary on *Aeneid* 6 aims to be sufficiently helpful in terms of grammar, syntax, and other translation issues to make the text easily accessible to students at the intermediate level of college Latin. It aims to provide a rich range of material that will enhance appreciation of Book 6, especially with respect to its importance for the *Aeneid* as a whole as well as for its place in the Western literary tradition. Book 6 is one of the key books of the *Aeneid*, and as such is often read apart from the other books. It profoundly influenced later works, such as Dante's *Divine Comedy*, particularly the *Inferno*, since Vergil there leads Dante into and through the underworld, just as the Sibyl of Cumae guides Aeneas in this book, also through the underworld.

I want to thank Randall Ganiban for organizing and editing these volumes, and for his many helpful suggestions along the way. I also want to thank Ron Pullins for initiating this project, and the staff at Focus Publishing for their meticulous editing.

P.A.J.

Introduction to Vergil's *Aeneid*

Vergil's lifetime and poetry

Publius Vergilius Maro (i.e. Vergil)[1] was born on October 15, 70 BCE near the town of Mantua (modern Mantova) in what was then still Cisalpine Gaul.[2] Little else about his life can be stated with certainty, because our main source, the ancient biography by the grammarian Donatus (fourth century CE),[3] is of questionable value.[4] The historical and political background to Vergil's life, by contrast, is amply documented and provides a useful framework for understanding his career. Indeed, his poetic development displays an increasing engagement with the politics of contemporary Rome, an engagement that culminates in the *Aeneid*.

Vergil lived and wrote in a time of political strife and uncertainty. In his early twenties the Roman Republic was torn apart by the civil wars of 49-45 BCE, when Julius Caesar fought and defeated Pompey and his supporters. Caesar was declared *dictator perpetuo* ("Dictator for Life") early in 44 BCE but was assassinated on the Ides of March by a group of senators led by Brutus[5] and Cassius. They sought to restore the Republic, which, they believed, was being destroyed by Caesar's domination and intimations of kingship.[6]

---

1   The spelling "Virgil" (*Virgilius*) is also used by convention. It developed early and has been explained by its similarity to two words: *virgo* ("maiden") and *virga* ("wand"). For discussion of the origins and potential meanings of these connections, see Jackson Knight (1944) 36-7 and Putnam (1993) 127-8 with notes.

2   Cisalpine Gaul, the northern part of what we now think of as Italy, was incorporated into Roman Italy in 42 BCE. Mantua is located ca. 520 kilometers north of Rome.

3   This biography drew heavily from the *De poetis* of Suetonius (born ca. 70 CE).

4   Horsfall (1995: 1-25; 2006: xxii-xxiv) argues that nearly every detail is unreliable.

5   Kingship was hateful to the Romans ever since Brutus' own ancestor, Lucius Junius Brutus, led the expulsion of Rome's last king, Tarquin the Proud, in ca. 509 BCE, an act that ended the regal period of Rome and initiated the Republic (cf. *Aeneid* 6.817-18). In killing Caesar, Brutus claimed that he was following the example of his great ancestor—an important concept for the Romans.

6   For the reasons behind Caesar's assassination and the fall of the Republic, see the brief accounts in Scullard (1982) 126-53 and Shotter (2005) 4-19.

The assassination initiated a new round of turmoil that profoundly shaped the course of Roman history. In his will, Caesar adopted and named as his primary heir his great-nephew Octavian (63 BCE-14 CE), the man who would later be called "Augustus."[7] Though only eighteen years old, Octavian boldly accepted and used this inheritance. Through a combination of shrewd calculation and luck, he managed to attain the consulship in 43 BCE, though he was merely nineteen years of age.[8] He then joined forces with two of Caesar's lieutenants, Marc Antony (initially Octavian's rival) and Lepidus. Together they demanded recognition as a Board of Three (*triumviri* or "triumvirs") to reconstitute the state as they saw fit, and were granted extraordinary powers to do so by the Roman senate and people. In 42 BCE they avenged Caesar's murder by defeating his assassins commanded by Brutus and Cassius at the battle of Philippi in Macedonia, but their alliance gradually began to deteriorate as a result of further civil strife and interpersonal rivalries.

Vergil composed the *Eclogues*, his first major work, during this tumultuous period.[9] Published ca. 39 BCE,[10] the *Eclogues* comprise a sophisticated collection of ten pastoral poems that treat the experiences of shepherds.[11] The poems were modeled on the *Idylls* of Theocritus, a Hellenistic Greek poet of the third century BCE (see below). But whereas Theocritus' poetry created a world that was largely timeless, Vergil sets his pastoral world against the backdrop of contemporary Rome and the disruption caused by the civil wars. *Eclogues* 1 and 9, for example, deal with the differing fortunes of shepherds during a time of land confiscations that

---

7   See below.

8   By the *lex Villia annalis* of 180 BCE, a consul had to be at least forty-two years of age.

9   Other works have been attributed to Vergil: *Aetna, Catalepton, Ciris, Copa, Culex, Dirae, Elegiae in Maecenatem, Moretum,* and *Priapea*. They are collected in what is called the *Appendix Vergiliana* and are generally believed to be spurious.

10   This traditional dating, however, has recently been called into question through re-evaluation of *Eclogue* 8, which may very well refer to events in 35 BCE. See Clausen (1994) 232-7.

11   Coleman (1977) and Clausen (1994) are excellent commentaries on the *Eclogues*. For a discussion of the pastoral genre at Rome, see Heyworth (2005). For general interpretation of the *Eclogues*, see Hardie (1998) 5-27 with extensive bibliography in the notes, Volk (2008a), and Smith (2011) 40-74.

resonate with historical events in 41-40 BCE.[12] *Eclogue* 4 describes the birth of a child during the consulship of Asinius Pollio (40 BCE) who will bring a new golden age to Rome.[13] By interjecting the Roman world into his poetic landscape,[14] Vergil allows readers to sense how political developments both threaten and give promise to the very possibility of pastoral existence.

The *Eclogues* established Vergil as a new and important poetic voice, and led him to the cultural circle of the great literary patron Maecenas, an influential supporter and confidant of Octavian. Their association grew throughout the 30s.[15] The political situation, however, remained precarious. Lepidus was ousted from the triumvirate in 36 BCE because of his treacherous behavior. Tensions between Octavian and Antony that were simmering over Antony's collaboration and affair with the Egyptian queen Cleopatra eventually exploded.[16] In 32 BCE, Octavian had Antony's powers revoked, and war was declared against Cleopatra (and thus in effect against Antony as well). During a naval confrontation off Actium on the coast of western Greece in September of 31 BCE, Octavian's fleet decisively routed the forces of Marc Antony and Cleopatra, who both fled to Egypt and

---

12   Octavian rewarded veterans with land that was already occupied.

13   This is sometimes called the "Messianic Eclogue" because later ages read it as foreseeing the birth of Christ, which occurred nearly four decades later. The identity of the child is debated, but the poem may celebrate the marriage between Marc Antony and Octavian's sister Octavia that resulted from the treaty of Brundisium in 40 BCE; this union helped stave off the immediate outbreak of war between the two triumvirs. For more on this poem, see Van Sickle (1992) and Petrini (1997) 111-21, as well as the commentaries by Coleman (1977) and Clausen (1994).

14   In addition to the contemporary themes that Vergil treats, he also mentions or dedicates individual poems to a number of his contemporaries, including Asinius Pollio, Alfenus Varus, Cornelius Gallus, and probably Octavian, who is likely the *iuvenis* ("young man") mentioned at 1.42 and perhaps also the patron addressed at 8.6-13.

15   For the relationship between Augustus and the poets, see White (2005). White (1993) is a book-length study of this topic. For an overview of literature of the Augustan period from 40 BCE-14 CE, see Farrell (2005).

16   In addition to the political conflicts, there were also familial tensions: Antony conducted a decade-long affair with Cleopatra, even though he had married Octavia, Octavian's (Augustus') sister, as a result of the treaty of Brundisium in 40 BCE (see n. 13 above). Antony divorced Octavia in 32 BCE.

committed suicide in the following year to avoid capture.[17] This momentous victory solidified Octavian's claim of being the protector of traditional Roman values against the detrimental influence of Antony, Cleopatra, and the East.[18]

Vergil began his next work, the *Georgics*, sometime in the 30s, completed it ca. 29 BCE in the aftermath of Actium, and dedicated it to Maecenas. Like the *Eclogues*, the *Georgics* was heavily influenced by Greek models— particularly the work of Hesiod (eighth century BCE) and of Hellenistic poets[19] such as Callimachus, Aratus, and Nicander (third–second centuries BCE). On the surface, it purports to be a poetic farming guide.[20] Each of its four book examines a different aspect or sphere of agricultural life: crops and weather signs (book 1), trees and vines (book 2), livestock (book 3), and bees (book 4). Its actual scope, however, is much more ambitious. The poem explores the nature of humankind's struggle with the beauty and difficulties of the agricultural world, but it does so within the context of contemporary war-torn Italy. It bears witness to the strife following Caesar's assassination, and sets the chaos and disorder inherent in nature against the upheaval caused by civil war (1.461-514). Moreover, Octavian's success and victories are commemorated both in the introduction (1.24-42) and conclusion (4.559-62) of the poem, as well as in the beginning of the third book (3.1-39). Thus once again, the political world is juxtaposed against Vergil's poetic landscape, but the relationship between the two is not fully addressed.[21]

---

17   For the history of the triumviral period, see the brief accounts in Scullard (1982) 154-71 and Shotter (2005) 20-7; for more detailed treatments, see Syme (1939) 187-312 and Pelling (1996). For discussion of the contemporary artistic representations of Actium, see Gurval (1995).

18   This ideological interpretation is suggested in Vergil's depiction of the battle on Aeneas' shield (8.671-713).

19   See discussion below.

20   Recent commentaries on the *Georgics* include Thomas (1988) and Mynors (1990). For interpretation, see the introduction to the *Georgics* in Hardie (1998) 28-52 with extensive bibliography in the notes, Volk (2008b), and Smith (2011) 75-103. Individual studies include Wilkinson (1969), Putnam (1979), Johnston (1980), Ross (1987), Perkell (1989), and Nappa (2005). For allusion in the *Georgics*, see Thomas (1986), Farrell (1991), and Gale (2000).

21   The overall meaning of the *Georgics* is contested. Interpretation of the *Georgics*, like that of the *Aeneid* (see below), has optimistic and pessimistic poles. Otis (1964) is an example of the former; Ross (1987) the latter. Other scholars, such as Perkell (1989), fall in between by discerning inherent ambivalence. For discussion of these interpretive trends, see Hardie (1998) 50-2.

Octavian's victory represented a turning point for Rome's development. Over the next decade, he centralized political and military control in his hands. He claimed to have returned the state (*res publica*) to the senate and Roman people in 27 BCE.[22] His powers were redefined, and he was granted the name "Augustus' ("Revered One") by the senate. It is true that he maintained many traditional Republican institutions, but in reality he was transforming the state into a monarchy. So effective was his stabilization and control of Rome after decades of civil war that he reigned as *Princeps* ("First Citizen") from 27 BCE to 14 CE, creating a political framework (the Principate) that served the Roman state for centuries.[23]

Vergil wrote his final poem, the *Aeneid*, largely in the 20s, during the first years of Augustus' reign, when the Roman people presumably hoped that the civil wars were behind them but feared that the Augustan peace would not last. The *Aeneid* tells the story of the Trojan hero Aeneas. He fought the Greeks at Troy and saw his city destroyed, but with the guidance of the gods and fate he led his surviving people across the Mediterranean to a new homeland in Italy.[24] As in the *Eclogues* and *Georgics*, Vergil interjects his contemporary world into his poetic world. In the *Aeneid*, however, the thematic connections between these two realms are developed still more explicitly, with Aeneas' actions shown to be necessary for and to lead ultimately to the reign of Augustus. (See below for further discussion.)

Vergil was still finishing the *Aeneid* when he was stricken by a fatal illness in 19 BCE. The ancient biographical tradition claims that he traveled to Greece, intending to spend three years editing his epic there and in Asia,

---

22   Augustus, *Res Gestae* 34.

23   For general political and historical narratives of Augustus' reign, see the relatively brief account in Shotter (2005); longer, more detailed treatments can be found in A. H. M. Jones (1970), Crook (1996), Southern (1998), and Everitt (2006) 186-320. A classic and influential book by Syme (1939) paints Augustus in extremely dark colors. For broader considerations of the Augustan age, see the short but interesting volume by Wallace-Hadrill (1993) and the more comprehensive treatments by Galinsky (1996, 2005). For the interaction of art and ideology in the Augustan Age, see Zanker (1988).

24   For general interpretation of the *Aeneid*, see the recent overviews provided by Hardie (1998) 53-101, Perkell (1999), Anderson (2005), Johnson (2005), Fratantuono (2007), Ross (2007), and Smith (2011) 104-49. For the literary and cultural backgrounds, see Martindale (1997), Farrell (2005), and Galinsky (2005).

but that early on he encountered Augustus, who was returning to Rome from the East, and decided to accompany him. Vergil, however, fell ill during the journey and died in Brundisium (in southern Italy) in September of 19 BCE. The *Aeneid* was largely complete but had not yet received its final revision. We are told that Vergil asked that it be burned, but that Augustus ultimately had it published. While such details regarding Vergil's death are doubted, the poem clearly needed final editing.[25] However, its present shape, including its sudden ending, is generally accepted to be as Vergil had planned.

Vergil and his predecessors

By writing an epic about the Trojan war, Vergil was rivaling Homer, the greatest of all the Greek poets. The *Aeneid* was therefore a bold undertaking, but its success makes it arguably the quintessential Roman work because it accomplishes what Latin poetry had always striven to do: to appropriate the Greek tradition and transform it into something that was both equally impressive and distinctly "Roman."

Homer's *Iliad* tells the story of the Trojan war by focusing on Achilles' strife with the Greek leader Agamemnon and consequent rage in the tenth and final year of the conflict, while the *Odyssey* treats the war's aftermath by relating Odysseus' struggle to return home. These were the earliest and most revered works of Greek literature,[26] and they exerted a defining influence on both the overall framework of the *Aeneid* and the close details of its poetry. In general terms, *Aeneid* 1-6, like the *Odyssey*, describes a hero's return (to a new) home after the Trojan war, while *Aeneid* 7-12, like the *Iliad*, tells the story of a war. But throughout the *Aeneid*, Vergil reworks ideas, language, characters, and scenes from both poems. Some ancient critics faulted Vergil for his use of Homer, calling his appropriations "thefts." Vergil, however, is said to have responded that it is "easier to steal his club from Hercules than a line from Homer."[27] Indeed, Vergil does much more than simply quote material from Homer. His creative use and transformation of Homeric

---

25   We can be sure that the poem had not received its final revision for a number of reasons, including the presence of roughly fifty-eight incomplete or "half" lines. See commentary note on 6.94.

26   These poems were culminations of a centuries-old oral tradition and were written down probably in the eighth century BCE.

27   *...facilius esse Herculi clavam quam Homeri versum subripere* (Donatus/Suetonius, *Life of Vergil* 46).

language and theme are central not only to his artistry but also to the meaning of the *Aeneid*.

Though Homer is the primary model, Vergil was also influenced by the Hellenistic Greek tradition of poetry that originated in Alexandria, Egypt in the third century BCE. There scholar-poets such as Apollonius, Callimachus, and Theocritus reacted against the earlier literary tradition (particularly epic which by their time had become largely derivative). They developed a poetic aesthetic that valued sophistication in meter and word order, small-scale treatments over large, the unusual and recherché over the conventional. Hellenistic poetry was introduced into the mainstream of Latin poetry a generation before Vergil by the so-called "neoterics" or "new poets," of whom Catullus (c. 84-c. 54 BCE) was the most influential for Vergil and for the later literary tradition.[28]

Vergil's earlier works, the *Eclogues* and *Georgics*, had been modeled to a significant extent on Hellenistic poems,[29] so it was perhaps a surprise that Vergil would then have turned to a large-scale epic concerning the Trojan war.[30] However, one of his great feats was the incorporation of the Hellenistic and neoteric sensibilities into the *Aeneid*. Two models were particularly important in this regard: the *Argonautica* by Apollonius of Rhodes, an epic retelling the hero Jason's quest for the Golden Fleece, and Catullus 64, a poem on the wedding of Peleus and Thetis.[31] Both works brought the great and elevated heroes of the past down to the human level, thereby offering new insights into their strengths, passions and flaws, and both greatly influenced Vergil's presentation of Aeneas.

---

28   Clausen (1987, 2002), George (1974), Briggs (1981), Thomas (1988, 1999), and Hunter (2006) display these influences, while O'Hara (1996) provides a thorough examination of wordplay (important to the Alexandrian poets) in Vergil.

29   The *Eclogues* were modeled on Theocritus' *Idylls*; the *Georgics* had numerous models, though the Hellenistic poets Callimachus, Nicander, and Aratus were particularly important influences. See above.

30   For example, at *Eclogue* 6.3-5, Vergil explains in highly programmatic language his decision to compose poetry in the refined Callimachean or Hellenistic manner rather than traditional epic. See Clausen (1994) 174-5.

31   On the influence of Apollonius on Vergil, see the important book by Nelis (2001).

Of Vergil's other predecessors in Latin literature, the most important was Ennius (239-169 BCE), often called the father of Roman poetry.[32] His *Annales*, which survives only in fragments, was an historical epic about Rome that traced the city's origins back to Aeneas and Troy. It remained the most influential Latin poem until the *Aeneid* was composed, and provided a model not only for Vergil's poetic language and themes, but also for his integration of Homer and Roman history. In addition, the *De Rerum Natura* of Lucretius (ca. 94-55/51 BCE), a hexameter poem on Epicurean philosophy, profoundly influenced Vergil with its forceful language and philosophical ideas.[33]

Finally, Vergil drew much from Greek and Roman[34] tragedy. Many episodes in the *Aeneid* share tragedy's well-known dramatic patterns (such as reversal of fortune), and explore the suffering that befalls mortals often as a result of the immense and incomprehensible power of the gods and fate.[35] As a recent critic has written, "The influence of tragedy on the *Aeneid*

---

32   Ennius introduced the dactylic hexameter as the meter of Latin epic. Two earlier epic writers were Livius Andronicus who composed a translation of Homer's *Odyssey* into Latin, and Naevius who composed the *Bellum Punicum*, an epic on the First Punic War. Both Naevius and Livius wrote their epics in a meter called Saturnian that is not fully understood. For the influence of the early Latin poets on the *Aeneid*, see Wigodsky (1972).

33   See Hardie (1986) 157-240 and Adler (2003). The influence of the Epicurean Philodemus on Vergil (and the Augustans more generally) is explored in the collection edited by Armstrong, Fish, Johnston, and Skinner (2004). For Lucretius' influence on Vergil's *Georgics*, see especially Farrell (1991) and Gale (2000).

34   The earliest epic writers (Livius, Naevius and Ennius; see above) also wrote tragedy, and so it is not surprising that epic and tragedy would influence one another. Latin tragic writing continued into the first century through the work of, e.g., Pacuvius (220-ca. 130 BCE) and Accius (170-c. 86 BCE). Their tragedies, which included Homeric and Trojan War themes, were important for Vergil. However, since only meager fragments of them have survived, their precise influence is difficult to gauge.

35   Cf., e.g., Heinze (1915, trans. 1993: 251-8). Wlosok (1999) offers a reading of the Dido episode as tragedy, and Pavlock (1985) examines Euripidean influence in the Nisus and Euryalus episode. Hardie (1991, 1997), Panoussi (2002, 2009), and Galinsky (2003) examine the influence of tragedy, particularly in light of French theories of Greek tragedy (e.g. Vernant and Vidal-Naquet (1988)), and draw important parallels between the political and cultural milieus of fifth-century Athens and Augustan Rome. On tragedy and conflicting viewpoints, see Conte (1999) and Galinsky (2003).

is pervasive, and arguably the single most important factor in Virgil's successful revitalization of the genre of epic."[36]

The *Aeneid* is thus a highly literary work. By considering its interactions with these and other models, or, to put it another way, by examining Vergil's use of "allusion" or "intertextuality,"[37] we can enrich both our experience of his artistry and our interpretation of his epic. However, no source study can fully account for the creative, aesthetic, and moral achievement of the *Aeneid*, which is a work until itself.

The *Aeneid*, Rome, and Augustus

While Aeneas' story takes place in the distant, mythological past of the Trojan war era, it had a special relevance for Vergil's contemporaries. Not only did the Romans draw their descent from the Trojans, but the emperor Augustus believed that Aeneas was his own ancestor.[38] Vergil makes these national and familial connections major thematic concerns of his epic.

As a result, the *Aeneid* is about more than the Trojan war and its aftermath. It is also about the foundation of Rome and its flourishing under Augustus. To incorporate these themes into his epic, Vergil connects mythological and historical time by associating three leaders and city foundations: the founding of Lavinium by Aeneas, the actual founding of Rome by Romulus, and the "re-founding" of Rome by Augustus. These events are prominent in the most important prophecies of the epic: Jupiter's speech

---

36   Hardie (1998) 62. See also Hardie (1997).

37   See Farrell (1997) for a full and insightful introduction to the interpretive possibilities that the study of intertextuality in Vergil can offer readers. For a general introduction to intertextuality, see Allen (2000). For the study of intertextuality in Latin literature, see Conte (1986), Farrell (1991) 1-25, Hardie (1993), Fowler (1997), Hinds (1998), and Edmunds (2001). For Vergil's use of Homer, see Knauer (1964b), Barchiesi (1984, in Italian), Gransden (1984), and Cairns (1989) 177-248. Knauer (1964a), written in German, is a standard work on this topic; those without German can still benefit from its detailed citations and lists of parallels. For Vergil's use of Homer and Apollonius, see Nelis (2001).

38   Augustus' clan, the Julian *gens*, claimed its descent from Iulus (another name for Aeneas' son Ascanius) and thus also from Aeneas and Venus. Julius Caesar in particular emphasized this ancestry; Augustus made these connections central to his political self-presentation as well. See, e.g., Zanker (1988) 193-210 and Galinsky (1996) 141-224.

to Venus (1.257-96) and Anchises' revelation to his son Aeneas (6.756-853). Together these passages provide what may be called an Augustan reading of Roman history, one that is shaped by the deeds of these three men and that views Augustus as the culmination of the processes of fate and history.[39]

This is not to say that the associations among Aeneas, Romulus, and Augustus are always positive or unproblematic, particularly given the ways that Aeneas is portrayed and can be interpreted.[40] To some, Vergil's Aeneas represents an idealized Roman hero, who thus reflects positively on Augustus by association.[41] In general this type of reading sees a positive imperial ideology in the epic and is referred to as "optimistic" or "Augustan." Others are more troubled by Vergil's Aeneas, and advocate interpretations that challenge the moral and spiritual value of his actions, as well as of the role of the gods and fate. Such readings perceive a much darker poetic world[42]

---

[39]   See O'Hara (1990), however, for the deceptiveness of prophecies in the *Aeneid*.

[40]   For general interpretation of the *Aeneid*, see n. 24 (above).

[41]   This type of reading is represented especially by Heinze (1915, trans. 1993), Pöschl (1950, trans. 1962), and Otis (1964). More recent and complex Augustan interpretations can be found in Hardie (1986) and Cairns (1989).

[42]   See, e.g., Putnam (1965), Johnson (1976), Lyne (1987), and Thomas (2001). Putnam's reading of the *Aeneid* has been particularly influential. Of the ending of the poem he writes: "By giving himself over with such suddenness to the private wrath which the sight of the belt of Pallas arouses, Aeneas becomes himself *impius Furor*, as rage wins the day over moderation, disintegration defeats order, and the achievements of history through heroism fall victim to the human frailty of one man" (1965: 193-4). For a different understanding of Aeneas' wrath, see Galinsky (1988).

and have been called "pessimistic" or "ambivalent."[43] Vergil's portrayal of Aeneas is thus a major element in debates over the epic's meaning.[44]

Randall Ganiban, *Series Editor*

---

43   For a general treatment of the optimism/pessimism debate, see Kennedy (1992). For a critique of the "pessimistic" view, see Martindale (1993); for critique of the "optimistic" stance and its rejection of "pessimism," see Thomas (2001). For the continuing debate over the politics of the *Aeneid* and over the Augustan age more generally, see the collections of Powell (1992) and Stahl (1998).

44   Indeed some readers also question whether it is even possible to resolve this interpretive debate because of Vergil's inherent ambiguity. See Johnson (1976), Perkell (1994), and O'Hara (2007) 77-103. Martindale (1993) offers a critique of ambiguous readings.

Introduction to Book 6:
Its Role in the *Aeneid*

Aeneid 6 provides a culmination to the first half of the epic. Book 1 began with the Trojans about to reach Italy and complete their search for a new home but, through Juno's intervention, a huge storm arose and drove them off course to Carthage, where they were welcomed by Dido to her new kingdom at the end of Book 1. Aeneas is the narrator of Book 2, recounting the fall of Troy, and of Book 3, tracing the Trojans' travels in their long search for a new home. Book 4 tells the tragic love story of Dido and Aeneas. At the end of Book 4 the Trojans depart from Carthage and head for Italy at the beginning of Book 5, but they are forced by an imminent storm to take refuge in Sicily. There they celebrate the funeral games for Aeneas' father, Anchises, who had died a year earlier (3.708-13). At the end of Book 5 they are again en route to Italy, when their helmsman, Palinurus, falls overboard and drowns. Consequently Aeneas takes the helm. Juno does not intervene with another storm, and Aeneas guides his fleet to Cumae, near the modern Bay of Naples.

At Cumae, Aeneas will visit the Sibyl, as he had specifically been instructed to do by the seer Helenus in 3.441-62, and again by the ghost of Anchises in 5.724-39. The Sibyl will guide Aeneas through the underworld to visit his father and learn the future of their descendants, who will become the Roman race. Book 6 narrates this journey; it can be divided into three parts. It begins (1-263) with the Trojans' landing at Cumae in Italy. Aeneas proceeds directly to visit the Sibyl, and together they prepare to enter the underworld. In the central portion of the book (264-678), the Sibyl guides Aeneas through the various regions of the underworld, where he sees and interacts with numerous shades. The book concludes (679-901) with Aeneas having reached the Fields of the Blessed in Elysium, where he finds the shade of his deceased father. Anchises reveals to him the future greatness of their descendants and of the Roman state they will establish, which will culminate in a golden age under Augustus.

Book 6 represents an important turning point in the epic. Here Aeneas will in some sense put the past behind him and bring to an end his wanderings in the "Odyssean" half of the epic. He will encounter many of the figures from earlier in the poem, and will, as a result, come to a better understanding of past events. At the same time, he will learn about the future. Prior to Anchises' prophecy, the Sibyl predicts a terrible conflict, one in which the Trojan War past threatens to be reborn in a new form, with Aeneas facing a new Achilles in Italy (6.83-94), thus providing a transition to the "Iliadic" half of the *Aeneid*, in which this new war will be depicted.

Aeneas' journey through the underworld draws upon many sources, making book 6 one of the richest of the *Aeneid*. The most important is Homer's *Odyssey* 11, where Odysseus travels to Hades to question the shades of the dead in order to learn how to return to his home in Ithaca. Vergil's underworld episode, however, is more complex than Homer's. Unlike Aeneas, Odysseus meets most of the shades at the entrance to the underworld, where they come to him. In addition, Homer's underworld does not look much further forward than Odysseus' lifetime, focusing instead more on past events; Vergil's underworld, by contrast, reveals a difference in the destinies of souls according to the lives they have lived on earth, and ultimately foretells the distant future.

In addition to Homer, there are many other literary, philosophical, and religious influences. Vergil's underworld reflects Orphic and Pythagorean accounts of punishment, rewards, and purgation in the afterlife, and of the transmigration of the souls (cf. with notes 132, 639, 645, 703-23, 724-51), so central to the Parade of Heroes at the end of the book. In addition, there are allusions to other literary/philosophical accounts of the afterlife, including the "Myth of Er" from Plato's *Republic* and the "Dream of Scipio" from Cicero's *Republic*, as well as the Stoic doctrine on the nature of the soul, which plays an important role (see 724-51 n.). Finally, the description of Elysium, where Anchises and other blessed souls are located, suggests the language of the happy existence of those initiated into the mystery religions, which were popular during the Hellenistic and Roman Imperial periods.

Up until now, Aeneas has dutifully fulfilled the demands of fate and the gods, not always with complete knowledge or understanding, but acting out of the piety that defines him (*pius Aeneas*). At the end of book 6, he receives from Anchises his first, full account of the greatness of the race he is destined to found. In the remainder of the poem, however, it is not clear that he is thinking in any detail about what Anchises has here revealed to him. To some readers, indeed, his departure from the underworld through the gate of ivory (from where false dreams exit) casts doubt onto everything he has witnessed (see 893-901 n.). Nonetheless from this point on Aeneas tends to act with greater determination and confidence.

Bibliography. For general interpretation, see MacKay (1955), R. D. Williams (1964), Segal (1966), Camps (1967-68), Solmsen (1972), Feeney (1986), Zetzel (1989), Horsfall (1995) 144-54, Fratantuono (2007) and O'Hara (2007) 170-2. For the influence of Homer and other sources, see Knauer (1964a), Camps (1967-68), and Nelis (2001). For the religious and philosophical elements, see Butler (1920) 1-36, Fletcher (1941) ix-xxviii, Solmsen (1972), and Braund (1997). For Herakles' descent as a model for that of Aeneas, see Clark (2000, 2009). For the Parade of Heroes, see Feeney (1986), Goold (1992), Hardie (1998) 96-7, and Reed (2007) 148-50. For the gate of ivory, see 893-901 n. For the importance of viewing and spectacle, see Leach (1999). For all aspects, see the landmark commentaries (in German) by Norden (1957, fourth edition), and (in English) by Austin (1977).

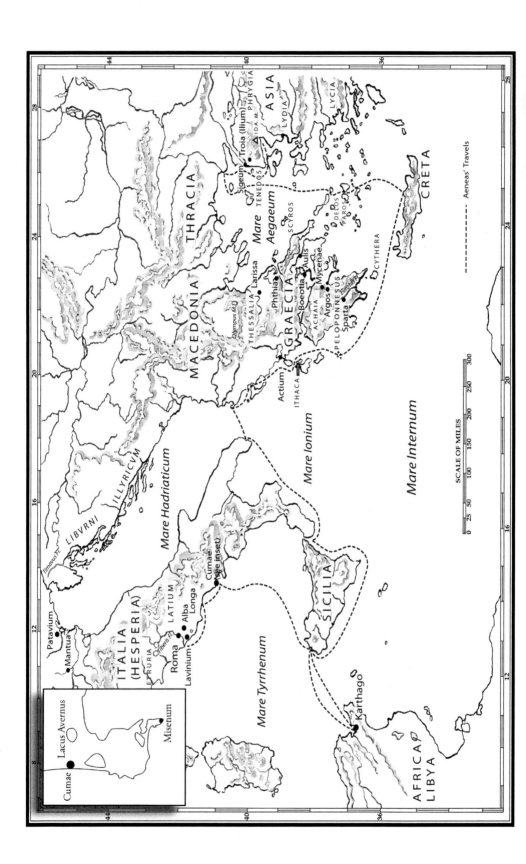

Liber Sextus

SIC fatur lacrimans, classique immittit habenas

1-263: The Landing at Cumae and Preparation to Enter the Underworld

After the Trojans land at Cumae, Aeneas quickly proceeds to the temple of Apollo, whose doors have been decorated by the master craftsman Daedalus. After gazing at the artwork, which is described at length (see 14-41 n.), Aeneas enters the cave of the Sibyl, where he hears a terrifying prophecy of the trials he will face in Italy. He also learns that before he can travel to the underworld, he must bury his companion Misenus (who, unbeknownst to him, lies dead on the beach, a victim of his own *hubris*) and find a golden bough which he is to present to Proserpina in the underworld. He quickly performs both tasks.

Aeneas' meeting with the Sibyl results from two earlier episodes: 1) the Trojan priest Helenus had instructed Aeneas to consult the Sibyl at Cumae and to learn about the wars he will have to fight (3.441-60), and 2) Anchises had appeared to Aeneas in a dream (5.722-39), prophesying the Italian war and also instructing him to travel to Elysium in the underworld, guided by the Sibyl, to meet with Anchises and learn from him the future of their descendants and of their city (i.e. Rome). Aeneas' meeting with the Sibyl in this section fufills the first task and initiates the second.

Throughout, Aeneas' *pietas* is emphasized – he is described as *pius* three times (9, 176, 232), an adjective that underscores the degree to which he has undertaken this task out of a sense of responsibility to the gods, the state, and his family; it also points to the difficulty and the heroic nature of his undertaking: he is a living being who hopes not only to descend to the underworld, but also to return from it alive – a far more difficult challenge. We shall also see the importance of burial (e.g. the case of Misenus), as well as the requisite mystical and ritual actions (e.g. performing sacrifices and finding the golden bough) mandated by the Sibyl. Such features make this section a rich and fitting prelude to Aeneas' descent to the underworld.

For the murals of Daedalus, see W. Fitzgerald (1984), Putnam (1998). For the golden bough, see Brooks (1953), Segal (1965, 1966), Clark (1992), West (1987; repr. 1990: 224-38), Weber (1995).

1—13. The Trojans land at Cumae in Italy and visit the Temple of Apollo.

1. **SIC fatur lacrimans:** because Aeneas' helmsman Palinurus died at the end of Book 5, Book 6 opens with Aeneas weeping for his lost comrade as he takes control of the helm or "reins" (*habenas*) of the ship to guide it to Cumae's harbor. **classi:** dative of reference. **immittit habenas:** a horse-racing metaphor which literally means "to loosen the reins"; here it refers to loosening the ship's cables so that the sails can be filled by the winds.

et tandem Euboicis Cumarum adlabitur oris.
obvertunt pelago proras; tum dente tenaci
ancora fundabat navis et litora curvae
praetexunt puppes. iuvenum manus emicat ardens   5
litus in Hesperium; quaerit pars semina flammae
abstrusa in venis silicis, pars densa ferarum
tecta rapit silvas inventaque flumina monstrat.
at pius Aeneas arces quibus altus Apollo

---

2. **tandem:** i.e. after long wanderings. **Euboicis...oris:** Cumae, just west of the modern city of Naples, was not founded until the seventh century BCE by settlers from the Greek city Chalcis on the island Euboea (cf. *Chalcidicaque* 17). Since Aeneas would have arrived five centuries earlier, the reference here is anachronistic*. Note that the gentle, lapping movement of lines 1-2, achieved by a mixture of soft vowels (*a, i*), and nasal (*m, n*) and liquid (*l, r*) consonants, creates a soothing effect, suggesting a dreamlike, gentle gliding into the harbor of Cumae.

3. **obvertunt pelago proras:** once in the harbor, they turn the prows to face the sea, so that the ships would be ready for immediate departure (cf. 901). **dente tenaci:** instrumental ablative.

4. **fundabat:** the imperfect tense indicates that the anchor was in the process of giving their ships a firm base on the shore, while the present tense (*praetexunt* 5) indicates the final result of their efforts.

5-6: **emicat ardens:** the Trojans dart forth (*emicat*) eagerly (*ardens*), in their desire to set foot on this long-sought land; the choice of words suggests a newly lit flame bursting forth. **litus in Hesperium:** Hesperia (lit. "the Western Land," i.e. Italy) has long been the goal of their quest, as Dido is informed by Ilioneus (1.530; 1.569) and Aeneas (4.355, etc.); cf. 2.781; 3.163, 185, and 503.

6-11. **quaerit pars...pars...rapit...at pius Aeneas...petit:** "Some seek..., others seize..., but pious Aeneas...."

6. **semina flammae:** the sparks ("seeds of flame") were believed to be hidden in the flint until it was struck. Cf. Homer, *Odyssey* 5.490; Vergil, *Geo.* 1.135; *Aen.* 1.174.

8. **rapit:** suggests a violent attack upon the woodlands, to find either wood for cooking or wild game.

9. **at:** strongly marks a change of subject. **pius Aeneas:** the epithet *pius*, most often applied to Aeneas, refers to his duty to the gods, the state, and his family; here his religious duties as well as his obligations to his father are emphasized. The phrase *at pius Aeneas* recurs at crucial junctures in the narrative (cf. 1.305; 4.393; 6.232; 7.5; 12.311). **altus Apollo:** Apollo is here identified with his lofty temple. This temple, however, is anachronistic since Apollo was not established at Cumae until 410 BCE; prior to that, the site was sacred to Hera. See Johnston (1998). The ruins of the historical Temple of Apollo still stand on the Acropolis of Cumae, above the city's ancient harbor; at a lower level, a few hundred feet away (*procul* 10), is the cave of the Cumaean Sibyl. Aeneas seems to climb up the hill from the harbor, and proceed through the sacred groves of Hecate (*Triviae lucos* 13), past the level of the cave itself to the entrance of the temple of Apollo, where he will be standing, admiring the temple doors (14-33), when the Sibyl (cf. 10 n.), having been previously summoned by Achates (34), suddenly appears and reproaches him for wasting time (37).

praesidet horrendaeque procul secreta Sibyllae,   10
antrum immane, petit, magnam cui mentem animumque
Delius inspirat vates aperitque futura.
iam subeunt Triviae lucos atque aurea tecta.

---

10. **Sibyllae:** the title of a priestess of Apollo; for her personal name see 36. She was thought to be the Sibyl from whom Tarquinius Superbus, Rome's last king, purchased the original Sibylline books. See Guarducci (1946-48); Parke (1988); Johnston (1998).

11. **cui:** the god "breathes (his reply) into" his seer (*cui*). **mentem animumque:** strictly speaking, *mens* is the "intelligence" or "insight" into the future which attends inspiration, while *animus* is the emotion associated with it. Both words are the direct objects of *inspirat*: "inspiration" is regarded as something almost material.

12. **Delius...vates:** Apollo was born on Delos, and hence he is the "Delos-born" prophetic god.

13. **iam subeunt:** "now they approach"; the use of the plural shows that Aeneas took companions with him to the temple of Apollo. **Triviae lucos:** cf. 9 n.; the grove surrounding the temple (*aurea tecta*) is described as sacred to Trivia, goddess of the "three-way-crossroads," an epithet for Hecate, the underworld goddess with the attributes of Apollo's twin sister, Artemis (= Roman Diana). The temple at Cumae may once have been associated with a cult of the dead. See Turcan (1992) 217-18, Pailler (1995) 111-26, Parker (1995) 485, Jimenez (2009). **aurea tecta:** by synecdoche*, a reference to the temple of Apollo (cf. 9 n.).

Daedalus, ut fama est, fugiens Minoia regna
praepetibus pennis ausus se credere caelo   15

14-41. The description of the temple and Daedalus' carvings on the doors

The action of the poem is suspended while Vergil describes in detail carvings Aeneas sees on the doors of the temple of Apollo. This literary device, known as *ecphrasis**, presents to the reader what the eyes of the characters are contemplating. (Compare *Aen.* 1.418-93, where Aeneas and Achates gaze at the paintings on Juno's temple in Carthage.) Here the artwork, created by the master craftsman Daedalus, tells the story of the slaying of the Minotaur, in which Daedalus himself played an important role. There are four main panels: the death at Athens of the Cretan prince Androgeos, son of king Minos (see 20-2 n.); the young Athenians chosen annually by lot to be sacrificed to the Minotaur at Crete to atone for Androgeos' death (see 20-2 n.); Pasiphae's mating with the bull that produced the Minotaur (see 23-6 n.); and Theseus' slaying of the Minotaur in the Labyrinth with Daedalus' help (27-30, see n.). As we learn at 30-3, sorrow prevented Daedalus from including the story of his son's death as they tried to flee Crete after the Minotaur's death.

This ecphrasis resonates with the main narrative. Aeneas and his companions contemplate mythical scenes of greed, passion, and murder, which hint at the pain of a father (Daedalus) whose son (Icarus) has not fulfilled his promise. The ecphrasis also provides a view of the tragedy in store for a father who fails what he has undertaken, and underscores the audacity—and promise—if he should succeed. Aeneas is thus reminded of his responsibilities to his own son and descendants (30-3), as well as to his father, Anchises, who had perished before the storm with which Book 1 begins.

The tale of Daedalus and Icarus was widely represented in ancient art. At Pompeii, for example, a fresco in the House of the Vettii depicts Daedalus' role in facilitating Pasiphae's mating with the bull, while his child Icarus sits on a bench nearby, playing with his father's tools. This important father-son theme recurs below, as in Aeneas' speech to the Sibyl (103-23), and in his subsequent encounter with his father in the underworld at the end of this book. The myth of Daedalus and Icarus is told in Ovid, *Metamorphoses* 8.183-235; it was frequently represented on Roman vases and gems and in wall paintings. Daedalus' connection with Cumae goes back to a history of Sicily written by Timaeus of Tauromenium (c. 350-260 BCE). For interpretations of the myth, see Otis (1964) 280-5, Segal (1965) 642-5, W. Fitzgerald (1984), Leach (1988) 356-9, Putnam (1998) 75-96, and Nyenhuis (2003).

14. **fugiens Minoia regna:** Daedalus, to escape from Crete and the anger of Minos, created for himself and his son *Icarus* (31) wings consisting of feathers joined by wax.

15. **praepetibus pennis:** "on swift wings." *Pennae* (lit. "feathers") here means "wings" by synecdoche*.

insuetum per iter gelidas enavit ad Arctos,
Chalcidicaque levis tandem super astitit arce.
redditus his primum terris tibi, Phoebe, sacravit
remigium alarum posuitque immania templa.
in foribus letum Androgeo; tum pendere poenas   20
Cecropidae iussi (miserum!) septena quotannis
corpora natorum; stat ductis sortibus urna.

---

16. **insuetum per iter:** *insuetum* because Daedalus was the first mortal to fly. **gelidas...ad Arctos:** "towards the icy Bears" (i.e. "north"). The Greater or Lesser Bears (*Arctos*) are the constellations that mark the celestial north pole. Daedalus and Icarus first flew northward, toward Samos, where Icarus fell, north of Crete. Daedalus then flew northwest, to Cumae. **enavit:** literally, "he swam out/forth"; here it is a metaphor for flying. For *ex* as a prefix meaning "upwards," "on high," cf. *elata* 23, *evadere* 128, *evexit* 130, *educere* 178, 630, and 3.567.

17. **Chalcidica...arce:** cf. 2 n. Daedalus arrived at Cumae safely after Icarus drowned in the sea, but in sorrow, and so he built this temple. The arrangement of epithet and noun framing the line is a neoteric feature. **levis...astitit:** not "alighted," but "came to a halt" or "hung hovering light(ly)." The next words, *redditus his primum terris*, describe his actual landing.

18. **sacravit:** the wings were dedicated as a thank-offering to Apollo (whom Vergil addresses by apostrophe*) for his safe arrival in Cumae (implying an analogy to the Trojans' safe arrival here, too, although there is no suggestion of a similar offering by the latter); the dedication also signaled that Daedalus was giving up flying (as the Trojans will give up their sea voyage). It was customary, when retiring from any profession, to dedicate one's instruments to the appropriate god; thus Antenor dedicates his weapons as a sign that his wars are over (1.248), and the poet Horace dedicates his lyre (*Odes* 3.26.3). Poetical inscriptions for such offerings are numerous in the *Greek Anthology*, a broad collection of Greek poetry assembled over a period of some 1,200 years, from the sixth century BCE to the sixth century CE.

19. **remigium alarum:** "oarage of wings." Cf. 1.301, where the phrase is used in describing the flight of the god Mercury. It is a mixed metaphor, because Daedalus was actually trying to "row" through air on artificial wings. **posuitque...templa:** the dedication of the wings in gratitude to Apollo was the main purpose for building the temple. The neuter plural (*templa*) suggests its magnificence; *immania* captures the viewer's awe.

20-2. To feed the Minotaur (see 14-41 n.), Minos ordered Aegeus, king of the Athenians (*Cecropidae* 21), to furnish annually seven young men and seven maidens selected by lot (*ductis sortibus* 22), though Vergil mentions only seven young men (*septena...corpora natorum* 21-2); Aegeus's son, Theseus, offered himself as one of these youths. Minos made this demand as punishment for the death of his son Androgeos, who was killed at the Panathenaic Games in Athens (in another version of the myth he was killed when he went to fight the bull of Marathon). **Androgeo:** a Greek genitive. **tum:** signals another scene—the sacrifice Minos exacted from the Athenians for his son's murder. **Cecropidae:** "descendants of king Cecrops," a mythical first king of Athens.

contra elata mari respondet Gnosia tellus:
hic crudelis amor tauri suppostaque furto
Pasiphae mixtumque genus prolesque biformis   25
Minotaurus inest, Veneris monimenta nefandae;
hic labor ille domus et inextricabilis error;
magnum reginae sed enim miseratus amorem

23-6. Minos, king of Crete (*Gnosia tellus* 23), had prayed for a perfect white bull to offer to the gods, but after receiving it, he could not bear to sacrifice it, so he substituted instead an inferior bull. To punish Minos, the gods caused his wife Pasiphae to become enamored of the white bull. To help her satisfy her passion, Daedalus created a wooden cow, into which she climbed and thus was mated (*supposta* 24) with the white bull. The offspring of this match was the *Minotaur*.

23. **contra elata mari:** on the opposing door (*contra*) are depicted the island of Crete "rising high (*elata*, cf. 16 n.) out of the sea," Pasiphae's passion for the bull, the Minotaur, and the Labyrinth built by Daedalus to house him. This door is said to "respond" (*respondet*) to the scenes depicted on the previously described door. **Gnosia tellus:** Crete is identified by its city, Cnossos.

24. **tauri:** objective genitive after *amor*. **suppostaque furto:** "mated by a trick." *Supposta* (lit. "placed beneath") is a contraction (syncope*) of *supposita* (cf. 14-41 n.).

25-6. **Pāsǐphăē:** consists of four syllables. **mixtum genus prolesque biformis...Veneris monimenta nefandae:** all in apposition to *Minotaurus* (26). **biformis:** describing *Minotaurus* ("the bull of Minos"), a creature half man, half beast.

27-30. Daedalus constructed a maze, the Labyrinth (*labor ille domus et inextricabilis error* 27), to enclose the Minotaur. When Theseus arrived in Crete, Minos' daughter Ariadne (*reginae* 28) fell in love with him and, with the help of Daedalus, provided him a sword and thread with which to retrace his steps from the Labyrinth after killing the Minotaur.

27. **hic:** "here." The Labyrinth is described in several ways: *labor ille...et inextricabilis error* (27, note the chiastic arrangement); *dolos tecti ambagesque* (29). **domus:** genitive singular.

28. **reginae:** the story has moved from Pasiphae to her daughter Ariadne, who is also a *regina*. Cf. Catullus 64.52-201 for the story of Minos and Pasiphae's daughter, Ariadne, who helped Theseus kill the Minotaur, and then was abandoned by him on the isle of Naxos. **sed enim:** "but in fact."

Daedalus ipse dolos tecti ambagesque resolvit,
caeca regens filo vestigia. tu quoque magnam 30
partem opere in tanto, sineret dolor, Icare, haberes.
bis conatus erat casus effingere in auro,
bis patriae cecidere manus. quin protinus omnia
perlegerent oculis, ni iam praemissus Achates
adforet atque una Phoebi Triviaeque sacerdos, 35
Deiphobe Glauci, fatur quae talia regi:
"non hoc ista sibi tempus spectacula poscit;

29-30. **ipse:** Daedalus *himself.* The "not-to-be-unraveled" (*inextricabilis* 27) maze was in fact unraveled (*resolvit*) by its own creator. **filo:** Ariadne provided Theseus the thread which enabled him to trace his way out. **vestigia:** of Theseus.

30-3. Daedalus, to escape from Crete (*fugiens Minoia regna* 14) and the anger of Minos, created for himself and his son *Icarus* (31) wings consisting of feathers joined by wax. Icarus, however, ignored his father's warning not to fly too near the sun. As a result the wax melted, his wings disintegrated, and he fell into the sea near Samos (therafter named "the Icarian Sea"), where he perished.

30-1. **tu...magnam | partem...<si> sineret dolor, Icare, haberes:** the present contrary-to-fact condition expresses Daedalus' inability to depict Icarus' story. For the story of Icarus' death, see the previous note. The dramatic break after *vestigia* (in bucolic diaeresis) provides an emotional pause before the pathetic apostrophe*.

32-3. **bis...bis:** the repetition of *bis* ("twice") (anaphora*) and the absence of a connective between the clauses (asyndeton*) help convey Daedalus' torment caused by Icarus' fall (*casus*). Compare 2.792-3, where a similar use of anaphora (*ter...ter*) reflects Aeneas' sorrow at the loss of Creusa. **conatus erat:** *pater* (i.e. Daedalus) is implied as the subject, from the adjective *patriae* (33). **omnia:** scan as a trochee (- ◡), by synizesis*, with consonantal *i*. Note the change of subject. There is an emotional pause after *manus,* and the narration moves from the picture on the doors to the Trojans gazing at them.

34-5. **perlegerent...adforet:** the contrary-to-fact construction here, as in 32, again reflects frustration—the Trojans' desire is to keep staring at Daedalus' art, which occupies their attention while they await the Sibyl's arrival (cf. 14-41 n.). **praemissus:** it appears that Achates had been sent ahead to summon the Sibyl. Cf. 9 n. **Triviae:** cf. 13 n.

36. **Deïphobe Glauci:** the Sibyl's name, Deïphobe, (daughter) of Glaucus, is here used. **regi:** i.e. Aeneas.

37. **ista:** the Sibyl's rebuke (cf. 9 n.) is consistent with her later responses to Palinurus (373-81). *Ista* is deictic and contemptuous, as she points scornfully to the *spectacula* at which they gaze— "such sights as those." A ritual offering must be made at once to Apollo and Trivia. It will consist of seven bullocks from a herd "untouched by the yoke" (*grege intacto* 38) (i.e. none of them have been used for toil) and seven sheep in their second year (*bidentes* 39). Norden notes here that the number seven had special significance in the cult of Apollo. **sibi:** reflexive, referring to *tempus.*

nunc grege de intacto septem mactare iuvencos
praestiterit, totidem lectas de more bidentis."
talibus adfata Aenean (nec sacra morantur   40
iussa viri) Teucros vocat alta in templa sacerdos.
    Excisum Euboicae latus ingens rupis in antrum,
quo lati ducunt aditus centum, ostia centum,
unde ruunt totidem voces, responsa Sibyllae.
ventum erat ad limen, cum virgo "poscere fata   45
tempus" ait; "deus ecce deus!" cui talia fanti

---

38. **mactare**: complementary infinitive after *praestiterit*.

39. **praestiterit**: "it would be better," potential subjunctive, used to express a wish (*pace tua dixerim, crediderim, affirmaverim*; cf. AG §447).

40-1. **nec sacra morantur | iussa**: "they do not delay (obeying) her commands." The parenthesis indicates that they perform the sacrifice as commanded, after which the Sibyl leads them into the temple and down to her cave.

42—76. *They approach the entrance to the Sibyl's cave, and the Sibyl instructs Aeneas to pray: he asks that she promise him at last a happy end to his wanderings and a home in Italy. As he prays, the Sibyl passes into the cave's recess, where the god Apollo takes full possession of her and issues his reply through her mouth.*

42-7. The Sibyl descends to her cave (*antrum inmane* 11, *antro* 77, *adyto* 98), hewn out of the face of the rock (42). It is at the threshhold of this cave (*limen* 45) where Aeneas actually consults the Sibyl. She is standing in front of its doors (*fores* 47) when she begins to feel "the power of the deity now nearer," and instructs Aeneas to offer prayer.

42. **Excisum Euboicae latus ingens rupis in antrum**: supply *erat* with *excisum* – "the huge side of the Cumaean (Euboean) cliff (had been) cut into a cave." Here we share the experience of Aeneas and his companions when they first come upon the great cave, whose passageway is a mix of light and dark because of the light shining across it at intervals from its lateral passageways. Lines 42-4 suggest the echoing sounds of a cave: *antrum...centum; ducunt, ruunt; Euboicae, Sibyllae.* For details of the cave, see notes on 9 and 42-7.

43. **quo**: "to where," "to which." **aditus centum, ostia centum**: *centum* is regularly used to represent an indefinite number, with grandiose effect. There is in fact only a single entrance; the *ostia* (lateral passages) are eight in number. See 81, where the "hundred" doors fly open spontaneously. In the repetition of *centum*, the metrical ictus* changes on the second repetition, as is often the case in Vergil.

45. **ventum erat**: "they had come." Intransitive verbs are frequently used impersonally in the passive voice. **fata**: "oracles"; literally, "the things said" (from *for, fari*) by the gods—and therefore destined to happen. Cf. 46 *fanti.*

46-9. **cui...color...comptae...comae...corda**: the alliteration underscores the Sibyl's struggle as the god takes possession of her.

46. **cui...fanti**: can be dative of possession or reference.

ante fores subito non vultus, non color unus,
non comptae mansere comae; sed pectus anhelum,
et rabie fera corda tument, maiorque videri
nec mortale sonans, adflata est numine quando   50
iam propiore dei. "cessas in vota precesque,
Tros" ait "Aenea? cessas? neque enim ante dehiscent
attonitae magna ora domus." et talia fata
conticuit. gelidus Teucris per dura cucurrit
ossa tremor, funditque preces rex pectore ab imo: 55
"Phoebe, gravis Troiae semper miserate labores,
Dardana qui Paridis derexti tela manusque
corpus in Aeacidae, magnas obeuntia terras
tot maria intravi duce te penitusque repostas

47-8. **non...non...non:** the three-fold repetition (anaphora*), paired with asyndeton*, is emphatic. **unus:** "the same" (as it had been before).

49. **corda:** "her wild heart swells" (the plural of *cor* is often used in a singular sense in poetry, as here). **maiorque videri:** supply *est* or *facta est*. *Videri* is an epexegetic infinitive: "she is greater to be looked upon," explaining in what sense *maior* is used, viz. not "greater" in dignity, age, or the like, but "greater in physical appppearance" (cf. 6.164 *praestantior ciere*, "more skilled to rouse"; 4.564 *certa mori*). Epexegesis* is the addition of one or more words to explain another word.

50. **mortale sonans:** *mortale* is a cognate accusative (cf. AG 390), but is equivalent to an adverb qualifying *sonans*. Cf. 201 *grave olentis*, "strong smelling"; 288 *horrendum stridens*, "hissing horribly"; 401 *aeternum latrans*, "ceaselessly barking"; 467 *torva tuentem*.

51. **cessas in vota precesque:** an unusual construction with this preposition. "Do you delay (to perform) your vows and prayers?" A "vow" (*votum*) is a promise to do something in case one's prayer is answered— "Grant me this (66)...then I will build (69)."

52-3. **Aenea:** vocative. **neque enim:** the Sibyl's indignant question (51-2) is really a command, and *enim* explains the reason for it. "Delay not to pray," she says, "*for* until (*ante*) you pray, the portals will *not* open." **attonitae...domus:** the "house" is spoken of as possessing sense and feeling, and the words *ora* and *dehiscent* are used to make the personification more vivid. **talia fata:** cf. 46 *talia fanti*.

54. **Teucris:** dative of reference.

56. **miserate:** vocative, "you who have pitied."

57. **derexti:** = *derexisti*; syncopated* forms in the perfect tense are common in Vergil.

58. **Aiacidae:** genitive, "of Aeacus' grandson" (i.e. "of Achilles"). The only part of Achilles' body that could be penetrated was his heel (hence the term "Achilles' heel"); Paris shot him in the heel, and thus the Greek hero perished. **obeuntia:** "bordering."

59. **duce te:** ablative absolute. **repostas:** syncope* for *repositas*; cf. *supposta* 24.

Massylum gentis praetentaque Syrtibus arva: 60
iam tandem Italiae fugientis prendimus oras,
hac Troiana tenus fuerit fortuna secuta.
vos quoque Pergameae iam fas est parcere genti,
dique deaeque omnes, quibus obstitit Ilium et ingens
gloria Dardaniae. tuque, o sanctissima vates,   65
praescia venturi, da (non indebita posco
regna meis fatis) Latio considere Teucros
errantisque deos agitataque numina Troiae.
tum Phoebo et Triviae solido de marmore templum
instituam festosque dies de nomine Phoebi.   70
te quoque magna manent regnis penetralia nostris:

---

60. **Massylum gentis:** the Numidians of North Africa, the inland neighbors of Carthage and Dido; cf. 4.132, 196 ff. **praetenta:** "stretched in front of," "bordering upon." **Syrtibus:** dative, governed by *praetenta*; the *Syrtes* are the sandy, desert flats between Carthage and Cyrene; the phrase *praetenta...arva* refers to the lands extending to them.

62. **hac...tenus...:** *hactenus* almost acquires a secondary sense of "this far but no farther," and this sense is here fully brought out by the perfect optative subjunctive *fuerit secuta*. "This far it may have followed us (but now may that following cease)." The "luck of Troy" was proverbial (cf. Aristotle, *Nichomachean Ethics* 1.10). Note the alliteration: *Troiana tenus fuerit fortuna.*

63. **vos:** the gods who had been Troy's enemies—Juno especially, but also Poseidon and Pallas (Minerva). **Pergameae:** an alternate adjective for *Troianus*, referring to Pergamum, the citadel of Troy. **iam:** emphatic. **fas est:** not "it is lawful," but "it is right." *Fas* and *nefas* represent the unchanging laws of right and wrong which are binding even on the gods. *Ius*, by contrast, would refer to law applicable to mortals.

66-7. **praescia venturi:** the objective genitive is common in poetry after adjectives implying knowledge, such as *conscius, inscius, nescius, doctus, docilis*; cf. AG §348. **da:** cf. 51 n. **non indebita...fatis:** an efficient form of expression in claiming the fulfillment of a promise; cf. 11.759, where Arruns, destined to be killed by Camilla, is called *fatis debitus.*

68. **agitata:** "storm-tossed."

69-70. **tum...:** here begins the vow the Sibyl called for in 51. The promises made anticipate events that will come long after Aeneas: the temple named here, according to Servius, is the one built in 28 BCE by Augustus to Apollo on the Palatine hill to commemorate the battle of Actium. (Cf. Horace, *Odes* 1.31; Propertius 2.31, 4.6.) The *festos dies* (70) of Apollo, *ludi Apollinares*, were actually instituted in 212 BCE, during the Second Punic War.

71. **penetralia:** the Sibylline Books (see 72-3 n.) were originally kept in the temple of Jupiter Capitolinus (Dionysius of Halicarnassus, *Antiquitates Romanae* 4.62) but were later moved into the *penetralia* of Augustus' new temple to Apollo on the Palatine (cf. 69-70 n.).

hic ego namque tuas sortis arcanaque fata
dicta meae genti ponam lectosque sacrabo,
alma, viros. foliis tantum ne carmina manda,
ne turbata volent rapidis ludibria ventis: 75
ipsa canas oro." finem dedit ore loquendi.
    At Phoebi nondum patiens immanis in antro
bacchatur vates, magnum si pectore possit

72-3. tuas sortis arcanaque fata: i.e. the Sibylline Books, which were said to be originally nine in number (Aulus Gellius, *Noctes Atticae* 1.19). When Tarquinius Superbus (Rome's seventh and final king) refused to purchase all of them from the Sibyl, she burnt three, and asked the same price for the six remaining. On his again refusing, she burnt three more, and asked the same price for the last three, which he then bought.

73-4. lectos...viros: the *quindecimviri sacris faciundis*, one of the four major priesthoods in Rome, were in charge of the Sibylline Books, and consulted them on occasions of national disaster (cf. Livy 5.13.6; 6.3.12; Cicero, *Epistulae ad familiares* 8.4.1). **foliis:** the seer Helenus (3.445) had warned Aeneas that the Sibyl's predictions were written on the "leaves" she carefully arranged, but that, when the doors of the cave were opened, the incoming wind would blow them about in confusion, with the result that those who sought a reply "departed unadvised and despising the Sibyl's dwelling." Vergil both here and in Book 3 appears to be referring to a well-known method of consulting the Sibylline books; his use of the term *sortes* suggests the chance selection of one of a number of oracles, each contained on a separate leaf. Vergil's own text was consulted for prophetic information as early as the second century CE (see *Scriptores Historiae Augustae*, *Hadrianus* 2.8) and thereafter. **ne...manda:** the use of *ne* with the imperative occurs in archaic Latin. In classical Latin prose, the subjunctive would normally be used (*ne mandes* or *ne mandaveris*). Cf. 614 *ne quaere*. **carmina:** "oracles," because they were delivered in hexameter verse; consequently, 76 *canas* = "utter your oracles"; cf. 3.155.

75. ne...volent: negative purpose clause.

76. ipsa: i.e. "with your own lips." Aeneas asks for the *spoken* and not the written word of prophecy. **canas:** cf. 73-4 n. **finem dedit:** "made an end."

77—97. While Aeneas speaks, the Sibyl, who has moved into the cave, begins to struggle against the god who is gaining possession of her. When she is finally subdued, she prophesies the Trojans will settle in Italy, but only after long wars.

77-80. The god gradually tames the priestess as one might tame an unruly steed (cf. 100-1). Cf. the madness of Cassandra in Aeschylus, *Agamemnon* 1150.

77. Phoebi nondum patiens: describing *vates* (i.e. the Sibyl), "not yet enduring Phoebus (to take control)." *Phoebi* is objective genitive. **immanis:** used adverbially, "violently."

78. si: "if" (i.e. "to see if"), "in the hope that."

excussisse deum; tanto magis ille fatigat
os rabidum, fera corda domans, fingitque premendo.   80
ostia iamque domus patuere ingentia centum
sponte sua vatisque ferunt responsa per auras:
"o tandem magnis pelagi defuncte periclis
(sed terrae graviora manent), in regna Lavini
Dardanidae venient (mitte hanc de pectore curam),   85
sed non et venisse volent. bella, horrida bella,

79-80. **excussisse:** "to have flung off the god"; the perfect tense is used in the strict sense, expressing her hope to be (completely) rid of him. **tanto magis ille fatigat:** supply *quanto magis illa bacchatur*—"the more she raves (*bacchatur*), so much the more he wears out…" **tanto:** ablative of degree of difference. **fatigat | os rabidum:** just as a strong curb would be used to "wear out" a horse, and if cruelly used, would fill its mouth with blood and foam. **fingitque premendo:** "and trains by restraining."

81. **ostia…domus…ingentia centum:** the *ostia* (cf. 43) now fly open spontaneously. The instant action is conveyed by the perfect tense (*patuere*). **domus:** genitive.

83. **o tandem…:** "O you who at last…" **defuncte:** vocative, from *defungor,* which governs the ablative case.

84. **terrae:** genitive after *graviora* (*sc. pericula*); parallels *pelagi* (83), both of which can also be construed as locative ("on the sea…on the land"). **Lavini:** the first syllable is short. Lavinium was Aeneas' first settlement in Italy. It lies on the coast of Italy, just south of Rome, at modern Pratica di Mare. This is the first time Aeneas hears this name; it is previously so named by Jupiter to Venus in 1.258-9 (*cernes urbem et promissa Lavini | moenia*) and 1.270; cf. 1.2; 4.236.

86. **sed non et venisse volent:** note the emphatic position of *non et,* emphasizing *venisse*: "they will wish they had *not even come.*" **bella, horrida bella:** the Sibyl now draws a parallel between the Trojan War and the coming war in Italy (which will be the subject of books 7-12, the so-called "Iliadic" half of the poem), only here the Trojans, not the Greeks, will be the invaders. There will be another Achilles (*alius…Achilles* 89), namely Turnus, king of the Rutulians: just as Achilles was the son of the sea-nymph Thetis, so Turnus was son of the goddess Venilia (90). Turnus' contest with Aeneas is central to the second half of the *Aeneid*. Aeneas, however, will also be partially modeled on Achilles in Books 7-12. The Sibyl's prophecy recalls the cyclic prophecy of that of *Ecl.* 4.34-6 *alter erit tum Tiphys et altera quae vehat Argo | delectos heroas; erunt etiam altera bella | atque iterum ad Troiam magnus mittetur Achilles.*

et Thybrim multo spumantem sanguine cerno.
non Simois tibi nec Xanthus nec Dorica castra
defuerint; alius Latio iam partus Achilles,
natus et ipse dea; nec Teucris addita Iuno   90
usquam aberit, cum tu supplex in rebus egenis
quas gentis Italum aut quas non oraveris urbes!
causa mali tanti coniunx iterum hospita Teucris
externique iterum thalami.
tu ne cede malis, sed contra audentior ito   95
qua tua te fortuna sinet. via prima salutis,
quod minime reris, Graia pandetur ab urbe."

87-8. Thybrim...Simois...Xanthus...Dorica castra: Vergil regularly uses the Greek spelling
for the river Tiber (here, in accusative case), with two exceptions (*Geo.* 1.499 and *Aen.*
7.715). The two rivers of Troy (*Simois, Xanthus*) and the Greek camps (*Dorica castra*) are
named metaphorically* in anticipation of the similar struggle that will take place in Italy
beside the local rivers Tiber and Numicus; the camps of Turnus and his followers will be
analogous to the Greek camps at Troy. **cerno:** i.e. in prophetic vision; cf. our word "seer."

89. **defuerint:** future perfect; there will be no lack of disasters similar to those which
characterized the fighting at Troy. **alius...Achilles:** see 86 n. **Latio:** ablative.

90. **Teucris addita Iuno:** "Juno added (i.e. to harass) the Trojans"; *addita* indicates that Juno
and her anger cannot be gotten rid of. For Juno's wrath, cf. 1.4 *saevae memorem Iunonis ob
iram;* 1.34-222; 7.286-340.

92. **quas gentis...quas...urbes!:** note the dramatic change to an exclamation.

93. **coniunx iterum hospita:** Helen, wife of Menelaus, originally welcomed Paris as a guest.
Here Lavinia, daughter of king Latinus, will be betrothed to Aeneas, and their engagement
will untimately lead to a war in Italy.

94. This is one of about 58 half-lines in the *Aeneid* that were not complete when Vergil died.
The only other half-line in book 6 is 835.

95. **ito:** second person singular, future imperative of *ire*; it conveys gravity.

96. **qua:** "by whatever path." Manuscript authority supports *quam* for *qua*: "yield not to
calamity, but face it more boldly *than* your Fortune will allow." Such an expression,
however, represents a defiance of fate, which, though perhaps rhetorically effective, is not
consistent with Aeneas' piety. For Vergil, even the gods can only achieve their goal *si qua
fata sinant* (1.18 and 6.146-7): within the limits of fate, free will and action have scope, but
they cannot surpass those limits.

97. **Graia...ab urbe:** i.e. Pallanteum, the city ruled by Evander, a Greek immigrant, who will
be allied with Aeneas in Books 8-12.

Talibus ex adyto dictis Cumaea Sibylla
horrendas canit ambages antroque remugit,
obscuris vera involvens: ea frena furenti   100
concutit et stimulos sub pectore vertit Apollo.
ut primum cessit furor et rabida ora quierunt,
incipit Aeneas heros: "non ulla laborum,
o virgo, nova mi facies inopinave surgit;
omnia praecepi atque animo mecum ante peregi.   105
unum oro: quando hic inferni ianua regis
dicitur et tenebrosa palus Acheronte refuso,

98—123. Aeneas accepts the struggle that awaits him, asking only that he first be allowed to pass through the entrance to the underworld at Avernus and visit his father there.

98. **Talibus...dictis:** ablative absolute, "with such words" (i.e. such things having been said). **adyto:** the *adytum* (lit. "not to be entered") is the inmost part of the cave, which serves as the sanctuary of a temple. Here it becomes clear that the Sibyl has been prophesying from within her sanctuary (*ex adyto*) while Aeneas stands at the entrance.

99-100. **horrendas canit ambages...obscuris vera involvens:** her prophecies are as obscure (*ambages*) and frightening (*horrendas*, causing one to shudder) as the Labyrinth itself (cf. 27-9), whose design causes one to wander in confusion. **remugit:** the echo from the cave suggests the lowing sound of cattle (*mugire*).

100-1. **ea frena...concutit et stimulos...vertit:** the horse-training metaphor* of 77-80 continues, as Apollo, against whose mastery the priestess was earlier represented as struggling violently, has gradually tamed her as one might gain control of an unruly steed, striking it with reins and goading it with spurs (*stimulos*). He now has absolute possession of her and keeps her wild excitement alive until she has finished delivering the oracle. **furenti:** present participle referring to the Sibyl raving under the influence of the god. Note the alliteration* of *frena furenti.*

102. **ut primum:** temporal clauses with *ut* govern the indicative (AG §543), "as soon as." **quiērunt:** = *quiēvērunt* by syncope*. The Sibyl's fury (*furor*) and her expression of that fury (*rabida ora*) finally abate.

103-4. **incipit:** the placement of the verb at the beginning of the sentence dramatically changes the subject to Aeneas. **Aeneas heros:** occurs only here; elsewhere he is called *Troius heros* (*heros* is a Greek nominative); cf. 192 *maximus heros,* 451 *Troius heros;* 8.18 *Laomedontius heros.* **laborum:** genitive governed by *non ulla...nova facies inopinave.* **virgo:** perhaps an allusion to the tale of the relationship between Apollo and the Sibyl. To win her favor, he promised to grant her wish for a long life, but she failed to also ask to stay young. She refused his advances, and so as she aged, she grew ever smaller, and finally looked like a cicada or a tiny bird. When children asked her "Sibyl, what do you want?" she replied, "I want to die." Cf. Petronius, *Satyricon* 48. **mi:** = *mihi,* dative of reference.

106-7. **quando...dicitur:** supply *esse.* **tenebrosa palus Acheronte refuso:** "the gloomy marsh where Acheron wells up." Lake Avernus is described as being an outlet (cf. 1.126 *stagna refusa*) for the subterranean waters of Acheron, one of the rivers of hell. Cf. 239.

ire ad conspectum cari genitoris et ora
contingat; doceas iter et sacra ostia pandas.
illum ego per flammas et mille sequentia tela   110
eripui his umeris medioque ex hoste recepi;
ille meum comitatus iter maria omnia mecum
atque omnis pelagique minas caelique ferebat,
invalidus, viris ultra sortemque senectae.
quin, ut te supplex peterem et tua limina adirem,   115
idem orans mandata dabat. natique patrisque,

108-9. **ire...contingat:** "(I ask that/let) it be my (happy) fortune to go...." *Contingit* is normally used of happy (as opposed to unhappy, *accidit*) occurrences. **ora:** more specific than *conspectum*. Aeneas wants not only to see his father (*cari genitoris*), but to meet with him face to face. **contingat...doceas...pandas:** subjunctives in indirect commands, governed by *oro* (106) (cf. AG §588).

110-14. Compare 2.707-8 and 711-14, where Aeneas, fleeing Troy, carries his father on his shoulders while escaping the flames and weapons (*mille...tela*) of the Greeks. Aeneas here summarizes the fall of Troy and his rescue of his father. Anchises accompanies Aeneas throughout *Aen.* 3 but dies at the end of the book. The depiction of Aeneas carrying his father out of Troy appears on many ancient works of art, including a denarius minted by Julius Caesar in 49 BCE. The seventeenth century artist Gian Lorenzo Bernini (1598-1680) closely modelled his famous statue of this event on these early depictions. Note Aeneas' emphasis on his own role in the escape from Troy (*meum...mecum*) and the rhetorical effect of the repetitions *omnia...omnis* and *-que...-que*, all culminating in the emphatic enjambment* of *invalidus* (114) to describe Anchises, who had been crippled by a thunderbolt. Elsewhere Anchises does not appear to be so weak (cf. 2.649).

110-12. **illum ego...ille meum:** the inversion reflects the link between father and son. The words are repeated at the beginning of consecutive sentences (anaphora*) but in different inflected forms (polyptoton*). **meum...iter:** object of *comitatus*, which describes *ille* (i.e. Anchises).

114. **ultra:** the preposition *ultra* governs the accusatives *viris* and *sortem*. **sortem...senectae:** the proper "lot of old age" is repose. Note the oxymoronic* juxtaposition of *invalidus* and *viris*.

115-16. **quin...idem...mandata dabat:** again Aeneas' actions are balanced by those of his father (*idem*), who in 5.731-9 instructed Aeneas to make these very requests. The Sibyl should thus take both father and son into consideration (*nati patrisque* 116). The adverb *quin* ("indeed") is used to add a point. **ut...adirem:** can be indirect command after *orans* or in apposition to *mandata*. **idem:** nominative singular; Anchises.

alma, precor, miserere (potes namque omnia, nec te
nequiquam lucis Hecate praefecit Avernis),
si potuit manis accersere coniugis Orpheus
Threicia fretus cithara fidibusque canoris,   120
si fratrem Pollux alterna morte redemit
itque reditque viam totiens. quid Thesea, magnum
quid memorem Alciden? et mi genus ab Iove summo."

117-18. **miserere:** imperative, second singular (deponent), governing the genitives *gnatique patrisque* (116). **potes namque omnia:** "for you have all power"; *omnia* is a cognate accusative (AG §390). **nec...nequiquam:** the double negative (litotes*) makes a strong positive statement. **lucis...Avernis:** Avernus here is an adjective, i.e. the woods around Avernus; cf. 106-7 n. and 4.552. **Hecate:** cf. 13 n.

119-23. To bolster his case, Aeneas offers two pairs of examples of heroes who traveled to the underworld. The first pair, Orpheus and Pollux, did so to perform acts of *pietas*; they support Aeneas' pious appeal *natique patrisque...miserere* (116-17). The second pair, Theseus and Hercules, were children of gods, as is Aeneas (*mi genus ab Iove summo* 123).

119-20. **si potuit...:** *si* with the indicative in an appeal implies no doubt of the fact, but rather irrefutable truth. The Thracian bard *Orpheus*, through the charm of his music (*fretus cithara fidibusque canoris* 120), was allowed to descend into the underworld to bring back his wife Eurydice (*coniugis* 119). Cf. notes on 645, 703-23. **Threicia... cithara:** the Thracians were a warlike people, and the Thracian women killed Orpheus in response to his devotion to the dead Eurydice. Vergil's choice of adjective here highlights a contradiction between Orpheus' music and the violent reputation of his people. **fretus:** "trusting in," "relying on," governs the ablatives *Threicia cithara* and *fidibus canoris*. **fidibus:** ablative plural of *fides*, which means "lyre string" but here (as elsewhere) signifies the entire instrument.

121-2. Pollux and Castor were sons of Leda, but Pollux was also the son of Jupiter, and therefore immortal. When Castor died, Pollux received permission to share his immortality with his brother, so that one day they were both dead and the next both were in the heavens. Thus "by alternate death" (*alterna morte*) Pollux redeemed his brother. **itque reditque viam:** *viam* is cognate accusative (cf. 50 n.), "both goes and returns (this) way."

122-3. **quid Thesea, magnum | quid memorem Alciden?:** *Thesea* and *Alciden* are Greek accusative forms; *Alcides* is a patronymic* describing Hercules, who was the (maternal) grandson of Alceus. For the actions of Theseus and Hercules in the underworld, see notes on 392 and 393. **Thesea, magnum:** though *magnum* is naturally taken with *Theseus*, some editors put a comma after *Thesea*, thereby linking *magnum* with *Alciden*. The debate goes back to Servius, who felt that *magnum* more appropriately described Hercules because Theseus behaved badly in the underworld and had to be rescued by Hercules. **memorem:** deliberative subjunctive (AG §443-4) in a rhetorical question* ("Why should I mention...?"). **mi genus ab Iove summo:** Aeneas was grandson of Jupiter through his mother, Venus. **mi:** = *mihi*; dative of possession (AG §373), supply *est*.

Talibus orabat dictis arasque tenebat,
cum sic orsa loqui vates: "sate sanguine divum,   125
Tros Anchisiade, facilis descensus Averno:
noctes atque dies patet atri ianua Ditis;
sed revocare gradum superasque evadere ad auras,
hoc opus, hic labor est. pauci, quos aequus amavit
Iuppiter aut ardens evexit ad aethera virtus,   130
dis geniti potuere. tenent media omnia silvae,

124-55. *The Sibyl tells him to seek the golden bough. Only the golden bough can provide the bearer a secure passage through the underworld. First, however, he must bury one of his companions, Misenus, who has just died, and then locate the mysterious golden bough. On the golden bough, cf. R.A. Brooks (1953), Segal (1965 and 1966), West (1987), Clarke (1992), Parvulescu (2005).*

124. **aras...tenebat:** a sign of supplication; cf. Iarbas praying to Jupiter, 4.219. The imperfect tense signifies action that was on-going when (*cum* 125) the Sibyl replied.

125. **sate:** vocative of perfect passive participle of *sero*, governing the ablative of origin (*sanguine*). **divum:** = *divorum*.

126-9: **facilis descensus...sed revocare gradum...hoc opus est, hic labor est**: an ironic statement, one that is often cited.

126. **Anchisiade:** "son of Anchises," patronymic*, cf. 122-3 n. The Greek vocative ending –*e* is long. **descensus**: this noun is rare in classical Latin, occurring in poetry only here, in Propertius 4.8.5, and in Manilius 5.5; cf. Statius, *Thebaid* 11.463 *descensuram Erebo*. **Averno:** "to Avernus" (dative after *descensus*) is an unusual construction. Servius explains: *id est ad Avernum*. Wellesley (1964) and Williams, however, interpret *Averno* as ablative, "by way of Avernus."

127. **noctes atque dies:** accusative showing duration of time—the doors never close. **atri ianua Ditis:** *Dis*, god of the underworld, is appropriately black. His name means "Wealthy" (cf. *dives*), since the seed that grows from under the soil is the source of agricultural wealth.

128-9. **revocare...evadere:** are substantive infinitives (AG §452) used as the subjects of the sentence. **hoc opus, hic labor:** polyptoton* (*hoc...hic*); the difference between the two nouns, which have no connective (asyndeton*), is probably the actual achievement (*opus*) as opposed to the toil itself (*labor*). **pauci:** emphatic by position; it is the subject of *potuere* (131). **aequus:** "level" should mean "impartial," as does "equal" in English, but from its constant opposition to *iniquus* ("hostile") it acquires the meaning of "favorable," "partial to."

130. **ardens...aethera:** very few mortals become gods; the most common example was Hercules (cf. Horace, *Odes* 3.3.9). Note the juxtaposition of these two words; the fiery spirit rises to that "aether" or elemental fire to which it is related. Cf. 761-2 *primus ad auras | aetherias Italo commixtus sanguine surget | Silvius...*

131. **dis geniti:** in apposition to *pauci* (129); *dis* is ablative of origin. **potuere:** emphatic by position; supply *evehi*. It repeats the *potuit* (119) of Aeneas' appeal, but to convey a warning. **media omnia:** "all the intervening space" between here and the underworld. **silvae:** the subject of *tenent*.

Cocytusque sinu labens circumvenit atro.
quod si tantus amor menti, si tanta cupido est
bis Stygios innare lacus, bis nigra videre
Tartara, et insano iuvat indulgere labori,   135
accipe quae peragenda prius. latet arbore opaca
aureus et foliis et lento vimine ramus,
Iunoni infernae dictus sacer; hunc tegit omnis
lucus et obscuris claudunt convallibus umbrae.

---

132. **Cocytus**: one of the rivers of the underworld. Others include the Styx, Lethe, Acheron, and Phlegethon, the river of Tartarus (551). The river Lethe (Greek "forgetfulness") suggests Orphic/Pythagorean influences (see 705, 749; cf. notes on 703-23 and 724-51). The rivers in Vergil's underworld are not mapped out very specifically; the Styx is the main waterway (cf. 295), and the other streams are named to add color. It should be noted that elsewhere (e.g. 323, 369, 414) Vergil calls the Styx a marsh, *palus*.

133-4. **quod si tantus amor**: supply *est*; cf. 2.10. *Quod si* is adversative, "but if"; *menti* is dative of possession. Note the rhetorical effect of the repetition of *si tantus...si tanta* without a connective here and in the next line. **bis...bis**: *bis* ("twice") is emphatic, since mortals normally descend to the underworld only once—at death. For the repetition (anaphora*) of *bis* with asyndeton*, cf. 32-3 n. **innare**: used with regard to flying at 16 (see n.).

135. **Tartara**: note the emphatic effect of the delayed naming of the object of the previous lines. **iuvat**: is impersonal, with *indulgere* as its complement, governing the dative *insano... labori*.

136. **quae peragenda**: supply *sunt* (thus forming a relative clause) or *sint* (an indirect question).

137. **aureus...ramus**: the phrase frames the line, "golden in both leaves and pliant stem (is) the bough (that lies hidden on the obscure tree)." Phrases describing the golden bough are placed in emphatic arrangements: here, 141 *auricomos...fetus*, 143-4 *alter | aureus*. **foliis... lento vimine**: ablatives of respect. Vergil gives the bough mystical qualities: it is made of gold; it quickly grows back when plucked; only those summoned by Fate may pluck it; and it has been established as the special offering owed to Proserpina. In 190-2 a special sign from the gods reveals its location, and it is instantly recognized and respected by Charon (406-10).

138-9. **Iunoni infernae**: = Proserpina (cf. 703-23 n.), who, with her husband, is as powerful in the underworld as Juno and her husband are in the world above, is often referred to by these terms. **tegit omnis | lucus...obscuris claudunt**: note the emphasis on the hidden nature of the bough.

sed non ante datur telluris operta subire   140
auricomos quam qui decerpserit arbore fetus.
hoc sibi pulchra suum ferri Proserpina munus
instituit. primo avulso non deficit alter
aureus, et simili frondescit virga metallo.
ergo alte vestiga oculis et rite repertum   145
carpe manu; namque ipse volens facilisque sequetur,
si te fata vocant; aliter non viribus ullis
vincere nec duro poteris convellere ferro.

140-1. **non ante datur...subire...quam qui decerpserit:** "it is not permitted to enter...except for the man who has plucked...." **ante...quam:** tmesis*, = *non datur subire...antequam....* **telluris operta:** *telluris* is partitive genitive. **auricomos...fetus:** "the golden-haired growth," which encloses the line, is a metaphor for "the golden branch"; *auricomos* is a compound epithet created by Vergil (neologism*); the metaphor of *coma* as applied to leaves is found as early as Homer. Cf. Catullus 4.11 *comata silva* or Lucretius 6.152 *lauricomos montis.* **qui:** the manuscripts vary; M reads *qui,* while P and R (accepted by Austin and Mynors) read *quis,* which is interpreted as <*ali*>*quis*: "before someone has plucked." For *qui,* cf. *Geo.* 1.201 *non aliter quam qui...subigit,* "just as when someone propels..."

142. **hoc...ferri:** indirect statement; Proserpina established that this be brought as her gift (i.e. for her). **sibi pulchra suum...Proserpina munus:** notice the emphatic interweaving of *pulchra...Proserpina* and *sibi...suum...munus.* Proserpina, queen of the underworld, claims it "for herself as her own special offering," and she does so by right of beauty. **suum munus:** in apposition to *hoc.* The enjambment* of *instituit* in 143 is emphatic.

143. **primo avulso:** supply *ramo*; ablative absolute.

144. **aureus:** note the emphatic enjambment* of *aureus* in this line; cf. also *aureus* in 136, and *auricomos* in 141. **frondescit...metallo:** "puts forth leaves of a similar metal." Vergil has similarly conjoined metal (which is not considered a living thing) with a growing plant in his *auricomos* (141), a striking oxymoron, not used before Vergil's time. **metallo:** ablative of material (AG §403).

145. **alte vestiga:** *altus* indicates something that is not at ground level. *Vestigo* (here imperative) usually refers to tracking footprints (*vestigia*) on the ground; *alte* is needed here to make its meaning clear. Some translate *alte* as "deeply," but here it refers to the branch's placement in a tree, "high up." **rite:** with *carpe manu. Rite* ("duly") is a religious word and suggests that there were certain forms and observances that Aeneas must respect. He is "duly" to pluck the bough with his hand and to use no other means, and this detail is added in explanation of the rule in 146-7: *ipse volens...sequetur...si te fata vocant.*

146-8. **manu:** "by hand." **ipse:** the bough itself will follow willingly, provided Aeneas' success is fated.

praeterea iacet exanimum tibi corpus amici
(heu nescis) totamque incestat funere classem,   150
dum consulta petis nostroque in limine pendes.
sedibus hunc refer ante suis et conde sepulcro.
duc nigras pecudes; ea prima piacula sunto.
sic demum lucos Stygis et regna invia vivis
aspicies." dixit, pressoque obmutuit ore.   155

---

149. **praeterea:** "in addition." The Sibyl now turns to the second of the preliminary tasks she mentioned at 136. **exanimum...corpus amici:** the dead body of a companion must be properly buried before Aeneas can approach the dwellings of the dead. **tibi:** ethical dative, showing the speaker's concern for the person affected and interested. Translate here as genitive: "of your friend."

150. **(heu nescis):** until now, Aeneas was unaware of the recent death of his friend and fellow Trojan, the trumpeter Misenus. An account of his death is given at 162-72. **funere:** here = "with his corpse."

151. **consulta:** a rare word except in the phrase *senatus consultum*, where it means "decree." Here, it means "consultation." **in limine:** at the entrance to the Sibyl's cave. **pendes:** here combines the idea of indecision with loitering.

152. **sedibus...refer...suis:** the dead man has a "home" or "resting-place" where he must be placed.

153. **nigras pecudes:** "black victims" were always offered to the gods of the underworld; here the Sibyl has switched to a new instruction, not related to Misenus' burial rites. **sunto:** future imperative (third person plural) form of *esse*, often used in legal formulae or in divine commands, here to reflect the authority of the Sibyl's instructions. "Let these be..." (AG §449).

154. **sic demum:** "in this way only." Cf. 330, 573 *tum demum*; 637 *his demum exactis*, "this being accomplished, and not before," "only when this was done." *Demum* is generally only used with pronouns (*is demum*, "he only") or with adverbs. **vivis:** dative after the adjective *invia* ("inaccessible").

155. **pressoque obmutuit ore:** *presso ore* and *obmutuit* are complementary. *Obmutesco* means "to become dumb" (cf. 4.279)

Aeneas maesto defixus lumina vultu
ingreditur linquens antrum, caecosque volutat
eventus animo secum. cui fidus Achates
it comes et paribus curis vestigia figit.
multa inter sese vario sermone serebant,   160

156-82. They find the drowned corpse of Misenus and prepare for his funeral.

The Misenus episode recalls Odysseus' encounter with the shade of Elpenor, who had
fallen off Circe's roof unnoticed and descended to Hades (Homer, *Odyssey* 10.552-60). But
whereas Elpenor's death was an accident anticipating Odysseus' descent to the underworld,
Misenus' boldness was responsible for his demise. Aeneas and his comrades lament
Misenus' death and prepare for his burial, but before the funeral rites are conducted (212-
35), Aeneas finds the golden bough (183-211). The death of Misenus reminds Aeneas of
his mortality and will resonate with Aeneas' encounter with the shade of his helmsman
Palinurus (337-83) who, like Misenus, is unburied.

156. **maesto defixus lumina vultu:** the phrase describes mingled mourning and meditation.
lumina: accusative of specification (AG §397b), limiting *defixus*, "fixed, with respect to
his eyes." The passive participle used this way is sometimes compared to the Greek middle
voice (which does not exist in Latin) with *lumina* (here) as a direct object, or explained as a
passive verb with a retained accusative. Cf. 184, 281, 470; 1.228, 481, 561, 579, 658, 713,
etc.

157-8. **caecos...eventus:** "the mysterious outcomes." He does not fully understand what he
has been told.

159. A beautiful line expressing the slow, melancholy pacing. Notice *figit*, "he plants," instead
of *ponit*, "places."

160-3. The structure is *multa...serebant...atque...vident*, "much were they debating...and
suddenly they see."

160. **sermone serebant:** an alliterative phrase that refers to the derivation (mentioned
by Varro, *Lingua Latina* 6.7.8 *sermo est a serie*) of *sermo* from *serere*, "to join together."
"Conversation" is the "linking" together of short remarks into one chain.

quem socium exanimum vates, quod corpus humandum
diceret. atque illi Misenum in litore sicco,
ut venere, vident indigna morte peremptum,
Misenum Aeoliden, quo non praestantior alter
aere ciere viros Martemque accendere cantu.   165
Hectoris hic magni fuerat comes, Hectora circum
et lituo pugnas insignis obibat et hasta.
postquam illum vita victor spoliavit Achilles,
Dardanio Aeneae sese fortissimus heros
addiderat socium, non inferiora secutus.   170
sed tum, forte cava dum personat aequora concha,
demens, et cantu vocat in certamina divos,

161-2. quem...quod corpus humandum \<sc. esse\> diceret: indirect question, (discussing) "what lifeless comrade...what body...the prophetess meant...."

162-4. Misenum...Misenum (164): the repetition, (cf. 495 *ora | ora*), a rhetorical device known as epanalepsis*, is used for emotional effect. **in litore sicco:** although Vergil's account gives the impression that Misenus lies on the beach below the Sibyl's cave, the promontory named after him (Monte Miseno, see 234-5 n.), where he was said to have been buried, actually lies some 5 miles to the south-southeast. Lake Avernus lies between Cumae and Monte Miseno. In the forests surrounding Lake Avernus grows the tree with the golden bough. **venere:** = *venerunt* (syncope*; third person singular perfect). **Aeoliden:** Misenus was probably son of Aeolus, god of the winds (1.50-64) rather than son of a Trojan Aeolus (cf. 12.542).

165. ciere...accendere: epexegetic* (explanatory) infinitives after *praestantior* (164), "more outstanding at summoning...and at inflaming" (cf. 49 n.). The line is chiastic*. Note the choppy assonance of this description of a bugle call.

166-7. Hectoris hic..., Hectora circum | et lituo...et hasta: note the alliteration of *h*. **Hectora:** Greek accusative.

168. illum: Hector; the alliterative *vita victor spoliavit Achilles* concludes the line with Hector's killer. **vita:** ablative of separation after *spoliavit*.

169. heros: Greek nominative singular, referring to Misenus.

170. non inferiora secutus: "not following inferior (fortunes)," i.e. Aeneas, whom Misenus then followed, was equal to Hector.

171. sed tum: resuming the narrative after the descriptive parenthesis; "but then," i.e. on the occasion when he met his death. **dum personat:** "while he made the sea re-echo." *Dum* takes the present even when referring to past time; cf. 338. **concha:** Misenus had mockingly challenged the sea-god Triton on his own instrument.

172. demens: the adjective, when placed emphatically at the beginning of the line, has almost the force of an interjection—"Madman!" **vocat in certamina divos:** similarly, Thamyris "challenged" the Muses and lost his sight, and Marsyas challenged Apollo with the flute and was flayed alive.

aemulus exceptum Triton, si credere dignum est,
inter saxa virum spumosa immerserat unda.
ergo omnes magno circum clamore fremebant, 175
praecipue pius Aeneas. tum iussa Sibyllae,
haud mora, festinant flentes aramque sepulcro
congerere arboribus caeloque educere certant.
itur in antiquam silvam, stabula alta ferarum;
procumbunt piceae, sonat icta securibus ilex 180
fraxineaeque trabes cuneis et fissile robur
scinditur, advolvunt ingentis montibus ornos.

---

173. **exceptum:** "caught." The word is especially used of "lying in wait for" and so "catching"; it is frequently used of hunters. **si credere dignum est:** in *Geo.* 3.391, in the tale of Pan and Luna, Vergil uses the phrase to indicate that the tale is a myth, not necessarily a true story—but the fact that Misenus drowned, as opposed to the circumstances associated with his death, is not in doubt.

174. **virum:** = *eum*, i.e. Misenus.

175. **omnes...fremebant:** the low, rumbling sound of Misenus' sorrowing companions suggests the sound of the sea, in which he drowned.

176-7. **iussa...festinant:** "quickly perform the commands"; *festino* is here used transitively in the secondary sense of "do hurriedly." **aramque sepulchro:** "the funeral altar." The tomb is shaped like an altar; literally, they build "an altar to serve as a tomb." Vergil's early commentators were perplexed by the phrase and changed it to *sepulchri*, found in M and R, and which Austin retains, while others, such as Mynors, retain *sepulchro*, found in P.

178. **caelo:** dative, "toward the sky."

179-82. Vergil's description of the felling of forest-trees has been compared with Ennius, *Annales* fr. 181-5 in Warmington, fr. 175-9 in Skutsch, quoted by Macrobius, *Saturnalia* 6.2.27. Both passages echo Homer's description (*Iliad* 23.114-22.) of the gathering of wood for Patroclus' funeral. This passage is echoed in *Aen.*11.135-8, and is itself recalled by Lucan 3.440-5, Statius, *Thebaid* 6.90-107, and Silius Italicus 10.527-34. For analysis of the passage, see Austin *ad loc.* and G. Williams (1968) 263.

179. **itur:** impersonal passive; "there is a going" = "they go."

181. **fraxineae:** adjectival form of *fraxinus*, an ash tree, used for spears and javelins.

182. **montibus:** ablative, "from the mountains." **ornos:** mountain-ash trees, which usually occur in Vergil with reference to their coming down from the mountains. In *Geo.* 2.111, they are said to be barren (*steriles saxosis montibus orni*); in *Ecl.* 6.71 and *Aen.* 4.491, their descent from the mountains is named as *adynata*, impossibilities, and in *Aen.* 2.626, the fall of Troy is compared to the fall of an aged mountain-ash. Cf. also *Aen.* 10.766.

Nec non Aeneas opera inter talia primus
hortatur socios paribusque accingitur armis.
atque haec ipse suo tristi cum corde volutat   185
aspectans silvam immensam, et sic forte precatur:
"si nunc se nobis ille aureus arbore ramus
ostendat nemore in tanto! quando omnia vere
heu nimium de te vates, Misene, locuta est."
vix ea fatus erat geminae cum forte columbae   190
ipsa sub ora viri caelo venere volantes,
et viridi sedere solo. tum maximus heros
maternas agnoscit avis laetusque precatur:
"este duces, o, si qua via est, cursumque per auras
derigite in lucos ubi pinguem dives opacat   195

183-211. While cutting wood for the funeral pyre, Aeneas is attracted by two doves, the sacred birds of Venus, which guide him to the golden bough.

183. **Nec non Aeneas...primus:** the double negative (litotes*) provides an emphatic transition, as Aeneas takes the lead (*primus*).

184. **hortatur:** he not only "encourages" them with words but by example, when he girds himself with weapons like theirs (*paribus...armis*). **accingitur:** "he girds himself." This usage mimics the Greek middle voice (cf. 156 n.).

185. **suo tristi cum corde volutat:** i.e. he does not convey his sadness to his men, but ponders in silence.

186. **sic forte precatur:** Aeneas prays and the two birds appear—which he interprets as a coincidence (*forte*). The manuscripts strongly support *forte*, "by chance." The Romanus (R) manuscript and some editors read *voce*, but *forte* recurs in 190. By repeating the word, two ordinary events become a remarkable coincidence occurring together, and hence Aeneas infers that the apparent coincidence is a divine phenomenon.

187. **si:** = *O si*, "Oh would that" or "if only that golden bough would show itself."

188-9. **vere | heu nimium...vates...locuta est:** observe the order, "truly—alas! too truly—did she speak."

190. **vix ea fatus erat...cum:** "he had scarcely spoken when..."; a formulaic phrase, signifying "and immediately."

191-2. **venere...sedere:** third person plural syncopated forms (cf. 163 *venere*). **solo:** ablative of place where, "on the ground," agreeing with *viridi*.

193. **maternas...:** "recognizes his mother's birds"; doves were sacred to Venus. **laetusque precatur:** note here the dramatic change of Aeneas' mood, from *tristi cum corde volutat* (185).

194. **este:** present imperative plural of *sum*.

195. **pinguem dives:** artistic juxtaposition, the "richness" of the produce suggests the "wealth" or "fatness" of the soil.

ramus humum. tuque, o, dubiis ne defice rebus,
diva parens." sic effatus vestigia pressit
observans quae signa ferant, quo tendere pergant.
pascentes illae tantum prodire volando
quantum acie possent oculi servare sequentum.   200
inde ubi venere ad fauces grave olentis Averni,
tollunt se celeres liquidumque per aëra lapsae
sedibus optatis geminae super arbore sidunt,
discolor unde auri per ramos aura refulsit.

---

196. **dubiis...rebus:** "fail not my precarious fortunes."

197. **vestigia pressit:** he stops so as not to startle the birds—or more likely, to await their instructions.

198. **tendere:** can mean not only to stretch but also to aim (e.g. a weapon or a glance). Here the latter meaning is used in an intransitive sense: "aim for" or "head toward." Cf. 1.204-5 *per tot discrimina rerum | tendimus in Latium.*

199-200. **prodire:** historic infinitive. (Cf. 256 *mugire*, 491 *trepidare*, and 557 *exaudiri.*) "They kept advancing in flight (*volando*)." **acie:** here "sight," "view." **possent:** the subjunctive (expressing purpose) suggests that this is the intent of the birds, namely, to stay within Aeneas' sight. **sequentum:** a generalizing plural ("of any who might follow").

201. **ubi venere ad fauces...Averni:** they have moved quickly to Lake Avernus from Misenum. The *fauces* may be the NNW passage from Lake Lucrinus to Lake Avernus, which is now a road beside a canal. Beside the canal is the volcanic Monte Nuovo, which did not exist in Vergil's time (it erupted in the sixteenth century CE). The mephitic or sulphuric fumes (*grave olentis)* that are said to rise from Lake Avernus would be volcanic in nature. Clark (1992, 1996) argues that Aeneas finds the bough upon a tree beside the underworld cave within the Avernus-crater, which he must leave to complete the burial. **grave:** cognate accusative. Cf. 50 n.

202. **tollunt se celeres:** "swiftly they fly up." The dactylic movement of this line contrasts with 201, capturing the upward and then downward movement (*lapsae*) of the birds. **liquidum:** describes the bright, clear quality of the air (*aera* is a Greek accusative).

203. **sedibus optatis:** ablative of place where, indicating the place Aeneas hoped they would reveal. **geminae:** cf. 190 (*geminae columbae*); some manuscripts, however, read *gemina*, which would describe *arbore* and mean "two-fold," since the foliage consists of both plant-life and metal.

204. **aura:** is several times used of the scent which is given off by anything (*Geo.* 4.417 *dulcis compositis spiravit crinibus aura*), but here it is here used of the "variegated (*discolor*) radiance" that glistens from the gold. The assonance of the phrase *auri...aura* heightens its strangeness. **refulsit** (*refulgeo*) is used of anything bright which stands out against a dark background.

quale solet silvis brumali frigore viscum   205
fronde virere nova, quod non sua seminat arbos,
et croceo fetu teretis circumdare truncos,
talis erat species auri frondentis opaca
ilice, sic leni crepitabat brattea vento.
corripit Aeneas extemplo avidusque refringit   210
cunctantem, et vatis portat sub tecta Sibyllae.

---

205. **quale...viscum:** the bough is here compared to mistletoe (*viscum*), whose fresh green leaves (*nova* 206) are contrasted with the bare leafless oak on which it grows. **brumali frigore:** the adjective comes from *bruma,* the winter solstice, the coldest day of the year; hence the phrase means "in the coldest part of winter."

206. **quod non sua seminat arbos:** other growth is produced from its own parent tree (*sua seminat arbos*), but with the mistletoe this is not so. Vergil probably refers to the belief that mistletoe is produced in some mysterious manner and not from seed at all. In fact it is a parasitic plant, the fruit of which is eaten by birds, and the seed is sown by their rubbing their beaks, with the seed adhering, on the bark of trees. In *Geo.* 2.82, he depicts a grafted tree as being amazed at "branches and fruit not its own" (*miraturque frondes et non sua poma*).

207. **croceo fetu…:** "and with its yellow growth embrace the shapely trunks." Page's explanation (cited also by Austin) is worth repeating: "The color of mistletoe is a yellowish green. When seen with the sun shining through it, the leaves are edged and veined with gold and the stem seems powdered with gold dust."

208-9. **opaca | ilice:** ablative "on the dark oak." The color of the gold is contrasted with that of the holm-oak, whose leaves are much darker than the common oak.

209. **sic leni crepitabat brattea vento:** "so the gold foil made a crackling sound in the gentle breeze."

210. **avidusque refringit:** emphasizing Aeneas' eagerness, first suggested by *corripit.*

211. **cunctantem:** "close-clinging"; the adjective is used in artistic opposition to *avidus,* but somewhat awkwardly when we remember the Sibyl's words in 147-8. Austin argues that the "delay" is a reflection of the nature of the clinging plant, not a contradiction of the Sibyl's words, but others have argued that the bough "delays" to show that Aeneas was not without blemish, as is evidenced by his behavior with Dido.

Nec minus interea Misenum in litore Teucri
flebant et cineri ingrato suprema ferebant.
principio pinguem taedis et robore secto
ingentem struxere pyram, cui frondibus atris 215
intexunt latera et feralis ante cupressos
constituunt, decorantque super fulgentibus armis.
pars calidos latices et aëna undantia flammis
expediunt, corpusque lavant frigentis et unguunt.
fit gemitus. tum membra toro defleta reponunt 220

212—35. Meanwhile, the Trojans perform funeral rites for Misenus.

Vergil gives a detailed description of the elaborate funeral rites for Misenus. These rites bear comparison with the funeral rites for Pallas in Book 11 (59 ff.), both of which are based on the funeral rites of Patroclus in the *Iliad* (23.163 ff.), but details from Roman rites have also been added, as Williams points out, such as the averted faces (224), the meal prepared for the rites (*dapes* 225), the funeral procession (*lustratio* 231), and the conclusion of the rite (*novissima verba* 231). These funeral rites establish the solemn mood necessary for 236 ff., where Aeneas will himself prepare to descend to the underworld.

212. **Nec minus interea:** a transitional formula—Aeneas now returns to the funeral of Misenus (cf. 177-8).

213. **flebant:** note the emphatic spondee followed by a pause (cf. *Ecl.* 5.21 *exstinctum nymphae crudeli funere Daphnim | flebant*), and also the heaviness of ...*-ebant*...*-ebant*, which frame the entire line. **suprema:** "last offerings."

214-15. **pinguem taedis et robore secto...pyram:** *robore* here is oak; *pinguem* governs the ablatives of respect *taedis*, "pine-trees" and *robore secto*. Pine-wood was regularly used for torches and firewood because of its resinous (and hence flammable) quality. For the construction, cf. 4.505 *ingenti taedis atque ilice secta*. **cui:** antecedent is *pyram*; dative of reference. Translsate closely with *latera*, "whose (or its) sides."

216-22. **intexunt (216)...constituunt (217)...expediunt (219)...coniciunt (222):** Austin points out that the ritual aspect of the service is emphasized by these words, each placed at the beginning of a line, with the heavy sounds accented by *unguunt* and *reponunt*, which end lines 219 and 220. Cf. Ennius, *Annales* fr. 157 in Warmington, fr. 147 in Skutsch "*Exin Tarquinium bona femina lavit et unxit.*"

216. **ante:** adverbial, "in front" (of the pyre). **cupressos:** always associated with death; cf. Horace, *Odes* 2.14.23 *invisas cupressos*; *Epodes* 5.18 *cupressos funebris*.

217. **super:** adverbial, "above."

218. **pars...pars (222):** "some...others," hence the plural verbs. (Cf. 491-2, 642-4). **aëna:** "bronze cauldrons."

219. **frigentis:** genitive, describing Misenus.

220. **toro:** the funeral bed; it would be placed on the *feretro* (222), the funeral bier, which would then be placed on the pyre. **defleta:** *deflere* is a technical word for "lamenting the dead"; cf. 11.59.

purpureasque super vestis, velamina nota,
coniciunt. pars ingenti subiere feretro,
triste ministerium, et subiectam more parentum
aversi tenuere facem. congesta cremantur
turea dona, dapes, fuso crateres olivo.   225
postquam conlapsi cineres et flamma quievit,
reliquias vino et bibulam lavere favillam,
ossaque lecta cado texit Corynaeus aëno.
idem ter socios pura circumtulit unda
spargens rore levi et ramo felicis olivae,   230
lustravitque viros dixitque novissima verba.

---

221. **super:** cf. 217 n. **nota:** apparently "purple robes" are spoken of as "well-known wrappings" of the dead, because they were commonly used at the burial of the great; cf. 11.72, where Aeneas wraps the corpse of Pallas in robes (*auroque ostroque rigentis*), and *Iliad* 24.796.

222-4. **pars...feretro:** "others (cf. 218 n.) shouldered the huge bier—a sad service." **triste ministerium:** a cognate accusative in apposition to the action of the previous line. **more parentum | aversi:** the point is, not that it was "the custom of their ancestors" to kindle the pyre, but to do so "with averted face." The face was also averted in performing magic rites.

225. Offerings to the *manes* of the dead man include *turea dona* (incense), *dapes* (a meal, perhaps some form of cake prepared specially for the ritual) and *fuso crateres olivo* (bowls of poured olive oil). **fuso crateres olivo:** the ablative phrase *fuso...olivo* describes the contents of the *crātēres* (a Greek nominative plural; the final *–es* is short).

226. **conlapsi:** supply *sunt*. The quiet dignity of the line closes with *quievit*. **cineres:** refers in general to the pyre.

227. **reliquias:** sums up the remains. **lavere:** i.e. *laverunt*. **favillam:** refers to the burning ashes of the body.

228. **ossa...lecta cado:** the remaining bones were gathered up in a funeral urn (*cado*).

229. **idem:** "same man" (i.e. Corynaeus). **socios pura circumtulit unda:** *circumferre* originally = "carry around," then came to mean "carry lustral water around," and then "purify." Servius says: *circumtulit, purgavit. Antiquum verbum est.*" Cf. Plautus, *Amphitruo* 2.2.153 *quin tu istanc iubes pro cerrita circumferri?* "Why don't you have her sprinkled with holy water as a madwoman?"

230. **rore...et ramo:** hendiadys*, "dew from a bough." **felicis olivae:** "fruitful olive." *Felix* signifies a good omen as well as fruitfulness.

231. **novissima verba:** "last words." This marks the formal end of the ritual. Servius says that the phrase refers to the word *ilicet*, with which the mourners were dismissed, but more likely it alludes to the last farewell to the dead. Cf. 11.7 *salve aeternum mihi, maxime Palla,* | *aeternumque vale*; or 4.650 *incubuitque toro dixitque novissima verba*, where Dido bids farewell to her own life.

at pius Aeneas ingenti mole sepulcrum
imponit suaque arma viro remumque tubamque
monte sub aërio, qui nunc Misenus ab illo
dicitur aeternumque tenet per saecula nomen.   235
   His actis propere exsequitur praecepta Sibyllae.
spelunca alta fuit vastoque immanis hiatu,
scrupea, tuta lacu nigro nemorumque tenebris,

---

232. **ingenti mole:** ablative of description with *sepulcrum*.

233. **imponit:** "places on top" (of the pyre). **suaque arma viro…:** "the hero's own equipment, an oar and a trumpet." The position of *arma* between the emphatic words *sua* and *viro* indicates that some special "arms" are intended by the word, and all ambiguity is at once removed by the addition of the words *remumque tubamque*, which are in apposition to and explain *arma*. Compare Elpenor's tomb in Homer, *Odyssey* 12.15.

234-5. **qui nunc Misenus ab illo | dicitur:** today known as "Misenum" or "Capo Miseno," it is a prominent landmark in the area. Similarly, the name "Palinuro" persists (cf. 381 n.). Capo Miseno is an isolated, flat-topped mass of rock forming the western cusp of the Gulf of Pozzuoli, 300 feet high and commanding a magnificent view of the Bay of Naples. The bulk of the Roman fleet was stationed here, as Pliny the Younger's letter (6.16) on the death of his uncle and the eruption of Vesuvius indicates. The practice of aetiological explanations of such place names is Hellenistic.

236—63. *Having completed the funeral rites for Misenus, Aeneas now prepares for his own descent to the underworld by sacrificing victims to the gods at the entrance to Avernus, as he had been instructed by the Sibyl to do. When the rites are complete, the Sibyl and Aeneas descend to the underworld.*

236. **praecepta:** Aeneas now turns to the final part of the "instructions" given by the Sibyl (153)—a sacrifice to the gods of the underworld.

237-8. **spelunca…scrupea:** it is a natural cave, and hence it is covered with sharp rocks (*scrupeus,* "composed of sharp rocks," from *scrupus*). No such cave has been identified beside Avernus, although a passageway, which was a man-made tunnel, survives at the site. The Sibyl's cave was thought to be located in this tunnel beside Lake Avernus until Amadeo Maiuri discovered, in 1932, the separate Cumaean cave beneath the temple of Apollo on the Cumaean acropolis (cf. Clark (1996)). **immanis hiatu:** note the broad, gaping *a*-sounds, here and in 493 *clamor frustratur hiantes,* and 576 *quinquaginta atris immanis hiatibus.*

quam super haud ullae poterant impune volantes
tendere iter pennis: talis sese halitus atris   240
faucibus effundens supera ad convexa ferebat:
[unde locum Grai dixerunt nomine Aornon.]
quattuor hic primum nigrantis terga iuvencos
constituit frontique invergit vina sacerdos,
et summas carpens media inter cornua saetas   245
ignibus imponit sacris, libamina prima,
voce vocans Hecaten caeloque Ereboque potentem.
supponunt alii cultros tepidumque cruorem

---

239. "Over which no birds (*volantes*) in safety could direct their way in flight." Vergil refers to the supposed derivation of Avernus from the Greek *aornos*, "birdless," as stated in 242, which most editions reject as a spurious explanatory note suggested by 239, since it is lacking in some manuscripts. Lucretius 6.740 gives the same account of birds not being able to fly across Lake Avernus, and also explains the fact as due to the sulfuric exhalations of the district (cf. 240-1). Austin *ad loc.* and Hardie (Appendix in Austin, pp. 279-86) attempt to rebut the entire notion, although it is clear that Vergil accepted this tradition. For the sulfuric emanations from Avernus, cf. 201. In the Middle Ages, the "Acherusian Swamp" was identified as what is now known as the nearby Lago Fusaro. Vergil seems to have blended Lake Avernus and the Acherusian Swamp.

240. **tendere iter pennis:** "go their way with wings," i.e. "fly"; cf. 1.656 *iter ad navis tendebat Achates.* **halitus:** "exhalation," cf. 239 n.

241. **supera…convexa:** the vault of heaven; cf. 4.451 *caeli convexa.*

242. The line is considered to be an interpolation incorporating the etymological explanation of Avernus (see 239 n.).

243. **nigrantis terga:** *terga* is accusative of respect, governed by the participial adjective.

244. **constituit:** "made (them) stand." **invergit vina:** *invergere,* "to pour upon." Servius says that this phrase was used when the libation was poured to the gods below. The *sacerdos* is the Sibyl.

245. **summas…saetas:** "topmost bristles." Cf. 4.698, where Dido is sacrificing white heifers, and Homer, *Odyssey* 3.445.

246. **libamina prima:** in apposition to *saetas* (245), "first offerings," from *libare,* to pour out a few drops of wine as an offering; it then comes to mean to offer a small portion of anything. The offering of a portion is a symbol of the dedication of the whole.

247. **voce vocans:** "calling aloud." Cf. 506; 3.68; 4.680. This religious phrase marks an *audible* (spoken aloud) invocation of a god. **Hecaten:** Greek accusative. Cf. 118; Hecate is Diana of the underworld (cf. 13 n. on *Trivia*). **caeloque Ereboque:** Hecate's two spheres of power.

succipiunt pateris. ipse atri velleris agnam
Aeneas matri Eumenidum magnaeque sorori   250
ense ferit, sterilemque tibi, Proserpina, vaccam.
tum Stygio regi nocturnas incohat aras
et solida imponit taurorum viscera flammis,
pingue super oleum fundens ardentibus extis.
ecce autem primi sub limina solis et ortus   255
sub pedibus mugire solum et iuga coepta moveri
silvarum, visaeque canes ululare per umbram
adventante dea. "procul, o procul este, profani,"
conclamat vates, "totoque absistite luco;
tuque invade viam vaginaque eripe ferrum: 260
nunc animis opus, Aenea, nunc pectore firmo."

---

249. **succipiunt:** "catch from below"; according to Servius an archaic form (*nam modo "suscipiunt" dicunt*). Archaic forms and words are commonly preserved in religious and legal formulae.

250. **matri Eumenidum:** Night. Cf. 7.331, where Allecto is called *virgo sata Nocte*; Aeschylus, *Eumenides* 416. **magnae...sorori:** Earth, sister of Night, contains the underworld.

251. **sterilem...vaccam:** cf. Homer, *Odyssey* 10.522, where Circe tells Odysseus to offer a barren heifer to the shades. Note the metrical effect of the apostrophe* to Proserpina (*tibi*).

252. **Stygio regi:** Pluto, ruler of the underworld, also known as Dis (from *dives*, cf. 127 n.). **nocturnas:** sacrifices to the gods below were offered at night; line 255 further indicates that this was taking place at night.

253. **solida...viscera:** "whole carcasses." This was by no means usual; the ordinary practice was to burn only inedible portions of the victim, the remainder belonging to the priests and being eaten or even sold.

254. **super:** prefix to *fundens*, separated by tmesis*. The final syllable of *super* is normally short, but is here lengthened by its position (at the beginning of a foot).

256. **mugire:** historical infinitive. **coepta moveri:** the passive of *coepi* is used with passive infinitives; see AG §205a.

257. **visae:** supply *sunt*. **canes:** the hounds of the underworld accompany Hecate.

258. **adventante dea:** ablative absolute, "with the arrival of the goddess." **procul, o procul este, profani...:** a religious formula. **este:** the imperative of *sum*. **profani:** the "uninitiated," a reference to Aeneas' companions. Aeneas, armed with the golden bough, will be the only mortal to enter the underworld.

260. **tuque:** emphatic pronoun marks Aeneas as an initiate, as opposed to the *profani*. **vaginaque eripe ferrum:** the Sibyl tells him to draw his sword, apparently so that he will feel protected, although when he later draws it against creatures in the underworld, she will prevent him from using it. Odysseus (*Odyssey* 11.48) used his sword, but Aeneas will not.

261. **opus:** sc. *est*, "there is need of" (with ablative).

tantum effata furens antro se immisit aperto;
ille ducem haud timidis vadentem passibus aequat.

---

262. **furens:** her frenzy returns as she flings herself into the cave. **antro...aperto:** now at last the way to the underworld is open. **se immisit:** underscores her swift movement.

263: **haud timidis...aequat:** the litotes* underscores Aeneas' boldness as he closely accompanies the Sibyl.

Di, quibus imperium est animarum, umbraeque silentes

264-678: The Underworld

Aeneas now begins his actual journey through the underworld. They pass through the darkness, encountering countless monsters and varied shapes of human misery as they approach the river Styx, beside which they meet numerous figures trying to gain passage. Among them is Palinurus, Aeneas' helmsman who died at the end of Book 5. Once they persuade the boatman Charon to convey them across the river Styx, they encounter Cerberus, the horrific dog of Hades, and then observe the various regions of the underworld among which the shades are distributed. There is Tartarus, where guilty shades are punished (548-627), Elysium, for the shades of the blessed (637-78), and a less clearly defined place, where shades are in a kind of limbo (426-547 n.), experiencing neither punishment nor a happy existence. Along the way Aeneas will meet important figures from his past, to some degree in reverse chronological order, beginning with his helmsman Palinurus (337-83) who died at the end of book 5, then Dido (450-76) who committed suicide at the end of book 4, and Deiphobus (494-547) who was killed during the fall of Troy, the subject of book 2. These encounters will force Aeneas to come to a fuller understanding of earlier events, and also to see that he must leave that past behind and turn his attention to the future (e.g. 535-9).

The topography of Vergil's underworld displays much originality. (In *Odyssey* 11, the underworld is not fully described.) Vergil provides many details, although the physical arrangement remains somewhat vague, apart from the location of the river Styx and the lower level of Tartarus. Vergil probably made use of depictions of the underworld from other works as well, such as those mentioned by Aristophanes in the *Frogs*, but that are now lost. We also know of a detailed painting of the underworld by the fifth-century BCE artist Polygnotus, which would have been in existence in Vergil's time; although it has not survived, it is described in great detail in Pausanias' *Description of Greece* (4.28), written in about 150 CE, long after Vergil. This painting may have influenced some of the details of Vergil's depiction of figures in the underworld, supplying details not found in Homer. Later poets, particularly the great Italian poet Dante Alighieri (1265-1321), relied heavily on Vergil's account of the underworld. In his *Inferno*, Dante refines the geographical layout of *Aeneid*'s underworld to contain a sequence of descending circles, and has Vergil act as Dante's guide, just as the Sibyl does for Aeneas in this book.

For discussion of the different regions of the underworld, and their literary and philosophical background, see Butler (1920) 19-36, Norden (1957) *ad loc.*, Norwood (1954), Otis (1964), Solmsen (1972), Austin (1977) 154, Feeney (1986), Horsfall (1995), and Braund (1997). For the journey through the underwold, see R.D. Williams (1964) 193-9, Johnson (1976) 82-4, 88-92.

264—7. Vergil prays to the powers of darkness for permission to attempt so profound a theme.

264. **quibus:** dative of possessor. **silentes:** the dead, as in 432 (*silentum*). Not only is there a reference to the silence of the grave, but the ghosts are also described as being actually voiceless or possessing only a thin, almost inaudible voice (492). Throughout the underworld everything loses the substance and reality of the upper world, and is *immanis,* "without measure" or "lacking proportion."

et Chaos et Phlegethon, loca nocte tacentia late,   265
sit mihi fas audita loqui, sit numine vestro
pandere res alta terra et caligine mersas.
    Ibant obscuri sola sub nocte per umbram
perque domos Ditis vacuas et inania regna:
quale per incertam lunam sub luce maligna   270
est iter in silvis, ubi caelum condidit umbra
Iuppiter, et rebus nox abstulit atra colorem.
vestibulum ante ipsum primis in faucibus Orci
Luctus et ultrices posuere cubilia Curae;
pallentesque habitant Morbi tristisque Senectus,   275
et Metus et malesuada Fames ac turpis Egestas,

---

265. Chaos: cf. 4.510, where Dido invokes *Erebumque Chaosque*. **Phlegethon:** this river stands in for the rivers of the underworld more generally.

266. sit mihi fas...sit numine vestro: *fas* is what is permitted under divine law (cf. 63 n.); *sit...sit* are optative subjunctives; *numine vestro* means "consistent with your divine will," i.e. "may it be lawful." **audita loqui:** "to speak the things I have heard."

268—94. *Aeneas and the Sibyl approach the vestibule and entrance of Dis, where they confront all forms of human misery, dreams that dwell in a great elm tree, and monsters gathered at the entrance.*

268-9. Line 268 consists of slow, heavy spondees, while the lightness of 269 suggests the insubstantiality of these *domos...vacuas* and *inania regna*.

270. per incertam lunam: for *per lunam* cf. 2.340 *oblati per lunam*. It is clear that *incertam lunam* means a moon that gives no sure sign of its presence; it is hidden and gives just enough light (*maligna*) to make sight possible but no more.

271-2. caelum...Iuppiter: note that Jupiter is also a personification of the sky. **umbra:** ablative.

273. Aeneas and the Sibyl arrive at the entrance to the "house of Orcus," which is described as if it were a Roman house. It is actually located where the road leads to Acheron (cf. 295). **vestibulum ante ipsum:** Outside the front door of a Roman house was a porch (*vestibulum*), which Vergil envisions as a narrow hall or passageway, which he calls *fauces*, "jaws" or "throat," and hence "a narrow entrance" into the underworld. Here (274-89) they encounter personified abstractions of human worries. **Orci:** the name of the god (*Orcus*), equivalent to *Dis/Pluto* (cf. 252 n.), is used to describe his realm, just as the genitive of the equivalent Greek god, Hades, is often named to designate his realm, i.e. the underworld.

274. ultrices: an interesting adjective to apply to *Curae* ("Cares").

275. pallentes...Morbi: disease causes one to waste away.

276. malesuada Fames: hunger makes one susceptible to bad advice. **turpis:** not "dishonorable" but "disfiguring" or "squalid."

terribiles visu formae, Letumque Labosque;
tum consanguineus Leti Sopor et mala mentis
Gaudia, mortiferumque adverso in limine Bellum,
ferreique Eumenidum thalami et Discordia demens   280
vipereum crinem vittis innexa cruentis.
    In medio ramos annosaque bracchia pandit
ulmus opaca, ingens, quam sedem Somnia vulgo
vana tenere ferunt, foliisque sub omnibus haerent.
multaque praeterea variarum monstra ferarum,   285
Centauri in foribus stabulant Scyllaeque biformes
et centumgeminus Briareus ac belua Lernae

---

277. **visu**: supine, ablative of respect. **Labos:** archaic form = *Labor*.

278. **consanguineus Leti Sopor:** "Death's twin-brother Sleep." Cf. *Iliad* 14.231.

279. **adverso in limine:** "on the threshold before them." War is especially placed in the very gate of death; note the chiastic* arrangement.

280. **ferrei:** a dissyllable by synizesis*. **Eumenidum:** although Vergil here places the Furies in the entrance to the underworld, he later mentions them (555, 570, 605) as being in Tartarus.

281. **vipereum crinem…innexa:** construe *vipereum crinem* as accusative of respect after the "middle" participle *innexa* (cf. 156 n.), which modifies *Discordia*, though the Furies are also often depicted with hair consisting of venomous serpents. Cf. 7.351, where the Fury Allecto's serpent enters Amata's breast, setting in motion her fury against the Trojans; there her spirit (*animam*) is called *viperam*.

282. **In medio:** they have now passed the entrance and entered an inner court—possibly an atrium (Page) or some kind of peristyle court (Austin), open to the sky, where they encounter a giant elm tree.

283-4. **ulmus opaca, ingens:** insubstantial dreams reportedly cling beneath the leaves of the giant elm tree, like creatures of the night. The tree has no known literary precedent. **vulgo:** can be taken with *ferunt*, "commonly," or can refer to the dreams, "everywhere."

285. **monstra:** subject of understood *sunt*. Aeneas and the Sibyl encounter all sorts of unnatural creatures, which are described in 286-9 and have as little substance as the dreams.

286. **Centauri:** they were half-man, half-horse. **Scyllae:** Scylla was a blend of woman and sea-creature (probably a giant squid). Here her name occurs in the plural, suggesting "monsters like Scylla," even though Scylla was unique, and was located at the straits of Messina, not in the underworld. Cf. Lucretius who also uses the plural *Scyllae* at 4.732 and 5.893. Scylla and the Centaurs are not traditionally found in the underworld before Vergil.

287. **Briareus:** a hundred-headed (i.e. *centumgeminus*, an adjective created by Vergil) giant, like the *belua Lernae*, the multi-headed Hydra, each of whose heads, when severed by Hercules, grew back in multiples.

horrendum stridens, flammisque armata Chimaera,
Gorgones Harpyiaeque et forma tricorporis umbrae.
corripit hic subita trepidus formidine ferrum   290
Aeneas strictamque aciem venientibus offert,
et ni docta comes tenuis sine corpore vitas
admoneat volitare cava sub imagine formae,
inruat et frustra ferro diverberet umbras.
     Hinc via Tartarei quae fert Acherontis ad undas.   295
turbidus hic caeno vastaque voragine gurges
aestuat atque omnem Cocyto eructat harenam.

---

288. **horrendum stridens:** *horrendum* is cognate accusative. Cf. 50 n. **Chimaera:** a monster that was part lion, she-goat, and snake. It was slain by Bellerophon.

289. **Gorgones:** Medusa, whose gaze turned people and creatures to stone, was the most famous of the three *Gorgon* sisters. **Harpyiaeque:** a blend of women and birds, often represented as death-spirits (cf. 3.209-77). **forma tricorporis umbrae:** Geryon, a monster with three bodies who lived in Spain, was slain by Hercules, who then led Geryon's cattle through the future site of Rome (cf. 8.201-4).

290-1. **hic:** "at this moment." **subita trepidus formidine...Aeneas:** Aeneas, momentarily terrified, reaches for his sword.

292. **docta comes:** the Sibyl in her wisdom knows better. **tenuis...vitas:** the shades are described as "thin lives," by which probably Vergil is referring to the theory that the principle of life consists of a substance or essence "thin" or "rarefied" beyond comparison. Cf. Lucretius 3.243 *qua neque mobilius quicquam neque tenuius exstat*; their "lives" are without a body but are disguised (*sub*) in a hollow semblance of shape. Notice how each word emphasizes the idea of insubstantiality, enforced by Aeneas' vain attempts to cut them down in 294.

293-4. **admoneat...inruat...diverberet:** note the vivid use of the present subjunctives instead of the more usual pluperfect subjunctives in this past contrary-to-fact conditional. **volitare:** expresses the rapid uncertain movement of anything without weight, cf. Homer, *Odyssey* 10.495. **umbras:** emphatic at the end of the line.

295—336. They approach the ferry over the Styx and the Sibyl explains that the throng of ghosts, eager but unable to cross, are the unburied, who must therefore wander a hundred years upon its banks.

295. **Hinc via:** supply *est*. **Acherontis:** the river Acheron flows (*omnem eructat harenam*) into the *Cocytus* (297), and then Cocytus and Styx form a single stream, over which Charon ferries the souls. Vergil is not concerned with an exact plan of the rivers, other than the Styx.

296. **hic:** an adverb, "here, by this way." **vastaque voragine:** ablative of description, governed by *gurges*.

297. **Cocyto:** dative of direction, equivalent to *in Cocytum*. **eructat:** cf. Lucretius 3.1012 *Tartarus horriferos eructans faucibus aestus*; cf. also the eruption of Mt. Etna in *Aen.* 3.576.

portitor has horrendus aquas et flumina servat
terribili squalore Charon, cui plurima mento
canities inculta iacet, stant lumina flamma,   300
sordidus ex umeris nodo dependet amictus.
ipse ratem conto subigit velisque ministrat
et ferruginea subvectat corpora cumba,
iam senior, sed cruda deo viridisque senectus.
huc omnis turba ad ripas effusa ruebat,   305
matres atque viri defunctaque corpora vita
magnanimum heroum, pueri innuptaeque puellae,
impositique rogis iuvenes ante ora parentum:
quam multa in silvis autumni frigore primo
lapsa cadunt folia, aut ad terram gurgite ab alto   310

298-9. portitor…Charon: the memorable description of Charon, properly "the ferryman" (*portitor*), may be based on a painting, possibly the one by Polygnotus, as later described by Pausanias (10.28) (cf. 264-678 n.). Charon does not appear in Homer; cf. Euripides, *Alcestis* 253 ff.; Aristophanes, *Frogs* 139 ff; Etruscans depicted him as "Charun," a winged monster. **cui…mento:** "on whose chin" (lit. "with reference to whom on his chin").

300. stant lumina flamma: "his eyes stand fixed with flame." *Stant* implies a fixed stare.

301. nodo: Charon's *amictus* is fastened on his left shoulder with a "knot" instead of the more usual *fibula* ("buckle").

302. conto subigit: "pushes along with a pole." The force of *sub-* in *subigit* is clear: he starts the boat by pushing against the bottom. Afterwards, when he gets away from the bank, he "attends to the sails."

303. ferruginea…cumba: ablative; *ferruginea* describes a dark color, either dark purple or violet, cf. 410 n. **subvectat:** *sub-* seems used of bringing *up* to the bank they wish to reach.

304. iam senior…: he is old, but old age for a god (*deo*) is different than for mortals; it is *cruda* ("full of blood," "vigorous") and *viridis* (a common epithet of youth).

305. huc omnis turba…ruebat: the "whole throng" of the dead rush to the river bank (*ad ripas effusa*) to cross the river Styx.

306. vita: ablative governed by *defuncta* (nominative plural).

307. magnanimum: genitive plural.

309-12. Here there is a double simile*, first of leaves falling in the woods, and then of migrant birds, as they are all affected by the coming winter. Cf. Homer, *Iliad* 3.2, 6.146, and Vergil, *Geo.* 4.473. Clark (2001) 112-13 also finds echoes in these similes of Pindar's and Bacchylides' allusions to the descent of Herakles. The "leaves" and "birds" selected in this comparison with ghosts and their movements recalls the description above (283-4) of *somnia vana*.

310. lapsa cadunt: the leaves slip and fall. **ad terram gurgite ab alto:** toward the land, from the deep sea.

quam multae glomerantur aves, ubi frigidus annus
trans pontum fugat et terris immittit apricis.
stabant orantes primi transmittere cursum,
tendebantque manus ripae ulterioris amore.
navita sed tristis nunc hos nunc accipit illos,   315
ast alios longe summotos arcet harena.
Aeneas miratus enim motusque tumultu
"dic" ait, "o virgo, quid vult concursus ad amnem?
quidve petunt animae? vel quo discrimine ripas
hae linquunt, illae remis vada livida verrunt?"   320
olli sic breviter fata est longaeva sacerdos:
"Anchisa generate, deum certissima proles,
Cocyti stagna alta vides Stygiamque paludem,

---

312. **fugat…immittit:** understand *eas* (i.e. *aves* in 311) as object of both verbs; *fugat* is transitive, from *fugare*, "put to flight." **terris…apricis:** = *in terras apricas* (cf. 297 n.). Note the contrast of *apricis* ("sunny") with the present setting. Cf. *Ecl.* 9.49, *Geo.* 2.522.

313. **orantes…transmittere cursum:** the usual construction with *oro* is *ut* + a subjunctive noun clause (indirect command); here the infinitive *transmittere* depends on the sense of desire contained in *oro*. **cursum:** an internal accusative.

314. **ripae ulterioris amore:** "in (passionate) longing for the farther shore."

315. **navita:** = *nauta*, i.e. Charon. The postponed connective (*sed*) is a Hellenistic usage.

316. **ast:** (archaic) = *at*. **summotos:** *summovere* is used technically to denote the action of the lictors who clear a way for the consul or make a crowd "move on." Cf. Horace, *Odes* 2.16.10 *summovet lictor…tumultus*; Livy 3.48 *i, lictor, summove turbam*. **harena:** ablative of separation.

317. **enim:** not "for," but adding emphasis to the word it follows, "Aeneas marvelling, indeed,…." Cf. *Geo* 2.508 *hunc plausus hiantem | per cuneos geminatus enim… | corripuit*, "redoubled, indeed"; *Aen.* 8.84 *quam pius Aeneas tibi enim, tibi, maxima Iuno, | mactat*, "to you, indeed, to you."

318. **quid vult:** = *quid sibi vult*, i.e. "what does this (gathering at the river) mean?"

319-20. **quo discrimine:** i.e. What is the distinction between those who can and those who cannot cross the river? **linquunt:** "leave," i.e. these ghosts (*hae*) are refused passage by Charon and therefore retreat from the banks of the river. **remis…verrunt:** i.e. the other ghosts (*illae*) cross the river. The dead serve as Charon's crew.

321. **olli:** the archaic form of *illi* provides a solemn effect; cf. 730 *ollis*.

322. **Anchisa:** ablative of origin, governed by vocative participle *generate*.

di cuius iurare timent et fallere numen.
haec omnis, quam cernis, inops inhumataque turba est;   325
portitor ille Charon; hi, quos vehit unda, sepulti.
nec ripas datur horrendas et rauca fluenta
transportare prius quam sedibus ossa quierunt.
centum errant annos volitantque haec litora circum;
tum demum admissi stagna exoptata revisunt."   330
constitit Anchisa satus et vestigia pressit
multa putans sortemque animo miseratus iniquam.
cernit ibi maestos et mortis honore carentis
Leucaspim et Lyciae ductorem classis Oronten,
quos simul a Troia ventosa per aequora vectos   335
obruit Auster, aqua involvens navemque virosque.

---

324. **iurare...numen:** *iurare* takes a cognate accusative (here *numen*) of the deity or thing invoked in an oath, "whose deity the gods fear to invoke." **et fallere:** i.e. "falsely." An oath taken in the name of the river Styx (323) was the most binding of all, for both men and gods. Cf. Homer, *Iliad* 15.37-8; *Odyssey* 5.185-6.

325. **inops:** "helpless," though it could also be taken as "poor," because the ghosts in this *turba* lack the coin usually placed between the lips of the dead with which to pay their passage.

326. **portitor ille:** supply *est.* **supulti:** supply *sunt.*

327. **datur:** impersonal verb; supply *ei* (or *Charoni*). The subject is the infinitive *transportare*, whose object is the dead thronging the shores.

328. **sedibus:** the last resting-place, i.e. the grave; cf. 152, 371.

329. **centum...annos:** accusative showing duration of time. **circum:** the preposition follows its object *haec litora* (anastrophe*).

330. **tum demum:** "then, and only then" do they return to this shore to seek passage.

331. **constitit:** Aeneas pauses to ponder (*putans*) their fate. **Anchisa satus:** for the construction, cf. 322 n.

332. **animo:** locative, "in mind." Page and other editors accept the variant reading *animi*, as a locative (cf. 10.686), but the original *animo* is read by all the manuscripts except M, which also includes the correction *animo.*

333. **mortis honore carentis:** "lacking the honor of death," i.e. of the rites owed to the dead; *careo* governs the ablative of separation (*honore*).

334. **Leucaspim...Orontem:** Leucaspis is not mentioned earlier; Servius assumes he was the helmsman of Orontes' ship, which sank at 1.113-17 as a result of the storm Juno sent against Aeneas and his ships.

335-6. Note the alliteration* throughout, and the whirl and rush of 336, depicting the rough seas in which the ship sank. A weak caesura after *Auster* is followed by the elision of the long *a* in *aqua*, while the *w* (= *v*) sound continuously recurs. **vectos:** "while voyaging."

Ecce gubernator sese Palinurus agebat,
qui Libyco nuper cursu, dum sidera servat,
exciderat puppi mediis effusus in undis.
hunc ubi vix multa maestum cognovit in umbra,   340
sic prior adloquitur: "quis te, Palinure, deorum
eripuit nobis medioque sub aequore mersit?
dic age. namque mihi, fallax haud ante repertus,
hoc uno responso animum delusit Apollo,
qui fore te ponto incolumem finisque canebat   345
venturum Ausonios. en haec promissa fides est?"
ille autem: "neque te Phoebi cortina fefellit,

337—83. The ghost of Aeneas' helmsman, Palinurus, approaches and relates the story of his death. He begs Aeneas to let him accompany them across the stream, but the Sibyl tells Palinurus this cannot be done; she promises that he will be buried and that the spot where he died will bear his name forever.

337. **sese…agebat:** "was approaching," "was making his way (to us)." For Palinurus' death, see 5.835-71.

338. **Libyco…cursu:** "on the voyage from Libya."

339. **mediis effusus in undis:** "falling overboard in mid-ocean." It took him three days (355) to reach land.

340. **vix:** adverb, "with difficulty," suggests the dimness of the light in the underworld.

341. **prior adloquitur:** Aeneas "first addresses (him)"; cf. 387 *prior adgreditur dictis,* and 834-5 *prior…proice,* "be first to fling away."

342. **nobis:** dative of disadvantage.

343-4. **dic age:** *age,* "come," used in this way is common in spoken Latin, and thus is frequently found in Roman Comedy. **mihi:** dative of reference; construe closely with *animum* (344). **fallax haud ante repertus…Apollo:** cf. Aeschylus, *Choephori* 559, where Apollo is addressed as "not previously false." **hoc uno responso:** this oracle is not described earlier in the poem.

345. **fore:** = *futurum esse.*

346. **Ausonios:** often used for "Italian." The Ausones were the indigenous people of Campania, the province to the south of Latium, where Cumae is located. The accusative *Ausones* after *venturum* indicates motion toward the Ausones and their land. **en…fides est?:** an exclamatory question.

347. **ille autem:** "but he (replies)." **cortina:** the cauldron on the tripod, on top of which the priestess at Delphi sat; here it signifies the Delphic oracle.

dux Anchisiade, nec me deus aequore mersit.
namque gubernaclum multa vi forte revulsum,
cui datus haerebam custos cursusque regebam,   350
praecipitans traxi mecum. maria aspera iuro
non ullum pro me tantum cepisse timorem,
quam tua ne spoliata armis, excussa magistro,
deficeret tantis navis surgentibus undis.
tris Notus hibernas immensa per aequora noctes   355
vexit me violentus aqua; vix lumine quarto
prospexi Italiam summa sublimis ab unda.

---

348. **Anchisiade:** vocative of the patronymic. **nec me…:** "nor did any god drown me in the deep," in answer to 341-2, but the emphasis must be placed on the words *aequore mersit*. Aeneas has referred to the ambiguity inherent in oracular language, which appears to say one thing and is subsequently found to have meant another, but was deeply respected in antiquity. An oracle such as this ("safe from the perils of the sea shall you reach the borders of Italy") is not merely considered free from fraud, but even deserving of admiration for the skill with which "it wraps truth in darkness" (cf. *obscuris vera involvens* 100).

349. **namque…:** in 5.838-56, the god Sleep first casts him into slumber and, because he still clings faithfully to the tiller (*gubernaclum*) while asleep, flings him rudder and all into the sea. The tiller was connected to the rudder (*armis*), which governs the ship's direction. Palinurus can only account for finding himself afloat on the rudder by saying that it was "torn away with much violence."

350. **cui:** dative governed by both *datus* and *haerebam*; antecedent is *gubernaclum* (349).

351. **maria aspera:** accusative with verb of swearing (*iuro*). "By the harsh sea (I swear that…)" (AG §388d) (cf. 458).

352-4. **non ullum pro me tantum cepisse timorem, | quam tua ne…navis…:** "I did not feel any fear for myself as much as (for you) that your ship…" **ne…deficeret…:** fear clause governed by *timorem* (352); *deficeret* here means "sink." **spoliata armis, excussa magistro:** participial phrases modifying *navis,* "robbed of its rudder and torn from its guide." For this meaning of *armis,* cf. 349 n.; for the usage of *excussa,* cf. 1.115 *excutitur magister,* "the helmsman is dashed overboard." The ablative absolute, *excusso magistro* would perhaps be more usual, but the form of the phrase here is due partly to Vergil's desire to make the phrase parallel to the preceding one. Observe the sibilant character of this line, expressive of the whistling of the wind; cf. Horace, *Odes* 1.2.1-2 *iam satis terris nivis atque dirae | grandinis misit Pater.* **tantis undis surgentibus:** ablative absolute.

355. **tris…hibernas…noctes:** accusative showing duration of time. *Hibernas* ("winter") is used metaphorically here to mean "stormy," since the ancients did not sail in winter.

356. **aqua:** ablative of place. **lumine quarto:** ablative of time when.

357. **summa…ab unda:** "from the crest of a wave." Cf. Homer, *Odyssey* 5.392

paulatim adnabam terrae; iam tuta tenebam,
ni gens crudelis madida cum veste gravatum
prensantemque uncis manibus capita aspera montis   360
ferro invasisset praedamque ignara putasset.
nunc me fluctus habet versantque in litore venti.
quod te per caeli iucundum lumen et auras,
per genitorem oro, per spes surgentis Iuli,
eripe me his, invicte, malis: aut tu mihi terram   365
inice, namque potes, portusque require Velinos;
aut tu, si qua via est, si quam tibi diva creatrix
ostendit (neque enim, credo, sine numine divum
flumina tanta paras Stygiamque innare paludem),
da dextram misero et tecum me tolle per undas,   370
sedibus ut saltem placidis in morte quiescam."
talia fatus erat coepit cum talia vates:

358-61. **iam...tenebam, | ni gens (359)...invasisset (361):** a mixed condition. "Already I was reaching safety (and would have), had not a barbarous people...attacked me." Cf. 870-1.

360. **montis:** here "rock" or "boulder."

361. **ferro invasisset praedamque...putasset:** "had attacked me and thought..." (i.e. "had attacked me, while thinking..."). The subject is still *gens crudelis* (359). **praedam:** being ignorant of the facts (*ignara*), they considered him a shipwrecked sailor, who would probably have secured some wealth on his person before his ship was destroyed.

363-4. **quod te...oro:** the relative pronoun *quod* sums up his preceding account, "because of this situation...I beg of you."

365-7. **invicte:** adding to the force of the appeal, "save me, for you are unconquerable." **aut tu...aut tu:** notice the exceedingly strong *personal* emphasis. **terram | inice...portusque require:** the natural sequence would be the reverse — Aeneas would first have to return to the harbor of Velia (see below), to the south of Cumae, before he could cast dirt upon Palinurus' grave. For a similar chronological inversion, cf. 361. The "sprinkling of earth" thrice over the dead (cf. Horace, *Odes* 1.28.36 *iniecto ter pulvere*) constituted technical burial. **Velinos:** adjectival form of *Velia* (= ancient Elea), a Phocean town founded in the sixth century BCE, so this reference is anachronistic*. **diva creatrix:** Venus.

370. **da dextram:** he requests this both literally and as a pledge. **misero:** dative, understand *mihi*. Note the subtle alliteration* of *d, m, t* in this line.

371. **ut ...quiescam:** "that I may rest..." Palinurus asks only that he find rest in the peaceful (*placidis*) dwellings on the farther shore of the Styx now that he is dead. *Saltem* ("at least") should be taken with <in> *sedibus...placibus*, not with *in morte*.

372. Although he has addressed Aeneas, it is the Sibyl who replies. **talia...talia:** a strong response—*this* is his request, but *this* is the reply he receives.

"unde haec, o Palinure, tibi tam dira cupido?
tu Stygias inhumatus aquas amnemque severum
Eumenidum aspicies, ripamve iniussus adibis?   375
desine fata deum flecti sperare precando.
sed cape dicta memor, duri solacia casus.
nam tua finitimi, longe lateque per urbes
prodigiis acti caelestibus, ossa piabunt
et statuent tumulum et tumulo sollemnia mittent,   380
aeternumque locus Palinuri nomen habebit."
his dictis curae emotae pulsusque parumper
corde dolor tristi; gaudet cognomine terra.

---

373. **tam dira cupido:** cf. 721; 9.185.

374-5. **tu...aspicies?:** an indignant form of question, "will you (alone of all men)...behold...?";
tu is meant to rebuke his unacceptable desire. **inhumatus...iniussus:** "unburied...
unbidden." **severum:** transferred epithet, grammatically modifying *amnem*, but in sense
describing *Eumenidum*.

376. **desine fata deum...:** by *fata deum* (*deum* is genitive plural) Vergil means those general
laws for the government of the universe, which are not only "laws of the gods" but "laws for
the gods" and which even they cannot alter.

377. **duri solacia casus:** in apposition to *dicta*; the Sibyl, though stern, also shows him pity.
Casus is genitive.

378. **nam:** "for I tell you," characteristic of Sibylline verses, further reflected in 379-81, where
three lines end with a verb in the future tense. **tua:** construe with *ossa* (379).

379. **ossa piabunt:** the corpse is outraged by being left unburied, and must be "appeased" by
burial and expiatory sacrifices.

380. **sollemnia mittent:** they will make ritual offerings annually.

381. **Palinuri nomen:** the promontory from which he fell is now known as Capo Palinuro, on
the coast of Italy just south of Velia. Cf. 235 *aeternum tenet per saecula nomen* (of Misenus).

382. The slow, spondaic meter—only the fifth foot is a dactyl—suggests Palinurus' gradual
realization that his anxiety is now being lifted. **emotae...pulsus:** supply *sunt...est*.

383. **gaudet cognomine terra:** Hirtzel, Mynors, and Austin, following Servius, also read
terra, and interpret *cognomine* as the ablative of the adjective *cognominis* ("having the same
name"), though the manuscripts read *terrae*. Thus: "he takes joy in the land (*terra*) named
after him (*cognomine*)." Note that the only pleasure left to these doleful spirits is living
vicariously through others—the most famous parallel being Achilles' ghost in *Odyssey*
1.487-540.

Ergo iter inceptum peragunt fluvioque propinquant.
navita quos iam inde ut Stygia prospexit ab unda   385
per tacitum nemus ire pedemque advertere ripae,
sic prior adgreditur dictis atque increpat ultro:
"quisquis es, armatus qui nostra ad flumina tendis,
fare age quid venias iam istinc, et comprime gressum.
umbrarum hic locus est, somni noctisque soporae: 390
corpora viva nefas Stygia vectare carina.
nec vero Alciden me sum laetatus euntem
accepisse lacu, nec Thesea Pirithoumque,
dis quamquam geniti atque invicti viribus essent.
Tartareum ille manu custodem in vincla petivit   395
ipsius a solio regis traxitque trementem;
hi dominam Ditis thalamo deducere adorti."

384—416. Resuming their journey, the Sibyl and Aeneas approach the river Styx and the gruff, grumbling ferryman Charon, who carries the dead across the river in his leaky boat. Charon at first refuses to let them board his craft, but when he sees the golden bough, sullenly ferries them across.

385-7. Charon (*navita*), without waiting for them to get nearer (*iam inde...ab unda*), speaks first (*prior*) and "scolds them unprovoked" (*increpat ultro*) (i.e. before they can speak). **quos:** connecting relative pronoun; i.e. *eos* (Aeneas and the Sibyl). **iam inde:** "already from a distance."

389. **fare age…:** "Come, say now why you come, from there where you are (*iam istinc*), and check your steps." Note the abruptness of the line.

390. Charon's language now becomes grandiose as he identifies this place. **soporae:** "sleep-inducing." His speech in 388-97 is influenced by Aeacus' reaction to Herakles' approach during his descent in Euripides' lost *Pirithous* (see Clark (2000)).

391. **corpora viva:** contrasts with *umbrarum* in 390. **nefas:** supply *est*; reflects Charon's disapproval.

392. **Alciden:** i.e. Hercules, cf. 122-3 n.; accusative object of *accepisse* (393 n.). The eleventh labor Eurystheus imposed on Hercules was to descend to the underworld and bring Cerberus to the world above (see 395-6); afterwards he returned Cerberus to Pluto.

393. **accepisse lacu:** "to have welcomed on my lake," cf. 412 *accipit alveo*; 3.78 *portu accipit.* **Thesea:** Greek accusative. Theseus aided his friend Pirithous in an attempt to abduct Proserpina; the two heroes were not permitted to leave the underworld until Hercules came and rescued Theseus, but he could not bring back Pirithous.

394. **dis:** ablative of origin; construe with *geniti.*

395. **Tartareum...custodem:** Cerberus; according to Servius he was kept in chains for a year. **manu:** "by force," i.e. with physical violence.

397. **hi:** i.e. Theseus and Pirithous. **dominam:** Proserpina.

quae contra breviter fata est Amphrysia vates:
"nullae hic insidiae tales (absiste moveri),
nec vim tela ferunt; licet ingens ianitor antro   400
aeternum latrans exsanguis terreat umbras,
casta licet patrui servet Proserpina limen.
Troïus Aeneas, pietate insignis et armis,
ad genitorem imas Erebi descendit ad umbras.
si te nulla movet tantae pietatis imago,   405
at ramum hunc" (aperit ramum qui veste latebat)
"agnoscas." tumida ex ira tum corda residunt.
nec plura his. ille admirans venerabile donum
fatalis virgae longo post tempore visum
caeruleam advertit puppim ripaeque propinquat.   410

---

398. **contra:** here this preposition follows its object *quae*, a connecting relative referring to Charon's words/speech. **Amphrysia:** an epithet of Apollo, here referring to his priestess, the Sibyl. The epithet denotes his tending the sheep of Admetus by the river Amphrysus (*Geo.* 3.2); this service was required of him to atone for having killed the Cyclopes, with whose lightning bolts Jupiter had killed Apollo's son, Aesclepius, who had employed his medical skills to bring the dead back to life.

399. **absiste moveri:** "cease to be troubled."

400-2. **licet...licet...:** as a particle of concession, *licet* here governs the subjunctive (cf. AG §527b); "Even though the huge door-keeper (i.e. Cerberus) may frighten the bloodless ghosts...and even though chaste Proserpina may keep watch over her uncle's threshold." She was the daughter of Jupiter, and the wife of his brother, Pluto. Cf. 703-23 n. The tone throughout is contemptuous, hence the "bloodless" ghosts, and the emphasis on *casta*. **aeternum:** adverbial. **exsanguis...umbras:** with this phrase the Sibyl seems to mock Cerberus.

403. She boasts of Aeneas' credentials to Charon.

404. **Erebi:** refers to the underworld in general.

405. **si te nulla movet tantae pietatis imago...:** emphatic, "if no vision at all of such piety moves you..."

406. **at:** suggests a pause after *imago*; "yet..." (**aperit...latebat):** a moment of high drama, enforced by the repetition of *ramum*.

407. **tumida...corda residunt:** Charon is calmed by the authority of the bough.

408. **nec plura his:** supply *dicta sunt*; "nor (was there) more than this (said)." The discussion has ended; Charon yields at once.

409. **fatalis virgae:** "fateful branch," cf. 147. **longo...visum:** there is no known evidence that it has been previously used for this purpose.

410. **caeruleam...puppim:** cf. *ferruginea cumba* in 303. In both cases the color means something like "dark." **advertit:** i.e. towards the Sibyl and Aeneas.

inde alias animas, quae per iuga longa sedebant,
deturbat laxatque foros; simul accipit alveo
ingentem Aenean. gemuit sub pondere cumba
sutilis et multam accepit rimosa paludem.
tandem trans fluvium incolumis vatemque virumque   415
informi limo glaucaque exponit in ulva.
  Cerberus haec ingens latratu regna trifauci
personat adverso recubans immanis in antro.
cui vates horrere videns iam colla colubris
melle soporatam et medicatis frugibus offam   420
obicit. ille fame rabida tria guttura pandens

---

411. **alias animas:** "the other ghosts." Aeneas is not a ghost, and so is contrasted to the ghosts. **iuga:** the benches on the boat; the regular Latin word is *transtra*.

412. **deturbat:** "pushes out of the way." **laxat...foros:** the *fori* would be the gate or entrance to the boat; "he lets down the gangplanks." **alveo:** here "hull"; disyllabic by synizesis*.

413. **ingentem:** Aeneas' size contrasts starkly with that of the ghosts.

414-16. **sutilis:** the boat is described as "stitched together" (*sutilis*); it would consist of hides sewn together and stretched on a framework of wood. The boat is old and "leaky" (*rimosa* 414); the water is a "marshy ooze" (*paludem* 414); the landing-place is not solid ground but "shapeless mud" (*informi limo* 416) and "grey sedge" (*glauca...ulva* 416; grass-like plants found in swamps). **tandem:** emphasizing the slowness of the journey. **vatemque virumque:** the seer and the hero have a special connection, as *–que...-que* emphasize. The sounds of this line emphasize the ooze of the swamp.

417—25. *After crossing the Styx, they encounter Cerberus, the three-headed dog guarding the entrance to the underworld; they render him harmless with a drugged honey-cake.*

417-19. **Cerberus:** first named by Hesiod (*Theogony* 311, 769-74); thereafter numerous writers refer to him. He is also depicted on a number of vase-paintings, often in the company of Herakles, one of whose tasks was to capture him, bring him to Eurystheus (cf. 392), and then return him to the underworld. Like Charon, Cerberus is part of the traditional machinery of the underworld: he is physically huge, and all three of his heads bark (cf. *latratu...trifauci* 417) so loudly that his sound as well as his size fills (cf. *personat* 418, with 171 n.) the cave and blocks the way. In Vergil's depiction, his necks are covered with serpents (*colubris* 419). Cf. 8.296, where he is called *ianitor Orci*.

420-1. **soporatam...offam:** the Sibyl hurls him a "morsel made drowsy" (i.e. steeped) with honey and drug-soaked grain, the purpose of which is to make *him* drowsy. **famē:** some nouns, such as *fames*, vary between third and fifth declension; the ablative of *fames* is always long. Cf. AG §76b.1, 105e.

corripit obiectam, atque immania terga resolvit
fusus humi totoque ingens extenditur antro.
occupat Aeneas aditum custode sepulto
evaditque celer ripam inremeabilis undae.   425
    Continuo auditae voces vagitus et ingens
infantumque animae flentes, in limine primo
quos dulcis vitae exsortis et ab ubere raptos

422-3. **obiectam:** supply *offam* (420). **immania…:** "relaxes his enormous back, sprawling on the ground." The participle *fusus* here means "lying at ease." *Resolvit* and *fusus* vividly express the effect of the drug; shortly before he received it, his back was rigid and every muscle was strained with excitement. **humi:** locative.

424-5. **occupat Aeneas aditum…| evaditque…ripam:** the tone is mock-heroic. **occupat:** "springs upon." **custode sepulto:** ablative absolute, "its guardian buried (in sleep)." Cf. 2.265 *somno vinoque sepultum.* **evaditque…ripam:** Aeneas now passes from the Stygian water to the inner part of Hades. **inremeabilis:** "that permits no return" (*remeare* = to return). Cf. 5.591, where the adjective describes the Labyrinth.

426-547. Aeneas and the Sibyl now proceed to a region inhabited by shades that are neither punished (like those in Tartarus at 548-627) nor happy (like those in Elysium at 637-78). The first three groups in this region—infants (426-9), those wrongfully killed (430), and suicides (434-9)—are discussed briefly. They are followed by the inhabitants of the Fields of Mourning (*Lugentes Campi*), who have died because of love (440-76), and finally by the shades of famous warriors, both Greek and Trojan (477-547).

   This first region of the underworld, a kind of limbo, raises difficult questions. For example, will any of the shades it contains eventually be sent to Tartarus or Elysium? Why do the shades of infants and of warriors inhabit this same general region? Vergil does not provide answers to such questions; he is more concerned with presenting Aeneas' painful encounters in this region with two people from his past. In the Fields of Mourning, Aeneas discovers Dido, whom he addresses for the last time (450-76, see n.), as he acknowledges that her death was brought about by his departure from Carthage. She refuses to respond to him and instead turns away in silence, retreating into the arms of her husband Sychaeus, thus bringing a bitter close to her tragic affair with the Trojan leader. Then among the famous warriors, Aeneas encounters Priam's son Deiphobus (Helen's final Trojan husband), who describes his brutal death at the hands of his wife Helen, her Greek husband Menelaus, and Odysseus on the night of Troy's fall (see 494-547 n.).

   Vergil does not indicate how long these souls must stay here, nor does he attempt to establish any doctrine about the fate of souls in the afterlife, although commentators have long attempted to find one here.

426-39: The first three groups are innocents, who died before their allotted time.

426. **voces:** "cries." **vagitus:** regularly of the "wail of infants." **et:** the *et* is postponed (hyperbaton*). Notice the assonance* in this line.

427-8. **in limine primo | quos…vitae exsortis:** *vitae* is governed by *exsortis* (accusative plural), though it still resonates with *in limine primo*. These ghosts were deprived of a share in life "from the very beginning" (*in limine primo*).

abstulit atra dies et funere mersit acerbo.
hos iuxta falso damnati crimine mortis.   430
nec vero hae sine sorte datae, sine iudice, sedes:
quaesitor Minos urnam movet; ille silentum
conciliumque vocat vitasque et crimina discit.
proxima deinde tenent maesti loca, qui sibi letum
insontes peperere manu lucemque perosi   435
proiecere animas. quam vellent aethere in alto
nunc et pauperiem et duros perferre labores!
fas obstat, tristisque palus inamabilis undae
alligat et novies Styx interfusa coercet.

429. **abstulit atra dies:** "a black day carried off and plunged in bitter death." *Dies atri* in the Roman calendar were unlucky days, marked with black, on which no legal business could be transacted. **funere...acerbo:** contrasts with *dulcis vitae* (428), but *acerbus* is especially used, even in prose, of premature, "untimely" death.

430. The second group—those who were unjustly condemned to death. **iuxta:** preposition + accusative (*hos*), "near to"; for the anastrophe*, cf. 329 n. **mortis:** genitive governed by *damnati,* "condemned to death" on a false charge.

431-3. **nec vero...sine sorte..., sine iudice...:** even if denied justice on earth, they find it here. The reference is to the *sortitio iudicum* ("appointment of the jury by lot") in a Roman court by the magistrate investigating the case (*quaesitor* 432), who here is *Minos*, a judge in the underworld; he "shakes the urn and casts judgment among the silent (*silentum concilium* 432-3), and examines the record of their lives (*vitasque et crimina* 432)." Geymonat, Mynors and Austin here read *consiliumque,* suggesting a general gathering of the dead to cast judgment. The Labyrinthine quality of the underworld (*inremeabilis* 425) as well as the presence of Minos recall the scene on the doors of the temple of Apollo (20-39). **urnam movet:** the names were placed on tablets, and the urn shaken until one "leapt out." Cf. 22 *stat ductis sortibus urna.*

434-9. The third group consists of suicides.

434. **deinde:** disyllabic, by synezesis*.

435. **peperere:** from *pario.* **manu:** "by their own hand"; cf. 395. **lucem perosi:** *perosus* from \<*per*\>*odi*; one who wants to die can no longer bear the light of day; cf. Dido's misery: *taedet caeli convexa tueri* (4.451). (Note that Dido is not in this group.)

436-7. **quam vellent...:** unfulfilled wish in the present (though *vellent* might also be construed as an independent potential subjunctive or as in the apodosis of an contrary-to-fact condition, "if they could now (*nunc*) choose...how they would want..."; cf. AG §447.1).

438. **fas obstat:** *fas* here almost = "fate." Cf. 4.440 *fata obstant*, of Anna's pleas to Aeneas. **tristis...undae:** genitive of description. Page, following Servius and later manuscripts, modifies the reading to the ablative *tristi...unda.* **inamabilis:** "unlovable," an example of litotes*, meaning "hateful"; construe with *palus.*

439. **alligat...coercet:** understand *maestos* (cf. 434), i.e. suicides, as object. **novies:** the number has a magical binding force, heightening the power of the Styx.

nec procul hinc partem fusi monstrantur in omnem   440
Lugentes campi; sic illos nomine dicunt.
hic quos durus amor crudeli tabe peredit
secreti celant calles et myrtea circum
silva tegit; curae non ipsa in morte relinquunt.
his Phaedram Procrimque locis maestamque Eriphylen   445
crudelis nati monstrantem vulnera cernit,
Evadnenque et Pasiphaen; his Laodamia
it comes et iuvenis quondam, nunc femina, Caeneus
rursus et in veterem fato revoluta figuram.

440—76. They now come to the Fields of Mourning (Lugentes campi), where the victims of cruel love wander at large. Seven mythical heroines wander here, setting the stage for Aeneas' meeting with Dido.

440. **partem fusi…in omnem:** the *Lugentes Campi* are vast, allowing solitude to their inhabitants. **fusi:** "spread" or "extending" (in every direction, *partem*).

442. **quos:** a collective masculine, even though Vergil names mainly women; its antecedent is an understood *eos,* object of *celant* (443)…*tegit* (444). **crudeli tabe:** "with a cruel wasting"; **peredit:** *edere* is to eat or consume; the prefix *per-* intensifies the persistence of the verb—it eats away at them continuously.

443. **secreti…calles:** "hidden haunts" or "remote passage-ways." **myrtea:** because the myrtle is sacred to Venus.

444. **curae:** "cares," " troubles."

445-6. **Phaedram**: wife of Theseus, daughter of Minos, slew herself because of her unrequited passion for her step-son Hippolytus (Euripides, *Hippolytus*). **Procrim:** Greek accusative. Procris jealously spied on her husband Cephalus while he was hunting and was accidentally killed by him when he mistook her for a wild boar (cf. Ovid, *Metamorphoses* 7.690 ff.). Her excessive passion (rather than lust) sets the stage for the reintroduction of Dido. **Eriphylen:** Greek accusative. Eriphyle was killed by her son Alcmaeon because she had been bribed by the gift of a necklace to persuade her husband Amphiaraus to join the expedition of the Seven against Thebes, where he perished. This appears to be Vergil's comment on women in power who betray their country for the sake of their own desires. Phaedra, Procris and Eriphyle were depicted in Polygnotus' painting of the underworld (cf. 264-678 n.).

447. **Evadnen:** Greek accusative. Evadne, the wife of Capaneus, who was also slain at Thebes (cf. 445-6 n.), flung herself on his funeral pyre. **Pasiphaen:** Greek accusative. Pasiphae was the mother of the Minotaur, cf. 23-6 with n. **Laodamia:** the wife of Protesilaus, who was the first Greek to die at Troy. She obtained permission for her husband to return to life for three hours and then died with him (Cf. Catullus 68.73-86; Ovid, *Heroides* 13).

448-9. **Caeneus:** had been a maiden, but was changed by Poseidon into a young man (cf. Ovid, *Metamorphoses* 12.172-209). Vergil has him become a woman again and a victim of cruel love.

inter quas Phoenissa recens a vulnere Dido   450
errabat silva in magna; quam Troius heros
ut primum iuxta stetit agnovitque per umbras
obscuram, qualem primo qui surgere mense
aut videt aut vidisse putat per nubila lunam,
demisit lacrimas dulcique adfatus amore est   455
"infelix Dido, verus mihi nuntius ergo
venerat exstinctam ferroque extrema secutam?
funeris heu tibi causa fui? per sidera iuro,
per superos et si qua fides tellure sub ima est,
invitus, regina, tuo de litore cessi.   460

450-76. Aeneas now encounters Dido. His words to her and her response ironically recall Aeneas' own failure to respond to Dido's pleas in 4.448-9: *sed nullis ille movetur | fletibus aut voces ullas tractabilis audit.* Compare 1.479-82, where Pallas Athena, depicted in the mural at Carthage, also refuses to respond to the pleas of the Trojan women—Vergil uses the same words there (1.482) as in his description of Dido here, in 469 (see n.). Others have suggested an allusion here to *Odyssey* 11.543-67, where the great warrior Ajax, who had lost the contest for Achilles' armor to Odysseus and committed suicide as a result, refuses to respond to his former rival. See Panoussi (2002 and 2009).

450. **recens a vulnere:** Dido's wound is still fresh: she had stabbed herself with Aeneas' sword when he departed; cf. 4.646.

451-4. **quam...obscuram:** i.e. Dido; accusative, governed by *iuxta* and *agnovit.* **obscuram, qualem <lunam 454>...aut videt aut putat <se> vidisse:** the figure of Dido is unclear, like a new moon, which is barely visible. The postponement of *lunam* to the end of the sentence emphasizes how distant from this world it is.

455. **demisit lacrimas:** now it is Aeneas who sheds tears, as he addresses her and tries to persuade her that he only left because he was commanded by the gods, *iussa deum* (461). (For Dido's tears, cf. 4.30, 314, 413, etc.)

456-7. **infelix Dido:** Vergil has often given her this epithet, even as early as 1.712, and she applies it to herself at the end of Book 4 (596); cf. 4.68, 450, 529. **verus mihi nuntius ergo:** "then the news was true (that)…." **extinctam...secutam:** supply *esse*; implied indirect statement after verbal idea in *nuntius.* The flames at the beginning of Book 5 had been the first signal to the Trojans of Dido's tragedy.

458-9. **funeris:** genitive after *causa.* **heu:** "alas!" **et si qua fides…:** "if there be any honor/ honesty...."

460. **invitus, regina...:** cf. Catullus 62.39 *invita, o regina, tuo de vertice cessi.* In Catullus, it is the frivolous outcry of the Lock of Hair (*coma*) which has been severed from its mistress's head, whereas here it is employed in a powerful moment of anguish, rendered more complex when the reader realizes that Dido's husband, Sychaeus, is standing near her. (For discussion, cf. Johnston (1987).) Note the slow, spondaic meter in the first half of the line, suggesting Aeneas' sincerity in this statement.

sed me iussa deum, quae nunc has ire per umbras,
per loca senta situ cogunt noctemque profundam,
imperiis egere suis; nec credere quivi
hunc tantum tibi me discessu ferre dolorem.
siste gradum teque aspectu ne subtrahe nostro.   465
quem fugis? extremum fato quod te adloquor hoc est."
talibus Aeneas ardentem et torva tuentem
lenibat dictis animum lacrimasque ciebat.
illa solo fixos oculos aversa tenebat
nec magis incepto vultum sermone movetur   470
quam si dura silex aut stet Marpesia cautes.

461-3. **me iussa deum, quae nunc...ire...cogunt...egere:** "the gods' orders, which now
compel me to go..., drove me (to leave then)...." *Egere* = *egerunt* (from *ago*, not *egeo*). **senta
situ:** "rough with neglect." *Sentus*, a rare word, means "uncared for"; cf. Terence, *Eunuchus*
2.2.5; Ovid, *Metamorphoses* 4.436; *situ* ("rust," "moldiness," "decay") indicates an absence
of activity or the *effect* of being left alone. **imperiis...suis:** suggesting that *dei*, not *iussa*, is
really the subject of *egere*.

463-5. Aeneas' words here sound more like a scolding than an expression of sorrow—that would
certainly explain Dido's apparent attempt to move away, causing him to say *siste gradum* (465).

466. **extremum...:** "it is fated that what I now say to you is the last." **quod:** cognate
accusative after *adloquor*.

467-8. **ardentem et torva tuentem...animum:** lit. "he was attempting to soothe her mind/
spirit....burning and giving him fierce looks" (*torva* is cognate accusative). **lenibat:** alternate
form of the imperfect (instead of *leniebat*), for metrical reasons; "was trying to soothe."
Many verbs may express an action which is incomplete or only attempted (conative,
from *conor*), particularly in the present (AG §467) or in the imperfect tense (AG §471c).
lacrimas...ciebat: conative imperfect would suggest the tears were Dido's, but Aeneas is
the subject of *lenibat* and of *ciebat*, suggesting that Aeneas is weeping, while Dido attempts
to turn away. Compare the ambiguity of *lacrimae volvuntur inanes* (4.448).

469. **illa solo fixos oculos aversa tenebat:** cf. 1.482 *diva solo fixos oculos aversa tenebat,* where
the same words depict Pallas Athena's hostility to the Trojans. In 4.331-2 Aeneas refuses
to be moved by Dido's words (*immota tenebat lumina*), and in 4.362 *talia dicentem...aversa
tuetur,* Dido refuses to be moved by Aeneas's words. In 4.448-9 Aeneas is again unmoved
by Dido's pleas (*sed nullis ille movetur | fletibus aut voces ullas tractabilis audit*).

470. **vultum:** accusative of specification, AG §397b.

471. **quam si dura silex:** an ironic echo of 4.366-7 (*duris genuit te cautibus...Caucasus*)
where Dido charges Aeneas with inhuman origins. **stet:** the monosyllabic verb is used in
preference to any of its compounds to express immovable fixity. Cf. Horace, *Odes* 3.3.42
stet Capitolium; Vergil, *Geo.* 4.208 *stat fortuna domus.* **Marpesia cautes:** Marpessus was a
mountain in Paros; Parian marble had a luminous glow.

tandem corripuit sese atque inimica refugit
in nemus umbriferum, coniunx ubi pristinus illi
respondet curis aequatque Sychaeus amorem.
nec minus Aeneas casu concussus iniquo   475
prosequitur lacrimis longe et miseratur euntem.
      Inde datum molitur iter. iamque arva tenebant
ultima, quae bello clari secreta frequentant.
hic illi occurrit Tydeus, hic inclutus armis
Parthenopaeus et Adrasti pallentis imago,   480
hic multum fleti ad superos belloque caduci
Dardanidae, quos ille omnis longo ordine cernens

---

472. **tandem corripuit sese:** "at length she rushed away"; *corripuit* suggests the sudden convulsive movement with which she breaks from her trance.

473-4. **coniunx...Sychaeus:** the first indication that her deceased husband Sychaeus now accompanies her, a violation of the rules of the *Lugentes Campi*, since he did not die of love, but was murdered. Many questions arise here: Is she happy now that she is with Sychaeus? Does *aequat amorem* mean he gives her the love she needs? Does Aeneas blame her situation on her fate (*casu...iniquo* 475) rather than on himself? Does he only pity her (*miseratur* 476), not love her?

475. **casu concussus iniquo:** "shaken by her unjust death."

476. **prosequitur...:** this word is used of escorting a person a part of the way as a mark of honor or esteem; cf. 898, where Anchises escorts Aeneas to the exit from the underworld.

477—93. *They now encounter those who fell in battle. First they see ghosts of soldiers who died at Thebes, then at Troy. The Trojans hurry eagerly to meet and question him, while the Greeks are terrified at the sight of him.*

477-8. **Inde datum molitur iter:** "from there he toils along the appointed path"; *molitur* suggests difficulty. **arva...ultima, quae...secreta:** these fields, "set apart" (*secreta*; cf. 443 *secreti calles*) comprise the last part of the neutral region (cf. 426-547 n.). **bello clari:** "men famous in war."

479-80 **illi:** dative; i.e. Aeneas. **Tydeus...Parthenopaeus...Adrasti:** these were three of the seven heroes who fought in the war against Thebes, which preceded the Trojan War. Adrastus, king of Argos, was their leader. **inclutus:** this archaic adjective meaning "renowned" or "celebrated" (echoing the Homeric epithet κλυτός) is more stately than the equivalent *clari* (478); cf. 562 and 781. There is an implicit irony in applying *inclutus armis* to Parthenopaeus, who ignored the prophecy that he would die a violent death and marched against Thebes anyway, where he was killed. Cf. Statius, *Thebaid* 4.246-50.

481. Here the Trojan dead appear. **multum fleti:** cf. 50 n. **ad superos:** = *apud superos* 568, "much lamented among those above," i.e. "upon earth" or "living." **bello...caduci:** "fallen in battle"; the adjective (*caduci*) is rarely applied to persons in this sense, but Tiberius Donatus on 10.622 suggests it implies premature death.

ingemuit, Glaucumque Medontaque Thersilochumque,
tris Antenoridas Cererique sacrum Polyboeten,
Idaeumque etiam currus, etiam arma tenentem.   485
circumstant animae dextra laevaque frequentes:
nec vidisse semel satis est; iuvat usque morari
et conferre gradum et veniendi discere causas.
at Danaum proceres Agamemnoniaeque phalanges
ut videre virum fulgentiaque arma per umbras,   490
ingenti trepidare metu; pars vertere terga,
ceu quondam petiere rates, pars tollere vocem
exiguam: inceptus clamor frustratur hiantis.

483-4. The Trojan warriors *Glaucus, Medon*, and *Thersilochus* are named in *Iliad* 17.216.
Polyboetes, a priest of Ceres, does not appear in Homer. Priests as fighting men (like
Chloreus, priest of Cybele, 11.768) appear to be a post-Homeric phenomenon.

485. **Idaeum:** was a herald and Priam's charioteer (Homer, *Iliad* 2.248; 24.325, 470). **etiam:**
= *et iam* "even yet," "still," a use fairly common even in prose; cf. *Geo.* 3.189 *invalidus
etiamque tremens etiam inscius aevi.*

486. **dextra laevaque:** ablatives of place where. These ghosts eagerly surround Aeneas.

487-8. **iuvat…:** "they delight to linger still, and to pace beside him, and to inquire the cause
of his coming."

489. **at Danaum:** the Greek reaction to Aeneas (the ghosts of the dead Greek warriors are not
named) contrasts with that of the Trojans. For contracted genitive plural, cf. *Pelasgum* 503,
Teucrum 562, *Graium* 588, and even *currum* 653.

490-1. **ut** = "when." **videre:** *viderunt.* **trepidare…vertere…tollere (492):** historical infinitives.

492-3. **ceu…rates:** the Greek ships were drawn up along the shore and fenced in; the Greeks
were several times driven by sallies of the besieged Trojans to take refuge behind this
stockade. **pars tollere:** observe the order: "some raised a shout—an insubstantial sound:
once begun, their war-cry (*clamor*) frustrates their gaping mouths." **exiguam:** "thin"; their
inability to utter the war-cry astonishes the ghosts. For the assonance of 493 cf. 237 above.
hiantis: accusative plural. Note the contrast with the Greek account of the same events:
through Aeneas, Vergil gives the impression that the Greeks were regularly driven back
to their ships, whereas in Homer the Trojans are represented as having been penned up in
their city for ten years. Fowler (1990) named Vergil's technique of exposing his audience
to a point of view that is not simply that of the poet or of the narrator within the poem
but that functions in conflict with the expected (here, the Homeric) context, "deviant
focalization."

> Atque hic Priamiden laniatum corpore toto
> Deiphobum vidit, lacerum crudeliter ora,   495
> ora manusque ambas, populataque tempora raptis
> auribus et truncas inhonesto vulnere naris.
> vix adeo agnovit pavitantem et dira tegentem
> supplicia, et notis compellat vocibus ultro:
> "Deiphobe armipotens, genus alto a sanguine Teucri,   500
> quis tam crudelis optavit sumere poenas?
> cui tantum de te licuit? mihi fama suprema
> nocte tulit fessum vasta te caede Pelasgum
> procubuisse super confusae stragis acervum.

494—547. Now Aeneas comes upon Deiphobus, Hector's brother, cruelly mangled, and hears the story of his death.

After the death of Paris, Deiphobus had competed successfully against his brother Helenus for Helen's hand in marriage, but was killed and mutilated by Menelaus (Helen's original Greek husband) and Odysseus on the night of Troy's fall. A briefer version of Deiphobus' story (whose exploits are recounted in *Iliad* 13) is told by the bard Demodocus at *Odyssey* 8.517-21 where we learn that Odysseus and Menelaus waged a fierce battle at Deiphobus' house, but neither Deiphobus' death nor his marriage to Helen is explicitly mentioned in Homer. Vergil's version, by contrast, not only makes Deiphobus' marriage and death clear, but also emphasizes the treachery of Helen in aiding the Greek warriors, and the inhuman and disgusting manner of his death. On Deiphobus, see Bleisch (1999).

494-5. Priamiden...Deiphobum: accusative, "Deiphobus, son of Priam." The first syllable of both words is long. Cf. 509 *Priamides* (nominative).

496-7. ora manusque ambas, populataque tempora...truncas...naris: accusatives of respect, governed by *lacerum* (495), "mangled, mutilated." **inhonesto vulnere:** *inhonesto* suggests something disgraceful, not the sort of treatment one Homeric warrior (*inclutus*—though in 479 the adjective is used of pre-Trojan War warriors) would inflict on another.

498-9. vix adeo...: Aeneas "hardly even" recognizes Deiphobus, as the latter cowers (*pavitantem*) and attempts to hide those hideous (*dira*) wounds; *adeo* underscores *vix*.

500. genus...: "O descendant of Teucer's lofty lineage."

501. quis...optavit: "Who chose to exact such cruel vengeance?" The indicative *optavit* indicates that it was the choice of such especially cruel vengeance that excites indignation.

502. cui tantum de te licuit?: "Who was permitted (to exact) such a price from you?" (*cui... licuit*, lit. "To whom was it permitted..."). **suprema | nocte:** as *suprema lux* or *supremum lumen* (735) would be "last day," "day of death," so the night that witnessed Troy's destruction is *suprema nox*.

503-4. fessum...te...procubuisse: "you, exhausted...had fallen down, dead"; accusative and infinitive construction dependent on *mihi fama...tulit*.

tunc egomet tumulum Rhoeteo litore inanem 505
constitui et magna manis ter voce vocavi.
nomen et arma locum servant; te, amice, nequivi
conspicere et patria decedens ponere terra."
ad quae Priamides: "nihil o tibi, amice, relictum;
omnia Deiphobo solvisti et funeris umbris. 510
sed me fata mea et scelus exitiale Lacaenae
his mersere malis: illa haec monimenta reliquit.
namque ut supremam falsa inter gaudia noctem
egerimus, nosti: et nimium meminisse necesse est.
cum fatalis equus saltu super ardua venit 515
Pergama et armatum peditem gravis attulit alvo,

505. **egomet:** emphatic, "with my own hands." **tumulum…inanem:** a monument in place of a tomb. **Rhoeteo litore:** Rhoeteum, on the shore north of Troy (cf. 3.108). It is also the place where Catullus' brother was buried (Catullus 65.7).

506. **magna manis ter voce vocavi:** the solemnity is enhanced by the double alliteration*. For the "last greeting" (231 *novissima verba*) to the dead which formed a part of the funeral ceremony, cf. 2.644 *positum adfati discedite corpus*; 3.68 *animam…supremum voce ciemus*.

507. **te, amice:** *te* in hiatus becomes short, as here.

508. **patria…terra:** construe this ablative phrase closely with *ponere*.

509. **nihil…, amice, relictum:** Deiphobus repeats Aeneas' friendly opening (507), "My friend, nothing has been neglected by you."

510. **omnia:** in contrast to *nihil* (509). **funeris umbris:** "for the ghost of the dead"; *funus* here is "corpse."

511-12. **Lacaenae:** genitive, "of the Spartan woman." It is a contemptuous reference to Helen: he will not name her. **his mersere malis:** as in 505, another echo of Catullus' sorrow for his brother: *accipe, qui<bu>s merser fortunae fluctibus* (68.13). The metaphor is of a shipwrecked sailor. **illa:** very emphatic, "*that* woman" (Helen). **haec monimenta:** deictic. Note the irony and antithesis* between the two halves of 511-12.

513-14. **ut…egerimus:** indirect question dependent on *nosti* (514); *ut* = "how." **falsa…gaudia:** their joy at the feigned departure of the Greeks was misinformed, as everyone now knows (*nosti* = *no<vi>sti*). When the city was buried in slumber, the warriors concealed in the belly of the horse descended and opened the gates to their comrades. **egerimus:** the -*i*- in the subjunctive ending was originally long, but here is short, "the earliest certain example of this prosody in the perfect subjunctive form" (Austin *ad loc.*, citing Norden).

515-16. **fatalis equus:** the Trojan horse, cf. 2.237-8 *scandit fatalis machina muros feta armis*. **saltu…venit:** cf. Ennius, *Alexander* fr. 80-1 in Warmington (a reference to Paris) *Nam maximo saltu superabit gravidus armatis equus | qui suo partu ardua perdat Pergama*, and Aeschylus, *Agammemnon* 825. The phrase vividly describes the horse as something living and animated with an eager desire for Troy's destruction. For the actual dragging of it into the city, cf. 2.234. **gravis:** cf. Ennius' *gravidus*, "pregnant" (see above); Vergil's *gravis* also suggests the *fatal* character of the offspring who were to come forth from that "heavy womb."

illa chorum simulans euhantis orgia circum
ducebat Phrygias; flammam media ipsa tenebat
ingentem et summa Danaos ex arce vocabat.
tum me confectum curis somnoque gravatum   520
infelix habuit thalamus, pressitque iacentem
dulcis et alta quies placidaeque simillima morti.
egregia interea coniunx arma omnia tectis
amovet et fidum capiti subduxerat ensem;
intra tecta vocat Menelaum et limina pandit,   525
scilicet id magnum sperans fore munus amanti,
et famam exstingui veterum sic posse malorum.
quid moror? inrumpunt thalamo, comes additus una

---

517. **illa:** i.e. Helen. **euhantis orgia:** "celebrating with Bacchic cries the (sacred) revels." Torchlight processions of women at night were common in the worship of Bacchus. **circum:** construe as adverb.

518. **flammam...tenebat:** in 2.256 the signal comes from the Greek ship to Sinon; in other versions, Sinon sends the signal to the Greeks, or Antenor is the traitor responsible. Other accounts say there were two signals, one from Sinon and one from Helen. Cf. Austin *ad* 6.519 for more details. Here Deiphobus accuses Helen of sending the signal. Cf. Austin *ad loc.* for more details.

519. **summa...ex arce:** "from the top of the citadel." This clashes with 2.567-88 (the spurious "Helen episode"), where Helen has taken refuge in the temple of Vesta.

523. **egregia:** in bitter scorn, "my excellent wife," cf. 4.93.

524. **amovet...subduxerat:** "removes all my weapons and had already slipped my trusty sword away from my head" (*capiti*, dative of separation). (He would have kept his sword near his head, ready to be used.) The change of tense in *subduxerat* indicates that this action had preceded the other, suggesting Helen had already planned to betray him before this opportune moment.

526. **scilicet:** strongly accentuates her pre-planned betrayal, which is also marked in *amanti* —"doubtless hoping that this would be a noble gift to her lover," a reference to her returning husband, Menelaus.

527. **famam exstingui...posse:** continuing the accusative and infitive construction after *sperans* (526).

528. **quid moror?:** a rhetorical question, summing up and anticipating the conclusion. **una:** adverb.

hortator scelerum Aeolides. di, talia Grais
instaurate, pio si poenas ore reposco. 530
sed te qui vivum casus, age fare vicissim,
attulerint. pelagine venis erroribus actus
an monitu divum? an quae te fortuna fatigat,
ut tristis sine sole domos, loca turbida, adires?"
    Hac vice sermonum roseis Aurora quadrigis 535
iam medium aetherio cursu traiecerat axem;
et fors omne datum traherent per talia tempus,
sed comes admonuit breviterque adfata Sibylla est:
"nox ruit, Aenea; nos flendo ducimus horas.

---

529. **hortator scelerum Aeolides:** i.e. Ulysses. He is called "child of Aeolus" intentionally, referring to the tradition that, although his mother was wife of Laertes, his real father was Sisyphus, son of Aeolus. Sisyphus was the least scrupulous, most cunning of mortals, and thus typifies badly-used cleverness. Ulysses is here characterized not as "the wise counselor," as in Homer but (as in later tradition, from Sophocles to Dante) as a manipulating scoundrel, who persuades others to carry out the crimes he dare not perpetrate himself. Cf. 2.164 *scelerumque inventor Vlixes*.

530. **instaurate:** *instaurare*, "renew," is a religious word. With *sacra* it signifies repeating a rite that was not duly carried out, hence it is used here in prayer. Here he is asking the gods to renew his sufferings, but they are to be inflicted this time upon the Greeks. **si:** = "as surely as." Deiphobus grounds his appeal on the "piety" of the mouth (*pio...ore*) that utters it.

531. **qui...casus:** nominative plural. **age, fare vicissim:** the imperatives reflect his impatience. "Come now, tell me..." In Vergil, an adverb (*vicissim*) at the end of the line is unusual.

532. **attulerint:** perfect subjunctive in indirect question. **pelagi...erroribus:** literally, "by wanderings on the open sea" (*pelagi* is locative); *erroribus* and *monitu* are ablative of means, governed by *actus*.

533-4. **an quae...:** "or what Fortune harries you to you approach these sad sunless halls, the dwelling of disorder?" **fatigat, | ut...adires:** indirect command; the secondary sequence of tenses after *fatigat* suggests "still harasses you (as it did harass you)...."

535-47. The Sibyl reminds Aeneas that he must not linger; they have reached the point where the path diverges in two opposing directions (540). Deiphobus bids farewell and returns to the shadows

535-6. **Hac vice sermonum:** "amid such interchange of speech." **roseis Aurora quadrigis...:** "Aurora in her rose-colored chariot had already passed the central pole in her journey through the heavens," i.e. on earth, it was past midday. **medium...axem:** the central axis or midpoint around which the heavens seem to revolve. *Aurora* = dawn (cf. metonomy*).

537. **fors...traherent:** much of the allotted time had already passed, and "perhaps (*fors*, adverb) they would now continue to spend all the allotted time (*traherent*, implied present contrary-to-fact apodosis)..." For this reason, the Sibyl interrupts them and brings their conversation to a close.

539. **nox ruit:** "night is rushing on," i.e. it is near nightfall. When "night falls" in Vergil (cf. 2.8 *nox praecipitat*), it is sinking to its close. **flendo:** gerund (ablative).

hic locus est partis ubi se via findit in ambas: 540
dextera quae Ditis magni sub moenia tendit,
hac iter Elysium nobis; at laeva malorum
exercet poenas et ad impia Tartara mittit."
Deiphobus contra: "ne saevi, magna sacerdos;
discedam, explebo numerum reddarque tenebris.   545
i decus, i, nostrum; melioribus utere fatis."
tantum effatus, et in verbo vestigia torsit.
     Respicit Aeneas subito et sub rupe sinistra

---

540. **partis...in ambas:** the word "both" can only be used when two things have been already mentioned, or where reference is made to things notoriously two in number, e.g. "with both eyes." Vergil's use of *ambas* assumes that every one knows the path here diverges in two directions.

541-2. **dextera quae <via>..., hac iter Elysium nobis:** "the path on the right hand which leads under the walls...by this one is our route to Elysium." *Elysium* is accusative after the idea of motion toward in *iter <est>*, cf. 3.507.

542-3. **at laeva <via> malorum | exercet poenas:** how the path on the left "exacts the punishment of evil-doers" is at once explained by the succeeding words. **impia:** the evil of its residents attaches to the place.

544. **ne saevi:** this use of *ne* + the imperative for a negative command is archaic; more usual would be the jussive subjunctive, *ne saevias*.

545. **explebo numerum:** "I will complete (i.e. fill) the number (of ghosts)" by going back and becoming one of them. Deiphobus had left the ranks of dead warriors in their "sunless dwelling" (534) and was following Aeneas, who was passing on to the sunny realms of Elysium. He retreats from this brighter path into the gloom and reoccupies the place he had left vacant.

546. This famous verse marks a turning point for Aeneas, as he ends his encounters with the past, and turns toward the future. After the following account of Tartarus by the Sibyl, Aeneas will meet with his father and take the first steps toward becoming a Roman (cf. 851-3).

547. **in verbo vestigia torsit:** "turned his tracks in mid-speech."

548—627. Aeneas, looking around, sees before him a vast and awful fortress from which come groans and sounds of woe. As he stares at the gates and buildings, the Sibyl explains that this is the abode of the damned, which she alone of those who are righteous has been allowed to enter, and then (562-620) in an extended ecphrasis*, she describes its inhabitants and their punishments. The description of Tartarus, like the description of the scenes Aeneas observes on Juno's temple in 1.446-93, is one of the major ecphrases* in the Aeneid.

548. **Respicit:** Aeneas, who has turned to the right towards Elysium, "looks back" (*sinistra <manu>,* ablative, "on the left") after the departing Deiphobus, and thus finds himself facing the gates of Tartarus.

moenia lata videt triplici circumdata muro,
quae rapidus flammis ambit torrentibus amnis,   550
Tartareus Phlegethon, torquetque sonantia saxa.
porta adversa ingens solidoque adamante columnae,
vis ut nulla virum, non ipsi exscindere bello
caelicolae valeant; stat ferrea turris ad auras,
Tisiphoneque sedens palla succincta cruenta   555
vestibulum exsomnis servat noctesque diesque.
hinc exaudiri gemitus et saeva sonare
verbera, tum stridor ferri tractaeque catenae.
constitit Aeneas strepitumque exterritus hausit.
"quae scelerum facies? o virgo, effare; quibusve   560
urgentur poenis? quis tantus clangor ad auris?"
tum vates sic orsa loqui: "dux inclute Teucrum,

549. **moenia:** here refers to the buildings of the city, whereas *triplici muro* refers to the actual walls; cf. 2.234 *dividimus muros and moenia urbis.*

550-1. **quae <moenia>:** accusative. **flammis torrentibus…Phlegethon:** the name of the River of Fire (Phlegethon) is derived from from the Greek *flegein,* "to burn" (cf. 616 *Phlegyas*). **ambit:** it surrounds Tartarus (*Tartareus,* adjective), like a moat.

552-4. **porta:** "confronting him (is) a mighty gate and doorposts of solid adamant." Adamant (*adamas*) is a legendary metal of extreme hardness. The doorposts are called *columnae* because of their size. The spondaic meter perhaps suggests the weight of the doors. **columnae, | vis ut nulla vir<or>um, non ipsi…caelicolae valeant:** a word like *tantae* is implied with *columnae,* and is followed by a negative result clause—"columns (so great) that…" **exscindere…valeant:** *vis nullla* and *ipsi caelicolae* are subjects of *valeant; eas* (i.e. *columnas*) is the understood object of *exscindere.* **stat:** "rising up" is implicit with *ad auras,* "to meet the breezes."

555. **palla succincta cruenta:** "girded with a bloody cape." Compare the description of *Tisiphone* below (cf. 570-1 n.), which anticipates the actions of Allecto in book 7.

556. **exsomnis…noctesque diesque:** the Fury never rests.

557-8. **hinc…:** "from here…" **exaudiri…sonare:** historical infinitives. **saeva sonare | verbera:** fierce lashes make the sound that lashes make (*sonare*). *Saeva verbera* is accusative of the inner object (cognate accusative). **tum…:** "then too (are heard) the creaking of iron and dragged chains."

559. **hausit:** he "drank in" or "devoured" the noise (*strepitum*). Some manuscripts read *haesit* instead of *hausit,* but this would require the dative instead of the accusative case.

560-1. Aeneas' questions have a staccato quality, a reflection perhaps of his shock and terror. **quis tantus clangor ad auris?:** supply a verb like *venit.*

562. The Sibyl now tells Aeneas of the sinners, their sins, and their punishments in Tartarus. **inclute:** a formal address (cf. 479). **Teucrum:** cf. 489 n.

nulli fas casto sceleratum insistere limen;
sed me cum lucis Hecate praefecit Avernis,
ipsa deum poenas docuit perque omnia duxit.   565
Gnosius haec Rhadamanthus habet durissima regna
castigatque auditque dolos subigitque fateri
quae quis apud superos furto laetatus inani
distulit in seram commissa piacula mortem.
continuo sontis ultrix accincta flagello   570
Tisiphone quatit insultans, torvosque sinistra
intentans anguis vocat agmina saeva sororum.
tum demum horrisono stridentes cardine sacrae

---

563. **nulli:** dative. **fas:** supply *est.* Note the slow rhythm as she begins her account with a skilful inversion of the rule that the guilty may not tread on holy ground: "No holy foot may tread that guilty threshold." The Sibyl explains that she, however, was an exception.

564. **cum:** temporal. **lucis…Avernis:** "the groves of Avernus (adjective)"; dative after *praefecit.* Although the Sibyl is *casta*, she was permitted by Hecate to enter Tartarus in order to learn what she needed to know as prophet.

565. **deum:** subjective genitive.

566. **Gnosius:** "of/from Cnossos," a city on the island of Crete. **Rhadamanthus:** Rhadamanthus, Aeacus, and Minos were the judges of the dead. According to Plato (*Gorgias* 524a), Rhadamanthus, the brother of Minos, judged the dead who came from Asia, Aeacus judged the dead from Europe. For Minos, see 431-3 n.

567. **castigatque auditque dolos subigitque:** Rhadamanthus chastises or reprimands them (*castigat*) and hears their confessions of fraud (*dolos*). The legal term *dolus malus*, "malice aforethought," constitutes the criminality of an action. The repeated *–que* links the actions closely so that they seem almost simultaneous.

568. **quae:** the antecedent *ea* is implicit, "(those things) which"; **quis:** = *aliquis.* **furto…inani:** a *furtum* is any fraudulent act; it will be rendered useless (*inani*) by the punishment.

569. **seram:** "late," "too late"; the opportunity for expiation is lost when death comes. **commissa piacula:** "crimes (they have) committed"; a *piaculum* is a crime requiring expiation.

570-1. **continuo:** as soon as Rhadamanthus has pronounced them guilty, "straightway vengeful Tisiphone, armed with a scourge, hounds the guilty (*sontis*), leaping upon them." **ultrix:** "avenging"; the root of Tisiphone's name, *tisis*, in Greek also means "avenger" (Servius *ad* 4.609). Note the alliteration of *t* and *s* in lines 570-2. Tisiphone, one of the three Erinyes (also called "Furies" and "Eumenides," e.g. in Aeschylus' *Oresteia*), avenges murder. **quatit:** the verb means "agitate," "keep in restless motion" and should be construed closely with *accincta flagello* and *insultans.* The picture is that of a brutal driver urging on a crowd of terrified animals; cf. 12.337-8 *equos…fumantis sudore quatit*; *Geo.* 3.132 *cursu quatiunt et sole fatigant.*

573. **cardine:** not a "hinge" but a pivot, with one socket in the sill, and the other in the lintel. Cf. 2.493 *emoti procumbunt cardine postes.*

panduntur portae. cernis custodia qualis
vestibulo sedeat, facies quae limina servet?   575
quinquaginta atris immanis hiatibus Hydra
saevior intus habet sedem. tum Tartarus ipse
bis patet in praeceps tantum tenditque sub umbras
quantus ad aetherium caeli suspectus Olympum.
hic genus antiquum Terrae, Titania pubes,   580
fulmine deiecti fundo volvuntur in imo.
hic et Aloidas geminos immania vidi
corpora, qui manibus magnum rescindere caelum
adgressi superisque Iovem detrudere regnis.
vidi et crudelis dantem Salmonea poenas,   585
dum flammas Iovis et sonitus imitatur Olympi.
quattuor hic invectus equis et lampada quassans
per Graium populos mediaeque per Elidis urbem
ibat ovans, divumque sibi poscebat honorem,

574-5. **custodia qualis...sedeat...servet?:** the rhetorical questions refer to Tisiphone, the single "watch" seen on this side of the door, in contrast to an (unseen) fifty-headed Hydra (576) with inky, black jaws that sits on the other side of the gate. This appears to be a different Hydra from the one in the *vestibulum* (287).

576. **Hydra:** cf. 574-5 n. For the onomatopoetic* sound of this line, cf. 237 above.

577-9. **Tartarus...bis patet in praeceps tantum...quantus ad aetherium caeli suspectus Olympum:** "Tartarus gapes open downward twice as far...as is the view of the sky upward...to heavenly Olympus." For the imagery, cf. 4.443.

580-1. The list of sinners now begins. **genus antiquum...Titania pubes:** the Titans, son of Earth and Sky, were defeated when they tried to overthrow Zeus and were cast into Tartarus. **volvuntur...:** "they writhe at the bottom of the pit." The passive form is the equivalent of the Greek middle voice (cf. 156 n.)—they are turning themselves.

582-4. **Aloidas geminos:** Otus and Ephialtes, twin Giants who piled Mt. Ossa on Olympus, and then added Mt. Pelion on top of that in an effort to make war on the gods in the heavens. Cf. Homer, *Iliad* 5.386; *Odyssey* 11.306; Apollodorus, *Library* 1.7.4; and Horace, *Odes* 3.42-80, where an analogy with Augustus' own wars against evil are suggested.

585. **Salmonea:** Greek accusative. Salmoneus, founder of a city in Elis, arrogantly thought he could imitate Jupiter's thunder (cf. 586-94).

586. **dum...imitatur:** in this prose construction, *dum* takes the present indicative ("historical present") to denote continued action in past time (cf. AG §469, 556)

588. **mediaeque per Elidis urbem:** "through the city in the middle of Elis." Olympia is located in Elis, hence the location is all the more insulting as it is the very place where the Olympian Jupiter was especially worshipped.

589. **ovans:** like an Olympian victor! **divum:** cf. 125 n.

demens, qui nimbos et non imitabile fulmen   590
aere et cornipedum pulsu simularet equorum.
at pater omnipotens densa inter nubila telum
contorsit, non ille faces nec fumea taedis
lumina, praecipitemque immani turbine adegit.
nec non et Tityon, Terrae omniparentis alumnum,   595
cernere erat, per tota novem cui iugera corpus
porrigitur, rostroque immanis vultur obunco
immortale iecur tondens fecundaque poenis
viscera rimaturque epulis habitatque sub alto
pectore, nec fibris requies datur ulla renatis.   600

590-1. **demens, qui...simularet:** "Madman! to mimic the clouds and inimitable
thunderbolt" (*qui...simularet* is relative clause of characteristic). **aere:** with bronze vessels, or
perhaps his chariot was made of bronze.

593. **contorsit:** he "whirled" his missile headlong. The emphasis is on the secure, steady spin
(*immani turbine* 594) of Jupiter's thunderbolt. **non ille:** Jupiter; *ille* is pleonastic* but is
added to emphasize strongly the contrast between *pater omnipotens* and Salmoneus.

594. **praecipitem:** "headlong," implicitly straight down into Tartarus.

595-6. **nec non...:** a connecting phrase, "and moreover"; the double negative (litotes*)
emphasizes the positive statement. **Tityon:** a son of Zeus and Elara. Fearing his wife's
jealousy, Zeus concealed Elara deep in the earth, from which Tityos emerged when he
was born. Tityos attacked Leto after she gave birth to Zeus' children Apollo and Artemis,
but Zeus struck him with his thunderbolt, and now a serpent or a vulture (two vultures
in Homer) consumes his liver, which continually grows back; cf. Hesiod, *Theogony* 523-
33. In other versions Apollo and Artemis killed him when he attacked Leto, and he fell to
earth, where his body covered nine *iugera*, or six acres (a *iugerum* is about 2/3 of an acre).
Terrae...alumnum: since he was nurtured and thus "borne" from the Earth.

596. **cernere erat:** impersonal construction, "it was also (permitted) to see."

597. **cui:** dative of reference; translate as "whose."

598. **tondens:** "trimming back" or "grazing upon the deathless liver and entrails rich
(*fecunda*) for (or in) punishment," i.e. the liver eternally produces fresh material to feed
upon. **poenis:** dative (or ablative).

599-600. **rimaturque epulis habitatque sub alto | pectore:** "pries open (the liver) for a feast
and settles deep in (the victim's) breast." **epulis:** dative of purpose. **renatis:** from *renascor*;
they grow again as fast as they are eaten.

quid memorem Lapithas, Ixiona Pirithoumque?
quos super atra silex iam iam lapsura cadentique
imminet adsimilis; lucent genialibus altis
aurea fulcra toris, epulaeque ante ora paratae
regifico luxu; furiarum maxima iuxta 605
accubat et manibus prohibet contingere mensas,
exsurgitque facem attollens atque intonat ore.

601. **quid memorem?:** the rhetorical question serves as another transition; *memorem* is a deliberative subjunctive. **Lapithas, Ixiona Pirithoumque:** Pirithous was the son of Ixion's wife and king of the Lapiths; he attempted, with the help of Theseus, to kidnap Proserpina (cf. 393 n.) from the underworld, but now is imprisoned there forever. The fight between the Lapiths and the Centaurs, which was depicted on the temple of Zeus at Olympia, occurred at the wedding of Pirithous, who invited the Centaurs to his wedding feast. Ixion attempted to rape Hera, but instead fathered, from the storm cloud Zeus had devised to look like Hera, the race of Centaurs. His traditional punishment in the underworld is to be whirled eternally on a wheel. In Vergil, however, the punishments of the Lapiths, Ixion and Perithous are more similar to those traditionally assigned to Tantalus, who in some accounts is eternally threatened by an unstable, overhanging rock (cf. 616-17, where other sinners also suffer this punishment), and in other accounts is desperately hungry and thirsty, and is tantalized by food and drink that move away when he attempts to taste them.

602. **quos super:** anastrophe*. **iam iam lapsura cadentique:** *iam iam* means "now, now," at every moment it is about to slip. Observe the accommodation of sound to sense—the overhanging syllable of the hypermetric* line (*cadenti- | qu[e] imminet*) suggests the overhanging rock.

603-4. **lucent...| aurea fulcra toris:** tall festal couches with "golden supports" that shine brightly (*lucent*) are piled high with cushions for participants in a sumptuous banquet. *Fulcra* are not "feet," but ornamental supports or rests for the cushions of a couch. **genialibus:** *genialis* usually refers to a bridal bed, but here it simply refers to the festal occasion.

605. **regifico:** "fit for a king." **furiarum maxima:** an unidentified Fury (partitive genitive governed by the superlative) stays close to them, enforcing their punishments.

606. **prohibet:** supply *eos* as object.

hic, quibus invisi fratres, dum vita manebat,
pulsatusve parens aut fraus innexa clienti,
aut qui divitiis soli incubuere repertis   610
nec partem posuere suis (quae maxima turba est),
quique ob adulterium caesi, quique arma secuti
impia nec veriti dominorum fallere dextras,
inclusi poenam exspectant. ne quaere doceri
quam poenam, aut quae forma viros fortunave mersit.   615
saxum ingens volvunt alii, radiisque rotarum
districti pendent; sedet aeternumque sedebit

608-14. **invisi fratres...pulsatusve parens...fraus innexa clienti...**: the next three pairs
of sinners, while based in part on Greek tradition, have committed violations against
particularly Roman social connections and ideas (see individual notes), including family
ties, legal obligations between patron and client, and the proper use of wealth (cf. 610-11).

608. **hic quibus...**: i.e. *hic (sunt ei) quibus.... Hic* is adverbial. **invisi:** supply *sunt.*

609. **pulsatus...innexa:** supply *est* and construe with *quibus* (608) as dative of agent. **fraus
innexa clienti**: "guile devised against a dependant," thus violating the Laws of the XII
Tables (the basis of early Roman Law), which say *Patronus, si clienti fraudem fecerit, sacer
esto* ("let him be cursed"). Conversely, the reciprocal duty of the client to his patron is
referred to below, in 613.

610. **divitiis....incubuere:** greed in a wealthy person is a serious fault; in *Geo.* 2.507, the greedy
miser is described as *defosso...incubat auro;* cf. Horace, *Satires* 1.1.70-1. **repertis:** not "found
by accident," for there could hardly be "a very great throng" of such discoverers of treasure,
but "gained" or "won" with trouble and difficulty after searching; cf. *repertus* in 718.

611. **posuere:** "set aside," possibly with the idea of investing. Those who have not set aside a
portion of their wealth for their relatives (*suis*) comprise the bulk of this group. Note the
simplicity of the words *quae maxima turba est.*

612-13. **quique ob adulterium caesi:** a woman caught in adultery could be killed by her
husband, but the adulterers could also be killed or punished. In 18 BCE (after the death
of Vergil) adultery was officially brought into the scope of the criminal law. **quique arma
secuti | impia nec veriti dominorum fallere dextras:** "those who took up arms in an
unholy cause or did not fear to violate the loyalty owed to their masters." *Arma impia*
implies civil war (cf. Horace, *Odes* 2.1.30 *impia proelia*), and *dominorum fallere dextras*
appears to be a reference to the war with Sextus Pompeius in 36 BCE, and particularly to
his enlistment of slaves in that cause.

614. **ne quaere:** an archaic construction (cf. 73-4 n. on *ne manda*).

615. **quam poenam:** sc. *exspectant* (614). **mersit:** the subjunctive of indirect question would be
more usual, but the indicative is more vivid, in keeping with the character of the Sibyl's words.

616-17. **saxum:** Sisyphus, who is doomed to roll a stone continually uphill which continually
rolls back again, is here suggested as a model for the others in this group. **volvunt alii...
pendent <alii>:** "some...others..." **radiisque rotarum:** Ixion is pinned on a revolving wheel
(cf. 601 n.). **districti:** "stretched out," from *distringere*.

infelix Theseus, Phlegyasque miserrimus omnis
admonet et magna testatur voce per umbras:
"discite iustitiam moniti et non temnere divos."   620
vendidit hic auro patriam dominumque potentem
imposuit; fixit leges pretio atque refixit;
hic thalamum invasit natae vetitosque hymenaeos:
ausi omnes immane nefas ausoque potiti.
non, mihi si linguae centum sint oraque centum,   625
ferrea vox, omnis scelerum comprendere formas,
omnia poenarum percurrere nomina possim."

618. **infelix Theseus:** in contrast with 122, where Hercules rescues him, Theseus is here doomed forever to some form of sedentary life. **Phlegyas:** father of Ixion. Apollo raped his daughter Coronis, and in revenge Ixion set fire to Apollo's temple at Delphi. **omnis:** accusative plural.

619. **testatur:** literally, "calls to witness"; he makes a solemn appeal to all to hear his words of warning (*admonet*). Of course the warning was useless in the underworld, but it is really being addressed by the poet to people on earth.

620. A chilling line and a warning to all. Read *moniti* (now that you have been warned) *discite iustitiam et non temnere...* **non temnere:** object infinitive after *discite*.

621-4. The wrongs in this group join treason with incest. Macrobius (*Saturnalia* 6.1.39) indicates that lines 621-2 are adapted from Varius: *vendidit hic Latium populis, agrosque Quiritum | eripuit, fixit leges pretio atque refixit*. Roman laws were inscribed on bronze tablets and set up in the forum; only a truly corrupt official would pass laws (*fixit*), and then, for a bribe (*pretio*), undo them (*refixit*).

621. **auro:** ablative of price.

623. Incest was a subject of literary interest in Republican and Augustan Rome. Vergil's Greek teacher Parthenius wrote a collection of love stories (*Erotika Pathemata*), dedicated to Vergil's friend Gallus, which included several such stories, and Ovid includes the stories of Myrrha (*Metamorphoses* 10.298-502) and of Byblis (*Metamorphoses* 9.454-665) in his poem. **hymenaeos:** the Greek word permits a quadrisyllabic ending to the line; cf. 4.99, 4.316; other examples: *elephanto* 6.895, 3.464; *cyparissi* 3.680; *hyacinthus* 11.69. So too with proper names: *Erymantho* 5.448 and *Adamasto* 3.614.

624. **ausi...:** "all dared an enormous wrong (*immane nefas*) and attained what they dared"; *potiti* (from *potior*) governs the ablative.

625-7. **non, mihi...ferrea vox...:** the Sibyl concludes her account of the punishments in Tartarus with a flourish; lines 625-6 are repeated from *Geo.* 2.43-4, where they summarize Vergil's praise of Maecenas—in sharp contrast to this context—and are based on *Iliad* 2.488-9 and Ennius, *Annales* 561-2.

Haec ubi dicta dedit Phoebi longaeva sacerdos,
"sed iam age, carpe viam et susceptum perfice munus;
acceleremus" ait; "Cyclopum educta caminis　　　　　630
moenia conspicio atque adverso fornice portas,
haec ubi nos praecepta iubent deponere dona."
dixerat et pariter gressi per opaca viarum
corripiunt spatium medium foribusque propinquant.
occupat Aeneas aditum corpusque recenti　　　　　635
spargit aqua ramumque adverso in limine figit.
　　　His demum exactis, perfecto munere divae,
devenere locos laetos et amoena virecta

628—36. The Sibyl and Aeneas now turn away from Tartarus, deposit the golden bough, and take the alternate path, toward Elysium.

628. **Haec...sacerdos:** compare line 321, of which this is a variation.

629. **carpe viam:** literally, "seize the path," i.e. "quickly pursue your journey." Cf. 634 *corripiunt spatium medium*; 5.316. **susceptum perfice munus:** "complete the duty undertaken," by bringing the golden bough as an offering to Proserpina (142).

630-1. **Cyclopum educta...moenia:** the entrance to Elysium was constructed (*educta*) by Vulcan and the Cyclopes in their forges. At this entrance (cf. 635-6 *aditum...adverso in limine*) Aeneas must deposit the golden bough. **adverso:** "facing," "opposite."

633. **per opaca viarum:** a favorite type of periphrasis* which really means "along the dark paths" but throws the emphasis on the substantive adjective *opaca* (cf. 2.332).

634. **corripiunt spatium:** they accomplish the journey they began in 629 (*carpe viam*) by covering the intervening distance.

635-6. **occupat Aeneas aditum:** repeated from 424. **corpusque recenti | spargit aqua:** a ceremony of purification on entering a sacred place or commencing a holy rite is usual.

637-78. They proceed to the groves of the blessed, where the souls of the blessed, the great and good dwell. The Sibyl inquires where Anchises is to be found, and Musaeus offers to guide them.

637. **His demum exactis:** "this done, then (but not before)"; cf. 154 n.

638. **virecta:** "green places." The word is coined by Vergil, from *virere*, "to be verdant."

fortunatorum nemorum sedesque beatas.
largior hic campos aether et lumine vestit   640
purpureo, solemque suum, sua sidera norunt.
pars in gramineis exercent membra palaestris,
contendunt ludo et fulva luctantur harena;
pars pedibus plaudunt choreas et carmina dicunt.
nec non Threicius longa cum veste sacerdos   645
obloquitur numeris septem discrimina vocum,

---

639. **fortunatorum nemorum sedesque beatas:** Vergil's Elysium is an extensive development of the concept found in Homer and Hesiod, both of whom speak of a place apart from mortal suffering, to which the heroes of Troy and Thebes were removed, apart from the grim underworld. Elysium is mentioned in Homer's *Odyssey* 4.561-8; Hesiod, *Works and Days* 167-73 describes it; cf. Pindar, *Olympian* 2.56 ff.; Plato, *Phaedo* 114c; Horace, *Epode* 16; Tibullus 1.3.57-66 and K.F. Smith's commentary *ad loc.*; for Orphic elements cf. Guthrie, *Orpheus and Greek Religion*. This idyllic place has much in common with the Golden Age, first described in Hesiod, *Works and Days* 109-120 as a privileged race free from pain and sorrow, which reappears in Vergil's Fourth *Eclogue* and *Geo.* 2.173-6. It appears again in *Aeneid* 7, where Latinus proudly announces that the Latin people are the Golden Race, but in *Aeneid* 8 Evander tells about the decline of this once-golden race. For further discussion, see Johnston (1980). Here Vergil's Elysium combines *otium* and *negotium*: the inhabitants enjoy poetry and leisure, but they continue to appreciate war-horses and chariots.

640-1. **largior...aether:** a "more generous aether/upper air"; the comparison can be to that of the air in the mortal world, or, alternatively, to the rest of the underworld. **lumine... purpureo:** the phrase may be descriptive ablative, describing the aether, "of dazzling light." Ancient purple had two characteristics—its rich color (the color of clotted blood) and its peculiar sheen or radiance. Hence *purpureus* means "purple" or, as here, "dazzling," "radiant," as in Vergil's description of Spring, *hic ver purpureum, Ecl.* 9.40. Cf. *purpureos flores* 5.79; 6.884; *lumenque iuventae purpureum* 1.590. **solemque suum, sua sidera norunt:** like Hesiod's Isles of the Blessed (*Works and Days* 167-73), Elysium enjoys its own fine weather. The inhabitants of this region are the subject of *no(ve)runt*.

642. **pars...pars (644):** "some...others."

644. **pars pedibus plaudunt choreas:** note the alliteration, mimicking the dance; *choreas* is cognate accusative.

645. **Threïcius...sacerdos:** "the Thracian seer" = Orpheus, who was not merely a poet but a prophet and the founder of the Orphic mysteries. Cf. 661-2 and 703-23 n. **longa...veste:** the "long robe" seems especially to have been worn by musicians. Cf. Horace, *Ars Poetica* 215 *tibicen, traxitque vagus per pulpita vestem*, and Ovid, *Fasti* 6.596. The *locus classicus* for the story of Orpheus and Eurydice is Vergil, *Geo.* 4.453-527.

646. **obloquitur numeris septem discrimina vocum:** the "differences of seven sounds" (*septem discrimina* is cognate accusative) are the seven distinct notes of the ancient lyre's seven strings, which Orpheus "utters as an accompaniment" (*obloquitur*) "to the rhythm" (*numeris*).

iamque eadem digitis, iam pectine pulsat eburno.
hic genus antiquum Teucri, pulcherrima proles,
magnanimi heroes, nati melioribus annis,
Ilusque Assaracusque et Troiae Dardanus auctor.   650
arma procul currusque virum miratur inanis.
stant terra defixae hastae passimque soluti
per campum pascuntur equi. quae gratia currum
armorumque fuit vivis, quae cura nitentis
pascere equos, eadem sequitur tellure repostos.   655
conspicit, ecce, alios dextra laevaque per herbam
vescentis laetumque choro paeana canentis
inter odoratum lauri nemus, unde superne
plurimus Eridani per silvam volvitur amnis.
hic manus ob patriam pugnando vulnera passi,   660
quique sacerdotes casti, dum vita manebat,

---

647. digitis…pectine: he played at times with his fingers (i.e. quietly), at times with his plectrum (i.e. loudly). The *pecten* (plectrum) was held in the right hand.

648-50. First named of the blessed race of heroes is *Teucer*, traditional ancestor of the Trojans (cf. 3.108); in another legend, *Dardanus* was already in Troy when Teucer arrived (cf. 3.167). *Ilus* was father of Laomedon and grandfather of Priam; Ilus' brother *Assaracus* was father of Capys and grandfather of Anchises.

651. procul: their weapons are a considerable distance away from them. **inanis:** not "empty," but "unreal," "ghostly."

653-5. quae gratia currum…: "the *same* delight in chariots…*that* was theirs in life, the same care to feed their glossy steeds" attends them now. The contracted genitive plural *currum* (for *curruum*) is rare. Cf. Martial 2.5.3 *duo milia passum*. Some manuscripts give *curruum*, the final syllable being elided with *armorum*. **cura…pascere:** poetic use of the infinitive, showing purpose; cf. AG §460c. **tellure repos<i>tos:** i.e. when buried.

656. dextra laevaque: ablative of place where.

657. vescentis…canentis: "eating and singing." **choro:** ablative, "in a choral dance." **paeana:** Greek accusative, modified by *laetum*. In Greek, a *paeon* is a hymn of gladness.

658-9. odoratum lauri nemus: *lauri* is genitive of specification (AG §349d). Ancient manuscripts, with one exception, read *lauri*, "fragrant with laurel"; Mynors and some other editors accept *lauris*, which is found in a fifth century manuscript and places the emphasis on the scent rather than on the trees. **unde superne…:** "from which source rolls the full flood of Eridanus through the forest into the upper world." Vergil identifies the Eridanus as the river Po (*Padus*).

660. hic: adverb. **manus:** bands of men (nominative plural), with *passi*. Note that warriors (659) and those who improved human life through their discoveries are here joined with poets and priests in Vergil's Elysium.

quique pii vates et Phoebo digna locuti,
inventas aut qui vitam excoluere per artis,
quique sui memores alios fecere merendo:
omnibus his nivea cinguntur tempora vitta.   665
quos circumfusos sic est adfata Sibylla,
Musaeum ante omnis (medium nam plurima turba
hunc habet atque umeris exstantem suspicit altis):
"dicite, felices animae, tuque, optime vates,
quae regio Anchisen, quis habet locus? illius ergo   670
venimus et magnos Erebi tranavimus amnis."
atque huic responsum paucis ita reddidit heros:

---

662. **vates:** the word (plural) means "poets" or "seers," since the two skills were considered to be one and the same.

663-4. "And those who enriched life by the discovery of skills and who by their services caused some people to remember them." (*Sui* is objective genitive, governed by *memores*.) **excoluere:** suggests *cultus*, which is the Latin word for "civilization," all that tends to make life less savage and barbarous. A widely accepted belief at Rome, which is reflected in Vergil's works, was that of the third century Alexandrian writer, Euhemerus, who wrote that all the gods were once mortal and were made gods after their deaths because they had improved human existence through their skills and discoveries; cf. Johnston (1980) 65-72.

665. **vitta:** the garland usually marks the sanctity of priests or poets; but note the *vittis cruentis* of the Furies in 281.

667. **Musaeum:** like Orpheus, Musaeus was a legendary poet and musician; cf. Plato, *Apology* 41a, *Republic* 363c. Austin (*ad loc.*) observes that it is rather strange that the crowd surrounds Musaeus rather than Orpheus but notes Lloyd-Jones' suggestion that it may be because of Musaeus' associations with the Eleusinian Mysteries (the most revered of the ancient mystery cults), which were based on the myth of the rape of Persephone (Roman *Proserpina*), daughter of Demeter (Roman *Ceres*): Persephone was seized by Hades (Roman *Pluto*), the ruler of the underworld, and was taken to his realm. Demeter, mourning the loss of her daughter, refused to allow plant life to grow until the gods relented and allowed her to return, for part of the year, to the world above. When Persephone returned to the world above, plants grew, but when she descended back to the underworld, plant life again died. Demeter then taught the rites of the Eleusinian Mysteries to the rulers of Eleusis (a suburb of Athens). Herakles (Latin *Hercules*) was inducted into the Eleusinian Mysteries before he descended to the underworld to bring back Cerberus (cf. notes on 119-23 and 392).

668. **umeris exstantem:** Musaeus is much taller than any of the crowd surrounding him.

669-71. The Sibyl's questions here are the last time she will speak in the book. Her request here is largely an act of courtesy toward Musaeus (cf. *tu* 669).

670-1. **Anchisen:** Greek accusative. **illius ergo | venimus:** *ergo* here is an archaic preposition, governing the genitive (like *causa* or *gratia*); "because of him have we come."

672. **paucis:** sc. *verbis*.

"nulli certa domus; lucis habitamus opacis,
riparumque toros et prata recentia rivis
incolimus. sed vos, si fert ita corde voluntas,   675
hoc superate iugum, et facili iam tramite sistam."
dixit, et ante tulit gressum camposque nitentis
desuper ostentat; dehinc summa cacumina linquunt.

---

673. **nulli**: dative of possession.

674. **riparumque toros…:** the banks form couches which seem to have been designed for this purpose; "cushions of river-banks and meadows fresh with streams." cf. 5.388 *viridante toro consederat herbae.*

675. **si fert ita corde voluntas:** "if the purpose in your heart is so inclined."

676. **hoc…iugum**: he points to a hill above them, from where they will see the path below.
   facili…sistam: he will place them on a path that will easily get them to their destination.

677. **ante tulit gressum:** "he took his step ahead (of them)," i.e. he led them.

678. **dehinc:** monosyllabic. **summa cacumina linquunt:** an elaborate way of saying that after they climbed the hill, they descended to the valley where Anchises resides (see 679).

At pater Anchises penitus convalle virenti
inclusas animas superumque ad lumen ituras   680
lustrabat studio recolens, omnemque suorum
forte recensebat numerum, carosque nepotes

679-901: Elysium and Anchises

In the third and concluding section of the book, Aeneas finally reaches the shade of
his father, Anchises, who first reveals how souls are regenerated and given new bodies
according to the lives they have lived on earth. He then proceeds to explain to his son
the hope and glory of their descendants, whose shades he points out as they wait in the
underworld to be born. Here, at last, the future will be revealed, in a parade of the great
Roman heroes to come, even though Aeneas will not fully comprehend their significance.
This development marks, for the first time, the transition from Trojan to Roman, as
Anchises describes the still-to-be-founded Roman state, which will impose law and order
on a chaotic universe and culminate in the emperor Augustus (792).

Anchises' revelation represents the most detailed account of Aeneas' future in the
epic. It also creates a strong contrast with Odysseus' experience in *Odyssey* 11. Homer's
underworld reflects largely on the past and on what is in store for him on his homeward
voyage. Aeneas, who has already completed that voyage, visits his father to learn not just
the immediate future, but the destiny of the new nation his descendants will build.

The encounter with Anchises, like so much of book 6, is also enwrapped in
mystery. Anchises' explanation of the regeneration of souls, taken by many as a kind
of philosophical core of the epic, is a complex blend of Orphic, Pythagorean, Platonic,
and Stoic ideas (see notes on 703-23, 724-51), although they do not fully mesh with the
Parade of Heroes that follows. Moreover, the book ends with the startling appearance of
the younger Marcellus (Augustus' nephew, son-in law, and presumed heir, but who died
young in 23 BCE, see 860-87 n.), and Aeneas' controversial exit through the Gate of
Sleep (893-901 n.). The issues raised by these episodes (and book 6 more generally) have
been interpreted as interacting in various ways with the overall prophecy, and thus affect
interpretations not only of this book, but indeed of the entire poem.

For overall discussions of this section, see Otis (1964) 299-301, Tarrant (1982), Gotoff
(1985), Feeney (1986), Goold (1992), Habinek (1989), Zetzel (1989), and Braund (1997)
216-18.

679-702. Aeneas and the Sibyl finally locate Anchises as he surveys the spirits destined to be reborn.
Here the purpose of Aeneas' journey through the underworld is fulfilled, as father and son come
face-to-face.

679. **At pater Anchises:** *At* marks a major turning point in the narrative. **penitus convalle**
    virenti: Anchises is deep in a green valley that is enclosed on all sides (*convalle*), watching
    the figures who are approaching the river Lethe prior to ascending to the upper world.

680. **animas superumque ad lumen ituras:** "souls destined to pass to the light above." Vergil
    later explains how they will do so.

681. **lustrabat studio recolens:** "was surveying them with eager contemplation."

fataque fortunasque virum moresque manusque.
isque ubi tendentem adversum per gramina vidit
Aenean, alacris palmas utrasque tetendit,   685
effusaeque genis lacrimae et vox excidit ore:
"venisti tandem, tuaque exspectata parenti
vicit iter durum pietas? datur ora tueri,
nate, tua et notas audire et reddere voces?
sic equidem ducebam animo rebarque futurum   690
tempora dinumerans, nec me mea cura fefellit.
quas ego te terras et quanta per aequora vectum
accipio! quantis iactatum, nate, periclis!
quam metui ne quid Libyae tibi regna nocerent!"
ille autem: "tua me, genitor, tua tristis imago   695
saepius occurrens haec limina tendere adegit;

---

683. **fataque fortunasque virum moresque manusque:** observe the balance and alliteration of this line—*virum* (genitive plural; = *eorum*) is framed by two pairs of alliterative nouns, the first pair the implicit outcome of the second pair (*moresque manusque*, "their character and their deeds").

684. **tendentem adversum:** describing Aeneas (685), "heading toward (him)."

685. **Aenean:** Greek accusative.

686. **genis:** *genae* are the cheeks or, as here, the sockets of the eyes and thus, metaphorically, "the eyes."

687-8. Anchises' welcoming words to his son reflect his long period of waiting but also his unwavering confidence in Aeneas' *pietas*, which has now *vicit iter durum* (688). The phrase marks the fulfillment of Aeneas' "Odyssean" quest of the first six books.

687. **parenti:** dative of agent.

688-9. **tueri...audire...reddere:** substantive infinitives, the subjects of *datur*. This is the kind of interaction Aeneas (1.409) laments not having with Venus, as she departs.

690. "This is what I kept planning in my mind and what I kept thinking would happen."

692-3. **quas...terras et quanta per aequora vectum...quantis iactatum...periclis!:** cf. 1.3-5 *multum ille et iactatum et alto...multa quoque et bello passus*; and 4.13-14 *heu, quibus ille iactatus fatis!* **quas...terras** : supply *per*.

694. **ne quid...nocerent:** *quid* (= *aliquid*) is cognate accusative with *nocerent* in a fear clause, "that the realms of Libya would do you some harm," i.e. that Dido might induce you to stay in Africa.

696. **tendere adegit:** the infinitive is due to the sense of compulsion contained in *adegit*, which takes *me* as object; cf. 567 *subigit fateri*. **haec limina:** accusative of place to which (without preposition).

stant sale Tyrrheno classes. da iungere dextram,
da, genitor, teque amplexu ne subtrahe nostro."
sic memorans largo fletu simul ora rigabat.
ter conatus ibi collo dare bracchia circum;   700
ter frustra comprensa manus effugit imago,
par levibus ventis volucrique simillima somno.
    Interea videt Aeneas in valle reducta
seclusum nemus et virgulta sonantia silvae,

700-2. Repeated from 2.792-4, where Aeneas tries to embrace Creusa.

700. **conatus:** supply *est*. **collo dare bracchia circum:** an elegant variation of the ordinary *circumdare bracchia collo*; *circum* and *dare* are separated by tmesis*.

701. **manus:** accusative plural, i.e. Aeneas' hands. **frustra:** construe with *comprensa*.

702. **somno:** stands in for *somnio*, "dream."

703—23. Aeneas notices a large number of spirits along the banks of Lethe and asks Anchises about them. Anchises says that they are souls waiting to be re-born, and that they have gathered here to drink the waters of forgetfulness before they move to a new life. He then explains the relationship between the soul and the body.

While the language in this passage recalls Lucretius' account of the Epicurean view of the destruction of the soul at death, the account itself is based on the Orphic and Pythagorean concepts of the purification and transmigration of souls and their rebirth in other bodies, including in the bodies of Aeneas' descendants. Orpheus (sixth century BCE) was said to have travelled to the underworld to recover his dead wife Eurydice but failed to bring her back (see Vergil, *Georgics* 4.315-527), and was torn apart by Maenads, followers of Dionysus (Bacchus). Orpheus was believed to be the author of a number of "gold leaves" found in Crete, Sicily and southern Italy which appeared to indicate that the dead person had been initiated into some kind of "mystic" cult (from Gr. *mystes*, "initiated"). Because he had been to the underworld, had spoken with Persephone (*Proserpina*) and returned, he was believed to have had the understanding to describe the underworld, the afterlife, and the origin of the gods. Pythagoras (sixth century BCE) is connected with two traditions, one religious—the transmigration of souls—and one scientific—among his important discoveries was the geometric theorem that still bears his name. His doctrine of the transmigration of souls led to a cult with periods of initiation, secret doctrines, passwords, special dietary restrictions and burial rites. Pythagoreans and adherents of Bacchic mystery cults adopted Orpheus as their figurehead. Plato and the later Neoplatonists discuss some of the Orphic/Pythagorean beliefs. Stoicism was a philosophical movement founded by Zeno of Citium in the third century BCE; divided into logic, physics and ethics, it was strongly influenced by Plato and Aristotle. Cf. 726 n.

On Anchises' speech, cf. Zetzel (1989); for the rebirth of souls, cf. Tarant (1982); Gotoff (1985); Feeney (1986); Habinek (1989).

704. **et virgulta sonantia silvae:** an elaboration of *seclusum nemus*, "the rustling thickets of a woodland."

Lethaeumque domos placidas qui praenatat amnem.   705
hunc circum innumerae gentes populique volabant,
ac velut in pratis ubi apes aestate serena
floribus insidunt variis et candida circum
lilia funduntur, strepit omnis murmure campus.
horrescit visu subito causasque requirit   710
inscius Aeneas, quae sint ea flumina porro,
quive viri tanto complerint agmine ripas.
tum pater Anchises: "animae, quibus altera fato
corpora debentur, Lethaei ad fluminis undam
securos latices et longa oblivia potant.   715
has equidem memorare tibi atque ostendere coram,
iampridem hanc prolem cupio enumerare meorum,
quo magis Italia mecum laetere reperta."
"o pater, anne aliquas ad caelum hinc ire putandum est
sublimis animas iterumque ad tarda reverti   720

---

705. **Lethaeum...amnem:** note how *Lethaeum...amnem* encloses *domos placidas*. In response to Aeneas' queries about the site (710), Anchises explains (713-18, etc.).

707-8. **ac velut...variis:** "even as when in the meadows the bees on a clear summer day settle on multicolored flowers." For the simile, cf. 1.430-6, describing the Carthaginians building their city; cf. also *Iliad* 2.87-9, where the Greeks hurrying to council are like bees, and Apollonius Rhodius, *Argonautica* 1.879-82, describing the Lemnian women gathering around the departing Argonauts.

710. **horrescit:** Aeneas shudders with surprise at the sight.

711-12. **quae sint...quive...viri comple<ve>rint...:** indirect questions after *causas requirit,* "and in ignorance (*nescius*) asks the reason, (asks) what is that river over there (*porro*), and what men filled the bank in such number."

713. This is the first information given to Aeneas concerning the rebirth of souls, which is first alluded to in line 680. **quibus:** dative. **fato:** ablative.

715. **securos latices..:** "waters that take away cares," and hence provide *longa oblivia,*" long-lasting forgetfulness"; cf. *longum bibebat amorem* 1.749.

716-17. **has <animas>...hanc prolem...:** the two clauses are connected by the emphatic repetition of *has* and *hanc*—"Of these truly (i.e. the souls on the Lethe's banks)...of this (specifically), the race of my children, have I long yearned to tell you."

718. **quo magis...laetere:** relative clause of purpose, "so that you may rejoice even more." **Italia...reperta:** ablative absolute.

719-20. **anne...putandum est:** "are we to think ...?" (lit. "must it be thought?"). **aliquas... animas...reverti:** accusative and infinitive construction after *putandum est.* **sublimis:** modifying *animas*, but translate as an adverb, "upwards."

corpora? quae lucis miseris tam dira cupido?"
"dicam equidem nec te suspensum, nate, tenebo"
suscipit Anchises atque ordine singula pandit.
   "Principio caelum ac terram camposque liquentis
lucentemque globum lunae Titaniaque astra   725

---

721. **lucis:** "light (of life)"; objective genitive, governed by *tam dira cupido* (cf. 373). **miseris:**
dative of possession. Aeneas' difficulty in understanding their (*dira*) longing for life reflects
the sufferings and sadness that have dominated his own life.

723. **suscipit:** "he (Anchises) takes up" these questions, or "replies."

*724—51. Anchises now explains what life is, and how it comes to pass that certain souls are
restored to their original purity and then, after drinking of Lethe, are again allowed to animate
mortal bodies.*

   The theory that Anchises puts forward here is a blend of the Stoic doctrine of the
anima mundi and the doctrine of rebirth in Platonic and Orphic-Pythagorean beliefs (cf.
703-23 n.; Plato, *Republic* 10.614, *Phaedrus* 248, *Gorgias* 493; and Vergil, *Geo.* 4.219-27). It
regards "life as something possessing substance" (cf. 292 n.); this vital substance permeates
the universe and is the source of life throughout; it is conceived of as analogous to air or fire
(Cicero, *de Natura Deorum* 2.15 *ignis ille corporeus, vitalis et salutaris omnia conservat, alit,
auget, sustinet sensusque afficit*). It is often identified with that fine and fiery element known
as *aether*, which, being lighter than earth, air, water, and fire, rises above them all to the
highest place, and so becomes the source of life for celestial bodies.

   United with this physical conception is an ethical one (derived from Plato, and
adopted much later by the nineteenth century Romantic writers) that in man the soul
becomes *infected by* the body, and finally loses its earlier, divine property. Hence after death
the soul must undergo purgation and purification, until all the taint is removed. Then, after
drinking of the waters of Lethe (the river of forgetfulness), the soul may again experience
rebirth. For the concept of the body as a prison of the soul, cf. Plato *Cratylus* 400c; *Phaedo*
66b. Vergil expresses these beliefs and explanations in consistently and pointed Lucretian
phrases and manner (cf. 624 *sedes beatae*; 724 *principio*; 759 *expediam dictis*), but Lucretius
had only scorn for the entire notion of an afterlife.

   This section can be seen as the philosophical core of the epic, and perhaps laying
a basis for the Parade of Heroes at 752-853. Some scholars, however, emphasize the
contradictions between this passage, particularly with its Platonic and Orphic background,
and the Parade of Heroes. For further discussion, cf. Bailey (1935) 275, Guthrie (1952) 186,
Otis (1964) 299-301, Solmsen (1968) 8-14, Tarrant (1982), Gotoff (1985), Feeney (1986),
Habinek (1989), and Zetzel (1989).

724. **Principio:** "In the first place"; a Lucretian term for beginning the sequence of a
philosophic argument; the argument continues *inde* (728), *hinc* (733), *non tamen* (736) *ergo*
(739). **campos...liquentis:** a periphrasis* for bodies of water.

725. **Titaniaque astra:** "the Titan's stars" can signify the Sun, the Moon, and Dawn, which
were the children of the Titan Hyperion; the Sun is frequently called *Titan*. Some editors
interpret the plural as a periphrasis* for the Sun alone, cf. Hesiod, *Theogony* 371-4.

spiritus intus alit, totamque infusa per artus
mens agitat molem et magno se corpore miscet.
inde hominum pecudumque genus vitaeque volantum
et quae marmoreo fert monstra sub aequore pontus.
igneus est ollis vigor et caelestis origo   730
seminibus, quantum non corpora noxia tardant
terrenique hebetant artus moribundaque membra.
hinc metuunt cupiuntque, dolent gaudentque, neque auras
dispiciunt clausae tenebris et carcere caeco.
quin et supremo cum lumine vita reliquit,   735
non tamen omne malum miseris nec funditus omnes
corporeae excedunt pestes, penitusque necesse est
multa diu concreta modis inolescere miris.

726. **spiritus...alit:** "a breath from within sustains." According to the Stoic principle, the universe is material and is pervaded by a fiery *anima* from which the human soul is detached until after death, at which time the soul returns to its original fiery element. This fiery *spiritus* is the warm air or ether that animates all living beings and sustains life.

727. **mens:** "mind (= Greek *nous*) sets in motion the whole mass, and mingles with its mighty frame."

728-9. **inde:** from this *spiritus* and *mens infusa* come all living creatures.

730. **igneus:** the nature of the *spiritus* or *mens* is the pure essence of fire. The particles of the divine fire are the *semina*; from each such "spark" or "seed" grows a separate human life. *Ignis* is the Stoic term to describe the *anima mundi*, the divine fire of the world soul and the source of life. **ollis:** = *illis* (*seminibus* 731), dative of possession. For the solemnity of the archaic *ollis,* cf. 321.

731-2. **quantum non...tardant:** "to the extent that they do not clog"; the seeds are, in their nature and essence, "fiery," but this fiery nature can only exhibit itself to a limited extent because it is clogged and dulled by the body. **tardant...hebetant:** supply *ea* (i.e. *semina*) as object.

733. **hinc:** from the union with material substance (i.e. with the the body). **metuunt cupiuntque, dolent gaudentque:** Vergil describes the four passions (*perturbationes*) which disturb the calmness and clearness of the pure soul. Cf. Cicero, *Tusculan Disputations* 4.6, Horace, *Epistles* 1.6.12. **auras:** the air above.

734. **clausae:** the souls are imprisoned in darkness; the concept of the body as a tomb or prison for the soul is Orphic; cf. Plato, *Cratylus* 400c, *Phaedo* 66b.

735. **supremo...lumine:** "on the last day of life."

736. **non tamen:** Vergil now turns to the doctrine of the purgation and transmigration of souls. **miseris:** dative of separation after *excedunt* (737).

737-8. **penitus...multa diu concreta...inolescere:** many long-accumulated contagions (*multa diu concreta*) have of necessity become deeply engrained (*inolescere,* "grow into"), and have to be expunged.

ergo exercentur poenis veterumque malorum
supplicia expendunt: aliae panduntur inanes   740
suspensae ad ventos, aliis sub gurgite vasto
infectum eluitur scelus aut exuritur igni —
quisque suos patimur manis; exinde per amplum
mittimur Elysium et pauci laeta arva tenemus —
donec longa dies perfecto temporis orbe   745
concretam exemit labem, purumque relinquit
aetherium sensum atque aurai simplicis ignem.
has omnis, ubi mille rotam volvere per annos,
Lethaeum ad fluvium deus evocat agmine magno,
scilicet immemores supera ut convexa revisant   750

739-42. exercentur poenis…: they are disciplined and assailed by three forms of punishment and purification—by air (*ventos* 741), water (*gurgite vasto* 741), and fire (*igni* 742).

740-1. panduntur…suspensae: some are "hung up" and "spread wide" to the winds. **aliis:** "out of others."

742. infectum eluitur scelus: "the guilty stain is washed out." **exuritur igni:** the metaphor is from purging away the dross from gold so as to leave it pure.

743. quisque suos patimur manis: "each of us endures his own ghost." **manis:** (accusative plural) in Vergil can refer to the collective spirits of the dead, to the place where they exist, or to the spirit of an individual. Here he extends the last of these meanings to include the purification process each must endure because of his or her past life. **exinde:** after this purification.

744. mittimur: implying all the souls in the process are being purified. **pauci:** those few who need only minimal purification (like Anchises, Orpheus, Musaeus) do not need to be reborn (as do the souls that crowd the banks of the Lethe in 706), and so they stay in Elysium.

745-7. donec longa dies….: the passage appears to mean that, when the purgatorial cleansing described in 739-42 is completed, thereafter (*exinde* 743) the soul passes into Elysium and dwells there "until the passage of time, the cycle at last completed, has removed the ingrown corruption and (so) leaves pure the ethereal sense and breath of elemental fire." **concretam…labem:** the solidified or hardened stain. **aurai simplicis ignem:** is a restatement of *aetherium sensum*. **aurai:** an archaic genitive; it is trisyllabic.

748. has omnis…: sc. *animas*; in contrast to *pauci*, those remaining in Elysium, the less fortunate are crowded on the bank of the Lethe and wait to be reborn "when they have rolled the wheel (of time) for a thousand years." The cycle is suggested by Plato, *Phaedrus* 249a, *Republic* 10.615a. **volvere:** = *volverunt*.

749-50. Lethaeum…scilicet immemores: "to Lethe's stream…forgetting, you see (*scilicet*)"; *scilicet* pointedly draws attention to the connection between the river Lethe and forgetting (cf. *immemores*). **deus:** may refer to Mercury, since Vergil uses this verb (*evocat*) with Mercury in 4.242. **supera…convexa:** "the heavenly vault," cf. 241.

rursus, et incipiant in corpora velle reverti."
    Dixerat Anchises natumque unaque Sibyllam
conventus trahit in medios turbamque sonantem,
et tumulum capit unde omnis longo ordine posset
adversos legere et venientum discere vultus.   755
    "Nunc age, Dardaniam prolem quae deinde sequatur
gloria, qui maneant Itala de gente nepotes,
inlustris animas nostrumque in nomen ituras,
expediam dictis, et te tua fata docebo.
ille, vides, pura iuvenis qui nititur hasta,   760

752—853. Anchises and the Parade of Heroes

Anchises, accompanied by Aeneas and the Sibyl, now ascends a mound and points out to Aeneas the souls of great Romans awaiting birth, who will build the glory of Rome: the Alban Kings and Romulus (760-87); the gens Iulia, and particularly Augustus (788-807), whose expansion of the Roman Empire will (implicitly) rival that of Alexander the Great, the early kings of Rome and early Republican leaders, Caesar and Pompey (826-35), and a series of other famous Romans.

Note that Vergil does not list these heroes in chronological order, but rather places Augustus midway between them, thus emphasizing his importance to Rome. Two other passages in the *Aeneid* parallel this one. The first is Jupiter's prophecy to Venus in 1.257-96, and the second is the description of the Shield made for Aeneas in 8.626-728.

While the main narrative of the *Aeneid* consists of Aeneas' wanderings and battles, this Parade of Heroes is an example of prolepses* (rhetorical anticipations) of and allusions to events in the future with respect to Aeneas' time, which later writers such as Lucan and Silius Italicus will elaborate in separate epic poems. For this open-ended aspect of epic poetry, see Fowler (1989, 1997) and Hardie (1993, 1997). The section ends with an epilogue that finally proclaims the special duty and responsibilities of Rome to the world.

752. **una:** adverb, "together."

753. **conventus:** accusative plural noun, "assemblies." **sonantem:** cf. 709 *strepit omnis murmure campus.*

754. **tumulum:** the height is here important, since it will enable Anchises to scan (*legere* 755) or identify them as they approach.

756-7. **Nunc age:** Anchises begins to speak. **Dardaniam prolem...Itala de gente nepotes:** the fusion of Trojan and the Italian stock is emphatic in his prophecy. **quae...qui...:** indirect questions dependent on *expediam* (759). **deinde:** "in the future."

758-9. **animas:** accusative, also dependent on *expediam*. **expediam dictis:** "I shall set forth in words," a favorite phrase of Lucretius; Vergil uses it to introduce a new aspect of Epicurean physical doctrine, and therefore, in using this phrase, is responding to his predecessor to introduce material that would be Epicurean blasphemy. **te tua fata docebo:** note that *docebo* governs two accusatives (of the person taught and of the thing taught).

760. **pura...hasta:** Servius says that this is a headless (*pura*) spear formerly given to a warrior who has won his first victory (*qui tum primum vicisset in proelio*).

proxima sorte tenet lucis loca, primus ad auras
aetherias Italo commixtus sanguine surget,
Silvius, Albanum nomen, tua postuma proles,
quem tibi longaevo serum Lavinia coniunx
educet silvis regem regumque parentem,   765
unde genus Longa nostrum dominabitur Alba.
proximus ille Procas, Troianae gloria gentis,
et Capys et Numitor et qui te nomine reddet
Silvius Aeneas, pariter pietate vel armis
egregius, si umquam regnandam acceperit Albam.   770
qui iuvenes! quantas ostentant, aspice, viris
atque umbrata gerunt civili tempora quercu!

---

761. **proxima ...lucis loca:** "holds by lot the place nearest to the light"; hence he will be the first to ascend.

763-78. **Silvius:** the first figure in Vergil's procession is Silvius, so-named from the site of his birth (*silvis* 765), the son of Aeneas by Lavinia, daughter of Latinus, king of Latium (*Italo commixtus sanguine*). Here we are told that he will found Alba Longa (766), which is regularly connected by legend with Aeneas' settlement in Italy. The name was thereafter borne by all the kings of Alba Longa (*Albanum nomen* 763). Aeneas Silvius (769) succeeded Silvius, whose successors included Capys and Procas, whose brother was Numitor, the father of Rhea Silvia (*Ilia mater* 778) and grandfather (*avo* 777) of Romulus and Remus.

763. **postuma:** not "born after the father's death," but as the next line shows, "last" or "latest-born."

764. **Lavinia:** see 763-78 n.

766. **Longa...Alba:** ablative.

768. **Numitor:** the final syllable is long. **te nomine reddet:** "shall recall you by his name."

769. **pariter...egregius:** the words recall the description of Aeneas in 403 (*Aeneas, pietate insignis et armis*) and mean "equally illustrious with you (either) in piety or valor," "whose fame for (either) piety or valor may be matched with yours." *Vel* is thus separated from *pariter* and is used naturally; *pariter* suggests that this second Aeneas is a counterpart of the first, not only in name but in nature.

770. **si umquam:** according to tradition he was kept out of his kingdom for 52 years. **regnandam:** "to be governed." Cf. 3.14. **acceperit:** future perfect.

772. **civili...quercu:** the *corona civica* (a crown of oak leaves), which was given to one who had saved the life of a citizen in war, and was assigned in 27 BCE as a perpetual honor for Augustus (cf. Ovid, *Fasti* 1.614; *Tristia* 3.1.36).

> hi tibi Nomentum et Gabios urbemque Fidenam,
> hi Collatinas imponent montibus arces,
> Pometios Castrumque Inui Bolamque Coramque.   775
> haec tum nomina erunt, nunc sunt sine nomine terrae.
> quin et avo comitem sese Mavortius addet
> Romulus, Assaraci quem sanguinis Ilia mater
> educet. viden, ut geminae stant vertice cristae
> et pater ipse suo superum iam signat honore?   780
> en huius, nate, auspiciis illa incluta Roma
> imperium terris, animos aequabit Olympo,

773-6. These are all early Latin towns near Rome (some of them deserted by Vergil's time), which were members of the Latin League headed by Alba Longa (cf. 763-78, above). *Nomentum* is about 14 miles NE of Rome; *Gabii* to the East; *Fidenae* (normally plural; the first syllable is long) 5 miles to the NE; *Collatia* (*Collatinus* is the adjective) is on the right bank of the Anio; *Pometii* is usually called Suessa Pometia and is in the territory of the Volsci to the south, as are *Cora* and *Bola*; *Castrum Inui* is to the south on the coast, near Ardea.

776: **nomina...sine nomine:** antithesis*.

777. **avo comitem sese...addet:** Romulus is introduced with the suggestion that he will be born during the lifetime of his grandfather (*avo*), Numitor. The adjective *Mavortius* is derived from *Mavors*, the archaic form of *Mars*.

778. **Ilia:** the Trojan name of Rhea Silvia, the Vestal Virgin who was the mother of Romulus and Remus. For Anchises' grandfather, *Assaracus*, cf. 648-50 n.

779-80. **viden:** = *videsne*, with second syllable shortened. The phrase is colloquial, found more often in comedy than in epic, and serves to provide a more immediate, conversational tone between father and son. **ut...stant:** this clause is paratactic*, with the verb in the indicative. Cf. AG §268. **geminae...cristae:** there is perhaps a reference to Mars here, but this phrase clearly indicates that Romulus has been marked as special by Jupiter (*pater ipse*) to become a god. Romulus, who was actually worshipped as "Quirinus." **superum:** genitive plural (= *superorum*).

781. **auspiciis:** "under his (i.e. Romulus') auspices." When Romulus and Remus were seeking a sign as to who should rule the new city, six vultures appeared first to Remus. Then twelve vultures appeared to Romulus. Remus' followers claimed priority, while Romulus' followers claimed number as the basis for choosing between the two. In the ensuing fight, Romulus killed Remus and thus obtained power. See Livy 1.6. (Note that Anchises—and possibly Vergil, too—minimizes this basic flaw in the founding in Rome, as does Jupiter in 1.267-8.) Romulus named Rome after himself; he was always represented in augural dress (alluded to by *auspiciis*), wearing a *trabea*, a short Etruscan garment, and holding a *lituus*, a trumpet-like instrument. **incluta Roma:** cf. 479 n.

782. Cf. Jupiter's prophecy, 1.287 *imperium Oceano, famam qui terminet astris*. Rome in her glory will extend her empire over the entire earth and her spirit to the heavens.

septemque una sibi muro circumdabit arces,
felix prole virum: qualis Berecyntia mater
invehitur curru Phrygias turrita per urbes   785
laeta deum partu, centum complexa nepotes,
omnis caelicolas, omnis supera alta tenentis.
huc geminas nunc flecte acies, hanc aspice gentem
Romanosque tuos. hic Caesar et omnis Iuli
progenies magnum caeli ventura sub axem.   790
hic vir, hic est, tibi quem promitti saepius audis,

---

783. **septemque una sibi:** note the juxtaposition of *septem* and *una* (i.e. *Roma*), emphasizing how a multiplicity of entities will become one (cf. *e pluribus unum*, the U.S. motto). The line is almost a repetition of *Geo.* 2.535 *septemque una sibi muro circumdedit arces.* **arces:** = "hills" of Rome.

784-7. **virum:** genitive plural. **Berecyntia mater:** Cybele, who was worshipped on Mt. Berecyntus in Phrygia, was brought to Rome in 204 BCE. She is called *Mater* as being identified with the earth and also with Rhea, the wife of Cronus and mother of Zeus, and so is commonly called *Magna Mater* ("the Great Mother") and *Mater Deum* ("Mother of the Gods"). In 2.788 Creusa becomes her servant; Anchises speaks of her lion-drawn chariot in 3.111; in 7.139 she is one of the deities Aeneas invokes on arrival at the site of Lavinium. In 9.82 she appeals to Jupiter to save the Trojans ships from burning, and in 10.234 she changes the Trojan ships into sea nymphs who go to summon Aeneas to assist Ascanius. Cf. also 9.619 and 10.252. Anchises here draws a comparison between her mural crown (*turrita* 785) (cf. Lucretius 2.606), and Rome's citadels surrounded by a wall, giving the effect of "a diadem of towers" (*muro circumdabit arces* 783), and again between the goddess "rejoicing in a brood of gods" (*laeta deum partu* 786) and Rome's similar pride in being "blessed with a race of heroes" (*felix prole virum* 784), culminating in the repetition of *omnis* (787).

789-807. Anchises now points out Augustus, who appears out of chronological order, immediately after Romulus (the founder of Rome), making him the "second founder" of Rome. On this, cf. Norden *ad loc.*; Stahl (1998); Grebe (2004).

789. **Caesar:** Augustus Caesar, not Julius Caesar, as is clear from 792. Julius Caesar was said to be a descendant of *Iulus* (an alternate name for Ascanius).

Augustus Caesar, divi genus, aurea condet
saecula qui rursus Latio regnata per arva
Saturno quondam, super et Garamantas et Indos
proferet imperium; iacet extra sidera tellus,   795
extra anni solisque vias, ubi caelifer Atlas
axem umero torquet stellis ardentibus aptum.
huius in adventum iam nunc et Caspia regna

792-3. **divi genus**: "son of a god." Julius Caesar, Augustus' adoptive father and great-uncle (his mother, Atia, was Caesar's niece), received divine honors after his death and was called *Divus*. **aurea condet | saecula…:** "who will again establish a Golden Age for Latium, amid the plough-lands once ruled by Saturnus." Saturnus was the mythological Roman god of sowing (the equivalent of the Greek Cronus) and the husband of Ops ("wealth"). He presided over a golden age that was based in agriculture, the source of all weatlth. After he was overthrown by his son, Saturnus is said to have brought his golden age to Latium, so-named because he was able to hide there safely (*hic quoniam latuisset* 8.323)—thus extending the Greek version of Zeus' defeat of Cronus, wherein Cronus was then cast into the underworld.

    In *Aen.* 7, Latinus tells Aeneas that the Latin people are the descendants of the race of Saturnus, a people who are spontaneously just, with no need of law (*neve ignorate Latinos | Saturni gentem haud vinclo nec legibus aequam, | sponte sua veterisque dei se more tenentem* 7.202-4), but in *Aen.* 8 Evander explains how the Golden Age was destroyed by the inferior race that succeeded it (*decolor aetas* 8.326), motivated as it was by war and greed (*belli rabies et amor…habendi* 8.327). (Compare Hesiod's account of the Myth of the Ages in *Works and Days* 110-201.) Here Anchises says that Augustus will be the founder of a new Golden Age, which will also be characterized by the simplicity of the Golden Age enjoyed under Saturnus. Cf. Johnston (1980) and Galinsky (1996).

794. **Garamantas**: Greek accusative plural ending, with a short vowel. The Garamantes (in modern Libya) were the most southern African nation known (*extremi Garamantes Ecl.* 8. 44), subdued in 19 BCE by L. Cornelius Balbus. India is said in the *Georgics* to lie at the farthest ends of the earth (*extremi sinus orbis* 2.123).

795. **iacet extra sidera tellus:** "earth (over which he shall extend his sway) lies beyond the stars." The sudden change of construction is dramatic: Anchises speaks as though he actually sees before him the land he is describing.

796. **extra…vias…:** the sun's apparent annual path through the stars (the Ecliptic), and the Zodiac, a belt on each side of this imaginary line. Beneath this belt, according to Vergil, lies a similar belt of earth, which is the world he knows, and the lands north and south of it are *extra sidera, extra anni solisque vias*. **caelifer Atlas:** Atlas is either a rebellious Titan condemned to support heaven, or Mt. Atlas in Mauretania, which is not unnaturally described as "heaven-supporting." Cf. 4.246-51.

797. This line, based on Ennius, is repeated from 4.482.

798. **huius in adventum:** "for (in expectation of) his coming."

responsis horrent divum et Maeotia tellus,
et septemgemini turbant trepida ostia Nili.   800
nec vero Alcides tantum telluris obivit,
fixerit aeripedem cervam licet, aut Erymanthi
pacarit nemora et Lernam tremefecerit arcu;
nec qui pampineis victor iuga flectit habenis
Liber, agens celso Nysae de vertice tigris.   805
et dubitamus adhuc virtutem extendere factis,

---

799. **responsis horrent:** the places themselves, and implictly their inhabitants, "shiver at the oracles," suggesting both a reaction to oracular response and also the chill of the Caspian Sea and the Crimea.

800. **septemgemini...Nili:** a reference to the Nile's delta, and hence an allusion to Augustus' victory over Egypt at Actium. **turbant:** here intransitive. **trepida:** in contrast to *horrent* (799), an excited state of fear, the hot haste of panic, as well as the warmth of Egypt (cf. *Geo.* 1.296 *trepidi aëni*, "a boiling caldron").

801-5. Hercules and Bacchus are cited here as models for Augustus. They were deified because, in addition to being half-divine, they extended the boundaries of civilization and thus improved the fate of the human race. Three of Hercules' labors involved capturing or slaying the "bronze-footed stag" (802) and the boar on Mt. Erymanthus in Arcadia (802), and destroying the many-headed Hydra at Lerna in Argolis (803). The progress of Bacchus in a car drawn by tamed tigers from Mt. Nysa (804-5) represents the advance and triumph of civilization. Augustus, too, by extending the boundaries of the Roman state, will improve the lot of the mortal race. Cf. Horace, *Odes* 3.3.9-16, where Augustus is compared to Hercules, Bacchus, and Quirinus.

801. **Alcides:** "Descendant of Alceus," i.e. Hercules. Cf. 122-3 n. **telluris:** partitive genitive, dependent on *tantum* ("so much").

802-3. **fixerit..paca<ve>rit...tremefecerit:** perfect subjunctives in concessive clause (cf. *licet*). **aeripedem cervam...Erymanthi...nemora...Lernam:** cf. 801-5 n.

804. **iuga flectit:** "guides his car."

805. **Liber:** i.e. Bacchus/ Dionysus. **celso Nysae de vertice:** Bacchus was said to have been raised by nymphs at Mt. Nysa, which is located variously in India, Ethiopia, Arabia, or Asia.

806. **et dubitamus...:** "and are we still (i.e. after contemplating the glory of Augustus) hesitating...?" Anchises concludes his prophecy with an exhortation based on the preceding *exempla*: now that he has seen the glorious vision, Aeneas should have no more doubts or hesitation. At the same time the use of the first person here suggests that Vergil is not so much thinking of Anchises and Aeneas as addressing an appeal with his own living voice to his fellow-Romans, raising the question whether Vergil, too, shares Anchises' imperialistic inclinations. **virtutem:** "manliness," "all that may become a man," "worth"; the phrase *virtutem extendere factis* means to develop one's *virtus* through one's deeds. Cf. Aristotle's statement in *Nicomachean Ethics* 1103-38 that virtue only exists when it is in action, i.e. one cannot be virtuous when one is asleep.

aut metus Ausonia prohibet consistere terra?
quis procul ille autem ramis insignis olivae
sacra ferens? nosco crinis incanaque menta
regis Romani primam qui legibus urbem   810
fundabit Curibus parvis et paupere terra,
missus in imperium magnum. cui deinde subibit
otia qui rumpet patriae residesque movebit
Tullus in arma viros et iam desueta triumphis
agmina. quem iuxta sequitur iactantior Ancus   815
nunc quoque iam nimium gaudens popularibus auris.
vis et Tarquinios reges animamque superbam

807. **prohibet:** understand *nos* as object.

808-12. Numa Pompilius (*regis* 810), second king of Rome, was a native of the little town of
Cures (811) in the Sabine territory; the Romans considered Numa the founder (*fundabit*
811) of their religious and legal institutions. Hence he is represented as a venerable
priest "offering sacrifice" and "decked with boughs of olive," the symbol of peace. For
the derivation of *Quirites* from Cures, cf. Austin *ad loc.*, Ogilvie *ad* Livy 1.18.1. **crinis:**
accusative plural. **menta:** "beard," an unusual plural for singular. **primam...urbem:**
"infant city"; *primam* may also be taken as a transferred epithet describing Numa (i.e. he
will first "found the city <based> on laws").

812. **cui:** "him"; connecting relative pronoun (dative after *subibit*, "will succeed," "come
after") referring back to Numa.

814. **Tullus:** Tullus Hostilius, third king of Rome; tradition emphasizes his military exploits.
For his destruction of Alba, see Livy 1.22-31.

815. **quem:** referring to Tullus; cf. 812 n. **Ancus:** Ancus Martius, fourth king; conqueror of
the Latins (cf. Livy 1.32-4).

816. **popularibus auris:** popular favor is compared to a breeze because of its fickle and
treacherous nature.

817-19. The fifth and seventh kings were Etruscan—Tarquinius Priscus and Tarquinius
Superbus. Tarquinius Superbus was banished in an uprising headed by L. Iunius Brutus
(510 BCE), the avenger (*ultoris* 818) of the outrage inflicted on Lucretia, the wife of T.
Collatinus by Superbus' son Sextus Tarquinius. Brutus recovered (*receptos* 818) for the
people the right of electing their own rulers, and he himself, along with T. Collatinus, were
elected the first *consules* (819); cf. Livy 1.49-2.21

817. **vis et...videre:** "do you also want to see...?" **superbam:** the transferring of the epithet of
Tarquin (Tarquinius Superbus) to Brutus is striking; Vergil normally uses this adjective in
the negative sense of excessive pride (e.g. Turnus, 10.514, 12.326; Mezentius 11.15, etc.),
but not always (e.g. Priam 2.556, etc). Here there is an ambivalence between admiration for
and criticism of the man who overthrew the tyrant but who also had his own sons executed
(821). On Vergil's attitude toward Brutus the assassin, cf. Jackson Knight (1944) 367 ff.,
Clark (1979) 174, Galinsky (2006), Johnston (2006).

ultoris Bruti, fascisque videre receptos?
consulis imperium hic primus saevasque securis
accipiet, natosque pater nova bella moventis 820
ad poenam pulchra pro libertate vocabit.
infelix! utcumque ferent ea facta minores:
vincet amor patriae laudumque immensa cupido.
quin Decios Drusosque procul saevumque securi
aspice Torquatum et referentem signa Camillum. 825

---

818. **fascis:** accusative plural. Twelve lictors preceded the kings and carried a bundle of rods
and an axe (*fasces*) as the token of their power to inflict scourging and death. Later the axe
was only carried with the *fasces* when the consul was at the head of an army in the field.

820. **natosque pater:** juxtaposition for emphasis. The sons of Brutus plotted to bring back the
Tarquins (cf. Livy 2.4), and consequently the father had to condemn his own sons to death
pulchra pro libertate (821).

822. **utcumque ferent…:** the simplest way to interpret these lines is to connect *infelix*
not with what precedes, but with what follows (as Augustine did, *de civitate Dei*
3.16):—"unhappy, however posterity (*minores*) will extol (*ferent* = *ferent laudibus*) that
deed." Then, after this parenthetic tribute to the father's grief, the poet returns to the
patriot's devotion (*vincet amor patriae* 823).

824. **Decios:** P. Decius Mus was the name of two plebeian consuls, father and son, who
solemnly devoted themselves to death in battle, the father (340 BCE, Livy 8.9) in a war
against the Latins, the son (295 BCE, Livy 10.28) in the battle of Sentinum against the
Gauls. **Drusos:** M. Livius Drusus Salinator was consul with C. Claudius Nero and defeated
Hasdrubal (brother of Hannibal) at the river Metaurus (207 BCE). The Drusi were one of the
famous families at Rome (its members included Augustus' wife, Livia Drusilla). See Feeney
(1986) on the "riddles" involved in the family plurals throughout the passage.

825. **Torquatum:** T. Manlius Imperiosus was called "Torquatus" after he slew a gigantic Gaul
(361 BCE) and took the chain (*torques*) he wore round his neck (Livy 7.10). Later, when
he was consul (340 BCE), he put his own son to death (*saevum securi* 824) for engaging in
combat with the enemy contrary to orders (Livy 7.8). **Camillum:** according to Livy (5.48-
50), M. Furius Camillus recovered the gold paid to the Gauls to ensure their withdrawal
from Rome in 390 BCE. Vergil modifies the story so that Camillus recovers not the gold
but the Roman standards (*signa*). Vergil's modification may reflect the recovery—or the
anticipation of the recovery—of the standards from the Parthians, achieved in 20 BCE.
The loss of the standards to the Parthians when they defeated Crassus in 53 BCE was a
major trauma in Vergil's time. See Augustus, *Res Gestae* 1.29; Horace, *Odes* 1.2.51, 1.12.53,
etc.

illae autem paribus quas fulgere cernis in armis,
concordes animae nunc et dum nocte premuntur,
heu quantum inter se bellum, si lumina vitae
attigerint, quantas acies stragemque ciebunt,
aggeribus socer Alpinis atque arce Monoeci   830
descendens, gener adversis instructus Eois!
ne, pueri, ne tanta animis adsuescite bella
neu patriae validas in viscera vertite viris;
tuque prior, tu parce, genus qui ducis Olympo,
proice tela manu, sanguis meus! —   835
ille triumphata Capitolia ad alta Corintho
victor aget currum caesis insignis Achivis.

826-7. **illae...paribus...armis...animae:** Caesar and Pompey. Pompey (*gener* 831) married Julia (the daughter of Caesar, *socer* 830), who died in 54 BCE (see Lucan, *Pharsalia* 111-19); he was defeated by Caesar at Pharsalus (48 BCE). **paribus...in armis:** i.e. both in Roman arms, indicating civil war; cf. Lucan *Pharsalia* 1.6 *obvia signis | signa, pares aquilas, et pila minantia pilis.* **fulgere:** second syllable is short, unusual for a second conjugation infinitive; cf. 4.409. **dum nocte premuntur:** i.e. while their unborn *animae* are still in the underworld.

830. The legions with which Caesar crushed Pompey were those that had served with him in Gaul (58-50 BCE). The Alps and promontory of Monaco (*arx Menoeci*) formed the "rampart" or "barrier" of Gaul in the North, from which Caesar invaded Italy.

831. **gener:** cf. 826-7 n. **adversis instructus Eois:** lit. "lined up with opposing Eastern (forces)." Pompey was associated with the East, because of his Mithridatic campaign (66 BCE) and his settlement of Judaea and Syria (63 BCE), but his forces were mainly gathered from Greece. Vergil presents the conflict between Pompey and Julius Caesar as a clash between East and West.

833. The alliteration of the repeated *v* expresses violence.

834. **tu...tu:** i.e. (the soul of) Julius Caesar is addressed.

835. **sanguis meus:** nominative for vocative. The *gens Iulia* claimed descent from Iulus, the grandson of Anchises. This is the first time Anchises addresses the ghosts, with special attention to his descendant. This and line 94 are the only incomplete lines in this book.

836-7. **ille...victor:** deictic, "that hero over there"—L. Mummius, surnamed Achaicus (*caesis insignis Achivis* 837), who destroyed Corinth in 146 BCE. **triumphata...Corintho:** *Corinthus* is feminine, and *triumphata* is intransitive; the construction is ablative absolute, "when Corinth has been defeated." **Capitolia ad alta...victor aget currum:** Roman triumphal processions had as their endpoint the temple of Jupiter Optimus Maximus on the Capitoline Hill.

eruet ille Argos Agamemnoniasque Mycenas
ipsumque Aeaciden, genus armipotentis Achilli,
ultus avos Troiae templa et temerata Minervae.   840
quis te, magne Cato, tacitum aut te, Cosse, relinquat?
quis Gracchi genus aut geminos, duo fulmina belli,
Scipiadas, cladem Libyae, parvoque potentem
Fabricium vel te sulco, Serrane, serentem?

838-9. ille Argos Agamemnoniasque Mycenas: Aemilius Paullus, who in 168 BCE at the battle of Pydna defeated Perseus (*Aeacides*), the last king of Epirus (Macedonia); Perseus is called *Aeacides* because he claimed descent from Achilles, grandson of *Aeacus*. *Argos* and *Mycenae* refer more generally to Greece, thus implying that the victory over Perseus served as retribution for the destruction of Troy.

840. templa et temerata Minervae: *et* is postpositive (= *et templa*). The temple was violated by Ajax son of Oileus, who on the night of the capture of Troy carried off Cassandra, who had taken refuge at its altar.

841. quis te: the apostrophe* provides a variation for the introduction of new names. **magne Cato:** M. Porcius Cato "the Censor," who died in 149 BCE at age 85; the famous opponent of Carthage. **tacitum:** in passive sense, "untold," "unsung." **Cosse:** Cornelius Cossus slew Lars Tolumnius, king of Veii, and won the *spolia opima* (854-9 n.) in 428 BCE.

842-3. Gracchi genus: the two most famous Gracchi were the great *tribuni plebis*, Tiberius Sempronius Gracchus, whose death by an aristocratic mob in 133 BCE marked the beginnings of the Roman Revolution that culminated in the fall of the Republic a century later. His brother Gaius was similarly killed a decade later (121 BCE); Vergil may also be thinking of an earlier Tiberius Sempronius Gracchus, twice consul (215, 212 BCE) in the Second Punic War, as well as their father, cos. 177 BCE. **duo fulmina belli:** P. Cornelius Scipio Africanus Major defeated Hannibal at Zama during the Second Punic War (202 BCE); his adopted son P. C. Scipio Africanus Minor (son of Aemilus Paullus) destroyed Carthage in 146 BCE during the Third Punic War. Cicero (*pro Balbo* 34) speaks of two Scipios as *fulmina nostri imperii,* and Lucretius 3.1034 has *Scipiades, belli fulmen, Carthaginis horror,* both allusions suggesting a play on the root meaning of the family name, *scipio,* "staff, support, prop."

843-4. parvoque potentem: "powerful with little." The contrast is between the *greatness* of Fabricius' public services and the *smallness* of his private means. Fabricius and Serranus are types of idealized old Roman generals, who left the ploughshare to lead an army and then returned to it after their victories. **Fabricium:** C. Fabricius Luscinus, consul 282 and 278 BCE in the war against Pyrrhus, was famous for the stern simplicity of his life and the firmness with which he refused the bribes of Pyrrhus. **Serrane:** C. Atilius Regulus Serranus, consul 257 BCE, defeated the Carthaginians off the Liparaean Islands, just off NE Sicily. Vergil here gives what was no doubt the popular etymology of his name Serranus, namely that he was found *sowing* (*sero*) when summoned to be consul. On coins the name is found as *Saranus,* and it is generally connected with Saranus, a town in Umbria.

quo fessum rapitis, Fabii? tu Maximus ille es,   ˙845
unus qui nobis cunctando restituis rem.
excudent alii spirantia mollius aera
(credo equidem), vivos ducent de marmore vultus,
orabunt causas melius, caelique meatus
describent radio et surgentia sidera dicent: 850

---

845. **quo…:** "Whither…?" or "To where…?" Anchises' question serves as a device for cutting short a list that is growing tedious. A long array of heroes of the great Fabian *gens* is supposed to claim the poet's attention, but the poet is "weary" and selects only him who was "the Greatest." **Maximus:** *Quintus Fabius Maximus Cunctator* ("the Delayer," cf. *cunctando* 846) was appointed dictator after the defeat at the Trasimene Lake (217 BCE), and wore out Hannibal by "delaying" and by continually hampering his movements while avoiding a pitched battle (cf. Livy 22.9, 48 *et passim*).

846. This line is based on Ennius' often quoted *unus homo nobis cunctando restituit rem* (*Annales* fr. 360 in Warmington, fr. 363 in Skutsch).

847-53. These seven lines, comprising the epilogue to Anchises' prophecy, convey Vergil's notion of Greco-Roman civilization, beginning with four lines summarizing the Greek accomplishment, and three climactic lines conveying the spirit of the *Pax Romana*. The formal structure is a list, known as a "priamel," in which there is an opening statement listing what others (*alii*) (here, the Greeks) will accomplish (*excudent…ducent…orabunt… describent…dicent* 847-50), followed by a contrasting statement of what, in this case, the Romans will accomplish (*tu* 851).

847. **excudent:** "will beat out." **alii:** clearly refers to the Greeks. **mollius:** the word indicates that the lines of the statue are soft, flowing, smooth, and natural; the opposite is *durius* (cf. Horace, *Satires* 2.3.22 *quid fusum durius esset*), which describes what is hard, stiff, unnatural.

848. **credo equidem:** the words have a concessive force: the concession is, however, only made in order to bring out more forcibly by contrast the claim which follows in 851-3. **ducent:** *ducere* is generally used of modelling any ductile material, such as clay, but here of "bringing out" the lineaments of the face from marble.

849. **caeli…meatus:** the movements of the heavenly bodies.

850. **radio:** the rod used for drawing astronomical or geometrical diagrams on sand, cf. *Ecl.* 3.41.

tu regere imperio populos, Romane, memento
(hae tibi erunt artes), pacique imponere morem,
parcere subiectis et debellare superbos."
    Sic pater Anchises atque haec mirantibus addit:
"aspice, ut insignis spoliis Marcellus opimis   855
ingreditur victorque viros supereminet omnis.
hic rem Romanam magno turbante tumultu
sistet, eques sternet Poenos Gallumque rebellem,
tertiaque arma patri suspendet capta Quirino."

851-3. "Remember, O Roman, to govern the nations with your command—these shall be *your* arts—to impose civilization (*morem*) on peace (*paci*)..." In these famous lines, the mission of Rome is clearly stated: to tame the proud and establish civilization through an orderly, just government.

852. **hae...artes:** parenthetical; the "arts" of government are opposed to the arts of sculpture, oratory, etc. **pacique:** some editors, based on a misreading of Servius, read *pacisque* ("the custom of peace") instead of *pacique*. *Pacisque,* however, has no manuscript authority. For the dative with *imponere,* cf. 2.619. Cf. Evander's description of the inhabitants of Italy before the arrival of Saturnus: *qui<bu>s neque mos neque cultus erat* (8.316).

853. **parcere..superbos:** "to spare those who submit and to thoroughly defeat those who are too arrogant." These Roman principles are also found in Cicero, *de officiis* (e.g. 1.35; Polybius 18.37.7; cf. Livy 30.42.17). Cf. Horace, *Carmen Saeculare* 51, where Augustus is described as *bellante prior, iacentem | lenis in hostem.*

854-9. Anchises points out one more hero, M. Claudius Marcellus.

854-9. M. Claudius Marcellus was consul five times; in his first consulship (222 BCE) he slew the leader of the Insubrian Gauls, and so won the *spolia opima,* which were the spoils taken when the Roman general slew the enemy's general (*quae dux duci detraxit* Livy 4. 20), and which according to tradition were only won three times—once by Romulus, once by Cossus (841 n.), and for the last time by Marcellus.

854. **mirantibus:** dative; i.e. Aeneas and the Sibyl.

857-8. **hic rem Romanam...sistet:** "this man will cause the Roman state to stand firm (*sistet*) when a great upheaval shakes it; as a horseman, he will trample (*sternet*)..." **tumultu:** specially used of a war *within* Italy or of an uprising by the Gauls. **sistet...sternet:** antithesis*, emphasized by assonance*. **sternet Poenos:** refers to Marcellus' role in the Second Punic (or Hannibalic) War.

859. **Quirino:** normally the spoils (cf. 854-9 n.) were dedicated to Jupiter Feretrius, but Vergil follows a tradition wherein the spoils normally dedicated to Jupiter Feretrius were instead dedicated to the deified Romulus (*Quirinus*), who is linked with Jupiter and was the builder of the temple of Jupiter Feretrius.

atque hic Aeneas (una namque ire videbat   860
egregium forma iuvenem et fulgentibus armis,
sed frons laeta parum et deiecto lumina vultu)
"quis, pater, ille, virum qui sic comitatur euntem?
filius, anne aliquis magna de stirpe nepotum?
qui strepitus circa comitum! quantum instar in ipso!   865
sed nox atra caput tristi circumvolat umbra."
tum pater Anchises lacrimis ingressus obortis:
"o nate, ingentem luctum ne quaere tuorum;
ostendent terris hunc tantum fata neque ultra
esse sinent. nimium vobis Romana propago   870
visa potens, superi, propria haec si dona fuissent.

860—92. Aeneas now draws his father's attention to a pale young man—Marcellus, the son of Augustus' sister, Octavia, and of C. Marcellus.

In 25 BCE Augustus gave Marcellus to his only child, Julia, in marriage, and promoted his brief political career. Marcellus, however, died in 23 BCE, at the age of 19. His death was a great blow to Augustus and his family. For Vergil's contemporary audience—and especially for Augustus and Octavia—this delicate eulogy is a very personal and a painful moment (see 878-82 n.). The Theatre of Marcellus in Rome was built in his memory. Why Vergil should end Anchises' revelation of the greatness of Rome on such a note of sorrow has long intrigued his readers. Cf. Brenk (1986), O'Hara (1990) 167-70 and Reed (2001).

860-2. The construction is "and at this point Aeneas (said), for he saw a youth walking beside him (*una*, i.e. with M. Claudius Marcellus)…, but his (the youth's) brow (was) very sad…"

863. **virum**: i.e. the Marcellus just described (854-9).

865. **instar:** the word is rarely used without a genitive and rarely with a modifier (*quantum*); here it means something like "presence," "bearing," "promise."

866. **sed nox atra:** the line describes night as hovering round him in a ghostly manner and already casting over his bright and youthful form the shadow of the grave.

869. **tantum:** adverb, "only." Fate will allow "only a glimpse" of him, nothing more.

870-1. "It seemed to you (*vobis visa <est>*), o gods, that the Roman race would be too great, if such gifts had been permanent (*propria*)." A mixed condition with the implied future tense of the apodosis (*nimium...visa potens*) overwhelmed by the contrary-to-fact protasis (*si... fuissent*). Cf. 358-61.

quantos ille virum magnam Mavortis ad urbem
campus aget gemitus! vel quae, Tiberine, videbis
funera, cum tumulum praeterlabere recentem!
nec puer Iliaca quisquam de gente Latinos   875
in tantum spe tollet avos, nec Romula quondam
ullo se tantum tellus iactabit alumno.
heu pietas, heu prisca fides invictaque bello
dextera! non illi se quisquam impune tulisset
obvius armato, seu cum pedes iret in hostem   880
seu spumantis equi foderet calcaribus armos.
heu, miserande puer, si qua fata aspera rumpas,
tu Marcellus eris. manibus date lilia plenis,
purpureos spargam flores animamque nepotis

872-3. **ille…campus:** in connection with "the city of Mavors," "that Field" (personified) is the Campus Martius. **virum:** syncopated genitive plural. **aget:** "will make."

873-5. **quae…funera:** Marcellus was buried with unusual ceremony in the mausoleum which Augustus had erected five years earlier (*tumulum…recentem*) in the Campus Martius for his family. *Funera* is strongly emphasized by its position and the pause that follows. **Tiberine:** the apostrophe* allows further variation in the personification of the river, who is also a god.

876. **in tantum spe tollet:** "will raise (our Latin descendants) so high (*tantum*) in hope." **tantum:** adverbial. **quondam:** "one day," "in the future"; cf. similar uses of *olim* at 1.289; 3.541.

878-82. **heu pietas, heu prisca fides…heu miserande puer (882)…rumpas:** Marcellus will embody the ideals of honor, piety, and bravery, but will not live to fulfill this promise. The heroes of the Roman race have just passed in review before the vision of Anchises and before Vergil's spellbound audience. The poet now concludes by focusing his skills upon this last figure. The final words, *tu Marcellus eris,* fall from Anchises' lips, in slow, measured, and almost ghostly accents. It was reported that Marcellus' mother Octavia (i.e. Augustus' sister) fainted as Vergil read these words (cf. *vita Donati* 32).

878. **prisca fides:** "ancient honor"; *priscus* suggests the goodness of "old-fashioned" ways. **invicta:** "invincible." Marcellus did participate in the Cantabrian campaign in 26 BCE (in Spain) with Augustus.

883. **tu Marcellus eris:** some editors place an exclamation point after *rumpas* to mark an emphatic change of tone, so that the words *tu Marcellus eris* form the climax of this scene. The mention of the name of Marcellus, reserved until the end of the sentence, however, gives these three simple words their full force. Cf. 878-82 n.

883-4. **manibus…flores:** "let me scatter bright/purple (*purpureos*) lilies with full hands." **date…spargam:** a mix of imperative and jussive subjunctive. **purpureos:** may mean "bright," "dazzling," or "purple" (the color of dried blood). Cf. 640-1 n.; 5.79.

his saltem accumulem donis, et fungar inani   885
munere." sic tota passim regione vagantur
aëris in campis latis atque omnia lustrant.
quae postquam Anchises natum per singula duxit
incenditque animum famae venientis amore,
exim bella viro memorat quae deinde gerenda,   890
Laurentisque docet populos urbemque Latini,
et quo quemque modo fugiatque feratque laborem.
     Sunt geminae Somni portae, quarum altera fertur

885-6. **fungar inani | munere:** *fungor* ("perform," "administer") governs the ablative case. This is the only time Vergil uses this verb. The pathos of *inani munere,* the "empty gift," is heightened by *saltem.*

887. **aëris in campis latis:** "in wide fields of air." Since Elysium is set in the underworld, Page attempts to associate this *aer* with the "mist" in Homer, *Odyssey* 20.64. Austin (*ad loc.*) rejects this notion, and instead, citing Norden, suggests the influence of such theories as that in "Plutarch's cosmological myth *de facie in orbe lunae visa* in which (943c) the soul after separation from the body is represented as wandering in the region between the earth and the moon," and then rises to the Elysian Plain, on the upper part of the moon.

890-1. Anchises' instructions now pertain to the immediate future. *Laurentisque...populos* (891) refers to Latinus and his people in Latium, whom the Trojans will meet in Book 7, while *bella...gerenda* (890) clearly anticipate the struggles that will dominate the final six books of the poem.

892. **quo...modo fugiatque feratque:** indirect questions.

893—901. Departure from the Gates of Sleep

The Gates of Sleep are a sudden break in the narrative. Just as Aeneas and the Sibyl entered the underworld aided by the golden bough, so now they depart mysteriously through twin (*geminae* 893) Gates of Sleep. One Gate is of horn (*cornea* 894), the other of ivory (*candenti...elephanto* 895), recalling Homer, *Odyssey* 19.562, where Penelope describes the gates of dreams. True dreams (*veris...umbris* 894) come through the gate of horn (*cornea*), while that of ivory (*candenti elephanto* 895) is for false dreams (*falsa...insomnia* 896) (cf. Plato, *Charmides* 173a; Horace, *Odes* 3.27.39).

cornea, qua veris facilis datur exitus umbris,
altera candenti perfecta nitens elephanto,   895
sed falsa ad caelum mittunt insomnia manes.
his ibi tum natum Anchises unaque Sibyllam
prosequitur dictis portaque emittit eburna,
ille viam secat ad navis sociosque revisit.
    Tum se ad Caietae recto fert litore portum.   900
ancora de prora iacitur; stant litore puppes.

The departure of Aeneas and the Sibyl through the Ivory Gate (*porta...eburna* 898) implies that they are "false dreams," but the significance of this detail has proved difficult to interpret. Earlier critics had tried to explain the problem in various ways: Norden interprets this as meaning that Aeneas and the Sibyl left the underworld before midnight, since "true dreams" appeared only after midnight. Austin suggests that they are not "true shades" so they cannot exit through the Gate of Horn. More recently, scholars have focused on the broader significance of the Gates of Sleep. For Tarrant their departure reflects the imperfection of man's corporeal state, while Gotoff argues that this fulfills the dramatic need for Aeneas not to remember his experiences in the underworld during during the second half of the epic (indeed, there is no indication in Books 7-12 that he does); cf. Horsfall (1995) 146. Others would emend the text (e.g. Kraggerud would eliminate line 896 altogether). In any case, there is some irony in the fact that the entire preceding Parade of Heroes was meant to inspire Aeneas, and yet his experiences in the underworld ultimately becomme associated with *falsa insomnia*.

    For further discussion see R.D. Williams (1964) 48; Thornton (1976) 61; Clark (1979) 224; Tarrant (1982) 51-5; Gotoff (1985); West (1987) 224-38; Habinek (1989) 253-4; O'Hara (1990) 170-2; Brenk (1992) 277-94; and Kraggerud (2002).

893. **fertur:** "is said"; supply *esse*.

897-8. **his...dictis porta...eburna:** "with these words then, Anchises escorts his son...and sends him forth by the ivory gate."

899. **viam secat:** the verb suggests that Aeneas is now cutting his way through a dense forest to reach the ships.

900. **Caietae:** Caieta (modern Gaeta) is in Latium, NW of Cumae. It will not actually be given this name until 7.1-6, where we learn that Aeneas' nurse Caieta died and is buried there, after which the port/town is named for her. **recto...litore:** Hirtzel, Page and Williams retain the manuscript reading *recto...litore*, "straight along the shore." Mynors, Austin, *et al.* accept the more recent manuscript reading, *recto ... limite*, thus avoiding the repetition of *litore*, as found in the next line (901 *stant litore puppes*). Cf. 3.277 *stant litore puppes*.

Appendix A: Vergil's Meter[1]

Dactylic Hexameter in English and in Latin

In English poetry, the meter and the natural accent of a word usually correspond:

"Áh to bé in Éngland, nów that Ápril's hére."

Consequently, English poetry is said to be "accentuative," because metrical patterns are based on the natural accents of words, and thus the ictus (i.e. the stress) of the poetic meter and the natural accent of individual words coincide. Greek and Latin meter, by contrast, is based not on word accent but on the length or "quantity" of each syllable (i.e. whether syllables are long or short, see below), and is therefore said to be "quantitative."

Latin and Greek epic poems are written in *dactylic hexameter,* which means that each line consists of six (*hex*) "measures" or "feet" (*metra*) with the defining metrical foot being the *dactyl,* which consists of one long syllable followed by two short ones. (*Dactyl* is a Greek word meaning "finger," which contains one long bone and two short bones.) In practice, however, the first four feet of a dactylic hexameter line consist of either dactyls or spondees (two long syllables), and the fifth foot is almost invariably a dactyl. The final foot is a spondee or a trochee (one long syllable and one short syllable). The basic schema for a dactylic hexameter line, accordingly, is:

$$ - \smile\smile / - \smile\smile / - \smile\smile / - \smile\smile / - \smile\smile / - \times $$

(Here, "/" separates metrical feet; "–" = a long syllable; " ⌣ " =
a short syllable; and "x" = an *anceps* ("undecided") syllable,
one that is either long or short.)

Very rarely a spondee is used in the fifth foot, in which case the line is called "spondaic."

Although dactylic hexameter is not often used in English poetry, some great English poets have employed it with interesting effect. The

---

1   For more on Vergil's meter, see Jackson Knight (1944) 232-42, Duckworth (1969) 46-62, Nussbaum (1986), and Ross (2007) 143-52.

American poet Henry Wadsworth Longfellow, for example, used this meter in "Evangeline," which begins:

> "Thís is the /fórest prim/éval, the /múrmuring /woóds and the /hémlock."

> dúm-da-da /dúm-da-da /dúm-da-da/ dúm-da-da / dúm-da-da / dúm-dum/

> [1ˢᵗ foot   2ⁿᵈ foot   3ʳᵈ foot   4ᵗʰ foot   5ᵗʰ foot   6ᵗʰ foot]

The meter of Longfellow's poem anticipates the grand, sweeping "epic" tale that will follow. The same meter can be used for a variety of other effects, however. In Alfred Lord Tennyson's "Northern Farmer," it conveys the repetitive motion of a laborer:

> "Próputty, / próputty, /próputty, /thát's what I /héär them/ sááy."

> dúm-da-da/ dúm-da-da /dúm-da-da /dúm-da-da/ dúm-da-da/ dúm-dum.

Here the forced division of what in English would ordinarily be one syllable into two syllables in the words "héär" and "sááy" to fit the meter has an almost comic or clumsy effect, which is probably what the poet intended for this topic.

Scansion

As noted above, Latin poetry is quantitative and thus based on the length of individual syllables. A syllable can be *long* in two ways: 1) *by nature*, if it contains a vowel that is inherently long or is a diphthong;[2] or 2) *by position*, if a short vowel is followed either by a double consonant (*x* or *z*) or, in most cases, by two consonants, even if they are not in the same word;[3]

---

2   One can determine if a vowel is long by nature by looking the word up in a dictionary to see if it has a macron over it or by checking inflected endings in a grammar (for example, some endings, like the first and second declension ablative singular (-*a*, -*o*), are always long; others, like the second declension nominative neuter plural (-*a*), are always short). Vowels long by nature are always marked with a macron; longs by position are not marked long as the reader is expected to recognize them from the rules of "long by position"; shorts are left unmarked. (Compare, for example, the differing lengths of –*e*- in *assevērātiō* , or of –*a*- in *amāritūdō*.)

3   An exception to this general rule: if a short vowel is followed by a mute consonant (*b, c, d, g, p, t*) and a liquid (*l* or *r*), the resulting syllable can be either short or long. Cf. 2.663 where the *a*'s in *patris* and *patrem* are short and long respectively: *natum ante ora pătris, pātrem qui obtruncat ad aras*. It should also be noted that *h* is a breathing, not a consonant; it therefore does not help make a vowel long by position.

consequently, the double consonant causes the short vowel to be lengthened.[4] In general, a long syllable takes twice as long to say as a short syllable.

If, however, a word ending in a vowel, diphthong, or –*m* with preceding vowel is followed by a word that begins with a vowel, diphthong, or *h* (which is silent), the vowel or diphthong at the end of that word is *elided* (and hence not pronounced) with the vowel beginning the next word, and the quantity of the remaining syllable is determined by the length of that syllable. Thus, in the first two lines of *Aeneid* 6 (see below), the final syllable of *classique* elides with *immittit* in line 1, while in line 2 the final –*dem* of *tandem* and the final -*rum* of *Cumarum* elide with the words that follow them. Since the remaining syllables (*im*- and *ad*-) contain vowels followed by two consonants, and *eu*- is a diphthong, they are all long, regardless of the lengths of the lost syllables (-*que, -dem, -rum*):

> *sic fatur lacrimans, classique immittit habenas* (6.1)
>
> sīc fā-/ tūr lă-crĭ-/ māns, clās/ sīque īm-/ mīt-tĭt hă-/ bē- nās
>
> dúm-dum /dúm-da-da /dúm-dum/ dúm-dum/ dúm-da-da /dúm-dum/

> *et tandem Euboicis Cumarum adlabitur oris:* (6.2)
>
> ēt tān- /dem Eū-bŏ-ĭ-/-cīs Cū-/ mā -rum ād-/lā- bĭ- tŭr/ ōr-īs.
>
> dúm-dum / dúm-da-da /dúm-dum/ dúm-dum /dúm-da-da /dúm-dum/

If, however, a long or short syllable is elided with a short syllable, the remaining syllable will still be short:

> partem opere in tanto, sineret dolor, Icare, haberes.   (6.31)
>
> pārtem ŏpě/-re īn tān /-tō,   sĭně /   -rēt dŏlŏr, / Īcăre, hă/ -bērēs.
>
> dúm-da-da /dúm-dum /dúm-da-da/ dúm-da-da /dúm-da-da /dúm-dum/

Word Accent in Latin

Despite the quantitative nature of Latin meter, the natural accent of words also plays an important role. Accentuation is fairly straightforward.

---

4   For example, compare the vowels in a word like *scrībĭt*: the first *ī* is naturally long and sounds more like "ee" in "meet" in contrast to the second *i* which is short and sounds like the *i* in "sit." Similarly, compare the vowels in *ămānt*. The initial *a* is short by nature and is not lengthened by position, while the second *a* is short by nature but lengthened by position.

Disyllabic Latin words have their accent on their initial syllable: *cáris, dábant, mólis*. If, however, words are three syllables or longer, the word accent falls on the penult[5] (second to last syllable) if it is long (*ruébant, iactátos*) but on the antepenult (the syllable preceding the penult), if the penult is short (*géntibus, mária, pópulum*). A word's accent in Latin, however, will not necessarily coincide with the *ictus* (or metrical stress) of a foot.

The management of the clash or coincidence of word accent and metrical *ictus* plays an important role in a poet's artistry. For example, coincidence of word accent and metrical stress can produce fluidity in the verse; clashing of word accent and metrical stress can create tension. In the following example, the syllable receiving the *ictus* is in bold, while the natural word accent is indicated with an accent " ´ ":

prāepĕtĭbūs pénnīs aúsūs sē **crē**dĕrĕ **cāe**lō (6.15)

Note how the tension in this line (created by the clash of metrical ictus and word accent in the first four feet) underscores the risky adventure undertaken by Daedalus when he invented wings and entrusted his own and his son's life to the sky to escape.

Caesura and Diaeresis

The flow of a line, finally, is affected not only by its rhythm but also by the placement of breaks between words, or "word breaks." A caesura (from *caedere*, "to cut") is a pause at the end of a word within a metrical foot.[6] If it coincides with a pause in the sense of the words (as at the end of a clause), it may be said to form a "main" caesura (indicated by "‖"). In dactylic hexameter the "main" caesura most often occurs in the third foot, as in the following example:

Daedalus, ut fama est, fugiens Minoia regna (6.14)
Dāe -dă- lŭs, / ūt fāma /ēst, ‖ fŭg-ĭ -/ ēns Mī- /nō-ĭ -ă/ rēg-nă.

(Note too that *caesurae* also occur here after *ut* and *fugiens*.) When a word break falls between metrical feet, the break is called a *diaeresis* (a

---

[5]   These words are compounds of *ultima* = "the last or final"; *paene*= "almost"; *ante* = "before." Hence *antepenultima* = "before the almost last (syllable)," *penultima* = the almost last (syllable)", and *ultima* = "the last (syllable)."

[6]   When a caesura falls after the first syllable of a foot, it is called "strong" (as after *ut* and *est* in 6.14); if it falls after the second syllable in a dactylic foot, it is called "weak."

"division").[7] In the above line, diaeresis occurs after *Daedalus* and *Minoia*. The two main breaks in this line are after *Daedalus* (as a diaeresis) and after *est* (the main caesura).

Vergil's use of the hexameter has always been much admired.[8] More than any other Latin poet, he was able to exploit the possible interplay between sentence endings and line endings, whereas in his predecessors the line and the sentence unit had tended to coincide. Like Milton's English blank verse, Vergil's Latin hexameter made new use of the kinds of emphasis possible through run-on words, mid-line pauses, and short staccato sentences. This resulted not only in extra emphasis in particular places, but in a great increase in the variety of narrative movement, with the result that the hexameter can retain the reader's attention over thousands of lines. Vergil also achieved the necessary variety by incorporating the metrical abnormalities and license of his predecessors. Finally, he understood and made use of the two rhythms inherent in this meter ever since it was first used by the early Latin poet Ennius (239-169 BCE). Ennius had applied the Greek hexameter meter to the more strongly stressed Latin language, which resulted in the imposition of an artificial scansion scheme on the normal stress pronunciation of Latin. Vergil employed the interplay of these rhythms for various aesthetic effects, and thus was able to make the sound suit the sense. This range of metrical movement triumphantly sustains the epic theme of the *Aeneid*.

---

7   When a *diaeresis* occurs just before the fifth foot, it is often called a *bucolic diaeresis* because this type of diaeresis was used frequently in pastoral poetry: e.g. *nos patriam fugimus; tu, Tityre,* || *lentus in umbra* (Vergil, *Eclogues* 1.4).

8   Williams (1972) xxvi-viii; cf. Wilkinson (1969).

Appendix B: Glossary

Terms of Grammar, Rhetoric, Prosody, Poetics

Vergil's skillful use of language is a defining element of his artistry. He often employs rhetorical figures and stylistic devices to reinforce the content of his poetry. Careful attention should therefore be paid both to what Vergil says *and* to how he says it. The following list defines many of the stylistic terms and features that are encountered in studying Vergil. For discussion of the examples cited from Book 6, see the commentary notes. For more information on the terms, see Lanham (1991) and Brogan (1994). Fuller information on Vergilian style can be found in Jackson Knight (1944) 225-341, Camps (1969) 60-74, O'Hara (1997), and Conte (2007) 58-122. Stylistic analyses of Vergilian passages are presented in Horsfall (1995) 237-48 and Hardie (1998) 102-14.

Alliteration (Lat. *ad* "to" + *littera* "letter"): the repetition of the initial consonant sound in neighboring words. In *pars pedibus plaudunt* (6.644), each word begins with *p*. In 6.335-6, *ventosa per aequora vectos/...aqua involvens navemque virosque*, note the repetition of the consonantal *u* (*v*).

Anachronism/anachronistic (Gr. *ana* "against" + *chronos* "time"): an error in chronology, especially a chronological misplacing of persons, events, objects, or customs in regard to each other. In 6.9, e.g., Vergil depicts Apollo as already established at Cumae when the Trojans arrive, but in fact Apollo was not a presence in Cumae until the late fifth century.

Anaphora (Gr. *ana* "up," "back" + *pherein* "to bring," "carry"; "bringing up again"): the repetition of a word at the beginning of consecutive sentences or clauses, bringing emphasis or emotional intensity, as in an oracular speech, prophecy or prayer:

non vultus, non color unus,
non comptae mansere comae (6.47-8)

bis conatus erat casus effingere in auro,
bis patriae cecidere manus (6.32-3)

Anastrophe (Gr. *ana* "up," "back" + *strophe* "a turning"; "a turning upside down"): the inversion of the normal word order, which may emphasize the words placed unusually. This often happens with prepositions: *volitantque haec litora <u>circum</u>* (6.329); cf. *hos <u>iuxta</u>* (6.430), *quos <u>super</u>* (6.602).

Apostrophe (Gr. *apo* "from" + *strophe* "a turning"): a turning away from one addressee to address another, usually to address an absent figure, as when Vergil addresses Apollo to describe the temple Daedalus built for him:

> *tibi, Phoebe, sacravit*
> *remigium alarum posuitque immania templa* (6.18-19)

Assonance (Lat. *ad* + *sonare* "to answer with the same sound"): the repetition of vowel sounds (in contrast to alliterative consonant sounds) in neighboring words or phrases. E.g., *noctes atque dies p<u>a</u>tet <u>a</u>tri i<u>a</u>nu<u>a</u> Ditis* (6.127).

Asyndeton (Gr. *a-* "not" + *syndein* "to bind together"; "not to be bound together"): the omission of connectives between words, phrases, or sentences. In the following example, the narrator tells how Daedalus attempted but failed to include the sad story of his son, Icarus, on the doors of the temple of Apollo (6.32-3):

> <u>bis</u> *conatus erat casus effingere in auro,*
> <u>bis</u> *patriae cecidere manus.*

Here there is no connective between the two clauses beginning with *bis*. Cf. 6.47-8, 134-5.

Caesura (Lat. *caedere* "to cut") is a word break within a metrical foot; in dactylic hexameter the *main* caesura (indicated by "||") usually occurs within the third foot:

> *Eumenidum aspicies,* || *ripamve iniussus adibis*   (6.375)

However, it can be elsewhere for a particular emphasis. For example:

> *"agnoscas."* || *tumida ex ira tum corda residunt*   (6.407, second foot)
> *praecipitans traxi mecum* || *maria aspera iuro* (6.351, fourth foot)

Chiasmus (Gk. letter *chi* or *X*) an arrangement of words whereby parallel constructions are expressed in reverse word order. E.g., *domos...vacuas et inania regna* (6.269). The sequence (*noun A, adjective A...adjective B, noun B*) has both the nouns on the outside, and both the adjectives on the inside of the phrase, producing a crossing ("X") pattern:

> *domos* [noun] ... *vacuas* [adj.]
>   *et* (X)
> *inania* [adj.] *regna* [noun]

Cognate accusative (Lat. *cognatus* "related"): when the object is of the same origin or of a meaning related to a transitive verb, it is called the cognate accusative. E.g., *vitam vivere*, "to live (one's) life." Sometimes the accusative is a substantive neuter adjective: *mortale sonans*, "making mortal sounds."

Dactyl (Gk. *dactylos* "finger"): this metrical foot has one long syllable and two short syllables (like the lengths of the bones of a human finger).

Diaeresis (Gr. *dia* "through" or "apart" + *haerein* "to take"; "division"): the coinciding of the end of a word with the end of a metrical foot. In dactylic hexameter, a "bucolic diaeresis" is when the diaeresis occurs at the end of the fourth foot (a reference to the bucolic poetry of Theocritus, where it occurs frequently). In the following example, *Daedalus* is a complete dactyl and forms a separate foot; it is followed by a *diaeresis*:

Daedalus,/ ut fa/ma est, fugi/ens Min/oia/ regna (6.14)

Ecphrasis (Gr. *ek* "out" + "*fradzein* "tell"; "description"): a passage describing, usually, a work of art, such as the description of the sculptures on the doors of the temple of Apollo in Cumae in Book 6.14-41. It does not advance the narrative plot, but may relate to the framing story either through parallels or contrasts.

Elision (Lat. *elidere* "to strike" or "knock out"): the omission of a vowel (or a vowel + *m*) at the end of a word before a word beginning with a vowel or *h*.

Ellipsis (Gr. *ek* "out" + *leipein* "leave"; "leaving out"): the omission of one or more words (nouns, pronouns, objects, finite verbs, clauses) necessary to complete the sense and that must be supplied by the listener or reader; this is particularly common with forms of *esse*:

quis, pater, <est> ille, virum qui sic comitatur euntem? (6.863)

Enjambment (Fr. *en* "in," "into" + *jambe* "leg"; "straddling," "spanning"): a "run-on" line, i.e., the continuation of the sense or syntactic unit from one line to the next (as opposed to "end-stopped" lines, where each linguistic unit corresponds with a single line). E.g., lines 6.142-3:

hoc sibi pulchra suum ferri Proserpina munus
instituit.

Enjambed lines are often followed by some kind of pause (here a strong caesura after *instituit*) that adds emphasis.

Epanalepsis (Gr. *epi* "in addition," "after" + *ana* "up"+ *lambanein/ lepsesthai* "to take"; "a taking up again"): the technically unnecessary repetition of a word or words whether for emphasis or for clarity. E.g., *Misenum...* *Misenum* (6.162-4), *ora / ora manusque ambas* (6.495-6).

Epithet (Gr. *epi* "on" + *tithenai* "to place"; "laid upon," "additional"): an adjective or other term applied to a person or thing to express an attribute: e.g., <u>auricomos</u> *fetus* (6.140-1); <u>Amphrysia</u> Apollo (6.398); <u>infelix</u> Dido (6.456).

Epexegetic (Gr. *ep-* "in addition" + *exegeisthai* "to lead or carry out," "tell at length"; "explaining or accounting in detail"): providing additional explanation. E.g., in *praestantior...ciere* (6.164-5), "more outstanding at summoning"; the (epexegetical) infinitive *ciere* specifies the limits of *praestantior.*

Etymology (Gr. *etumos* "true" + *logos* "the word" or "that by which the inward thought is expressed"): the derivation of a word, reflecting its original meaning. In a *false* etymology, the assumed meaning of a word is mistakenly thought to derive from incorrect sources: e.g., the name of Lake Avernus (6.239) was thought to derive from the Greek *aornus,* "without birds," while in fact it probably derives from the Italic word *for* birds (*aves*). Similarly, the name of the god "Sāturnus" (6.794), who ruled over the Golden Age in Italy, which was agriculturally based, was thought to derive from *sero, serere, satus,* "to sow," but in fact the stem of Sāturnus has a long *-a-,* while the *-a-* in the verb's perfect participle is short.

Hendiadys (Gr. *hen* + *dia* + *duoin* "one through two"): the expression of one idea through two terms joined by a conjunction. E.g., in *spargens <u>rore levi et ramo</u> felicis olivae* (6.230) the dew (*rore*) is on the branch (*ramo*), so the phrase would mean "sprinkling them with *gentle dew from the branch* of a fruitful olive tree."

Hyperbaton (Gr. *hyper* "beyond" + *bainein* "to go beyond") words that naturally belong together are separated from each other for emphasis or effect (especially when emphasis is thereby put on an important idea by placing the words at the beginning or end of a sentence). E.g., 6.136-8:

> *latet arbore opaca*
> **aureus** *et foliis et lento vimine* **ramus,**
> *Iunoni infernae dictus sacer*

Here the separation of *aureus* and *ramus,* which enclose line 137 emphasize the importance of the object being described.

Hyperbole (Gr. *hyper* "beyond"+ *bole* "a throw," "casting"): an exaggeration, as in 6.16, where it is said that Daedalus *gelidas enavit ad Arctos,* to indicate he flew northward from Crete, but he would certainly not have flown as far as the North Pole in order to reach southern Italy.

Hypermetric line (Gr. *hyper* "beyond" + *metron* "measure") an extra syllable at the end of the line, often *-que,* which elides with the first letter of the following line, emphasizing its connection to the next line. E.g., 6.602-3:

> *quos super atra silex iam iam lapsura cadentique*
> *imminet*

Ictus (Lat. *ictus* "stroke" or "blow"): the metrical foot accent; in dactylic hexameter the *ictus* falls on the first syllable of the foot, whether a dactyl or a spondee. Counterpoint between *ictus* and word accent in the first four feet and resolution in the last two feet is characteristic of Vergil's hexameters, providing both tension and harmony.

Interlocking word order (or **synchysis**): an arrangement of two phrases that interweave their members in an abAB pattern (e.g. adjective a, adjective b, noun A, noun B) or AbaB (e.g. noun A, adjective b, adjective a, noun B), with the result that the two phrases are interlocked

> abAB: *Excisum* (a) *Euboicae* (b) *latus* (A) ... *rupis* (B) (6.42)
> AbaB: *portitor* (A) *has* (b) *horrendus* (a) *aquas* (B)(6.298)
> AbaB: *unde genus* (A) *Longa* (b) *nostrum* (a) *dominabitur Alba* (B) (6.763)

Irony (Gr. *eironeia* "dissembling"): when one thing is said but its opposite is somehow implied or understood. There is rich irony in the Sibyl's statement to Aeneas that there is no difficulty in going to the underworld—the problem is in returning (6.126-9)

> *facilis descensus <est> descensus Averno ...*
> *sed revocare gradum superasque evadere ad auras*
> *hoc opus est.*

Litotes (Gr. *litos* "simple"; "simplicity"): making a positive statement by negating its opposite, as in <u>*nec non* Aeneas *primus*</u>, "Aeneas is the leader/first" (183); *haud mora*, "there is no delay" (i.e., they moved quickly) (6.177); or <u>*non inferiora* secutus</u> "pursuing not lesser things" (i.e., pursuing equally noble things) (6.170).

Metaphor (Gr. *meta* "over" + *pherein* "to carry"; "transference"): the application of a word or phrase from one field of meaning to touch upon another, thereby suggesting new meanings, as in *stabula alta ferarum* (6.179), "the lofty abodes/stables of wild creatures/birds," referring to the lofty trees that are being cut down for Misenus' funeral.

Metonymy (Gr. *meta* "after" + *onoma* "name"; "change of name"): the representation of one thing by another with which it is associated, such as *Aurora* for dawn (6.535), or *Ceres* for bread (7.113). Closely related is **synecdoche**, the representation of a part for the whole, as when *unda*, a single wave, represents an entire body of water in *Stygia prospexit ab unda* (6.385); cf. *aurea tecta* (6.485), where the "roof" represents the entire temple of Apollo.

Onomatopoeia (Gr. *onoma* "name" + *poiein* "to make"; "the making of a word or name"): the use or formation of words that imitate natural sounds, as in *quinquaginta atris immanis hiatibus Hydra* (6.576), where repeating *i* and *s* sounds suggest the hissing of the creature.

Oxymoron (Gr. *oxus* "sharp" + *moron* "foolish"; "pointedly foolish"): the juxtaposition of seemingly contradictory words. E.g., *animum pictura pascit inani* (1.464). Here the idea of feeding (*pascit*) on something that is empty (*inani*) seems contradictory.

Paronomasia (Gr. *para* "by" or "from the side" + *onoma* "name"; "slight alteration of name"): a wordplay or pun. E.g., *Vrbs antiqua fuit (Tyrii tenuere coloni) / Karthago* (1.12). Here there seems to be a wordplay, since the word *Karthago* meant *nova urbs* in Punic.

Pathos (Gr. *pathein* "to suffer") a quality or power of arousing pity, sympathy, or sorrow, such as Aeneas's speech to Dido in the underworld as he tries to make her understand why he abandoned her (6.456-66).

Patronymic (Gr. *pater* "father" + *onoma* "name"): a name derived from the name of a father or an ancestor, especially with the addition of a suffix such as *–des*, "son of." Cf. *Alcides*, "descendant of Alceus," or *Anchisiades,* "son of Anchises."

Periphrasis (Gr. *peri* "around" + *fradzein* "to speak"; "circumlocution"): the use of more words than is necessary to express an idea, e.g., *septena...corpora natorum* (6.21-2) instead of "seven sons"; *Tartareum...custodem* (6.395) for Cerberus; *Amphrysia vates* (6.398) for the Sibyl.

Personification (Lat. *persona* "mask," "character," "person"): the representation of inanimate things as if they were human. E.g., *Jupiter* for the sky (6.271-2); *Aurora* for dawn (6.535); the personified gods at 6.273-81.

Pleonasm, pleonastic (Gr. *pleonasma* "superfluity"): redundancy, especially for emphasis. E.g., *pater omnipotens...ille* (6.592-3): *ille* is unnecessary, but is added to emphasize the contrast between Jupiter and Salmoneus (6.585).

Polyptoton (Gr. *polu* "many" + *ptosis* "falling," "modification" of a word, hence "(grammatical) case"; "with or in many cases"): the repetition of a word in its inflected cases. E.g.,

<u>ausi</u> omnes immani nefas <u>auso</u>que potiti (6.604).

Prolepsis (Gr. *pro* "before" + *lepsesthai* (future tense of *lambanein*): "to take"; "anticipation") the introduction of a word or epithet before it is appropriate, thus anticipating what is to come:

alma, precor, miserere ... si potuit ... (6.117-19)

Here Aeneas implores the Sibyl to guide him; in seeking her pity (*miserere*), he anticipates that she will be *alma*, "kind, gracious."

Simile (Lat. *similis* "similar"): an explicit, figurative comparison between two different things, introduced by "like" or "as" (*sicut, ac veluti*, etc.).

> *hunc circum innumerae gentes populique volabant:*
> *ac veluti in pratis ubi apes aestate serena*
> *floribus insidunt variis et candida circum*
> *lilia funduntur, strepit omnis murmure campus.* (6.706-11)

Here the figures in the underworld gathering around the river Lethe are compared to honeybees gathering nectar from flowers. Cf. 6.309-10 and 6.310-12, which comprise a double simile.

Synchysis (Gr. *sun* "with" + *chein* "to pour"): see **interlocking word order.**

Syncope (Gr. *sun* "with" + *kope* "a cutting"; "cutting up into small pieces"): the omission of a letter or short syllable from within a word, such as *repostus* for *repositus*, or *complerint* for *compleverint*. *Syncope* is particularly frequent in verbs in the perfect tenses.

Synecdoche (Gr. *sun* "with" *ekdechesthai* "to take or receive from another": a part is used for the whole; see **metonymy.**

Synizesis (Gr. *sun* "with" + *idzanein* " to sit"; "subsidence," "collapse"): the running together of two syllables without full contraction. E.g., *ferrei* (6.280) is pronounced as two syllables, not three; as is *alveo* (6.412).

Tmesis (Gk. *temnein* "to cut"): the separation of a compound word into two parts. E.g., in *pingue super oleum fundens ardentibus extis* (6.254), *oleum* separates *super-fundens*, which translates as if it had not been separated. Cf. *hac...tenus* (6.62); *circum...ducebat* (6.517).

Tricolon (Gr. *tri-* "three" + *kolon* "limb," "clause"): the grouping of three parallel clauses or phrases. When the third element is the longest, the resulting *tricolon* is called *abundans, crescens*, or *crescendo*, as in 6.47-48, when the Sibyl goes into a trance:

> i) *subito non vultus,*
> ii) *non color unus,*
> iii) *non comptae mansere comae,*

When Anchises gives Aeneas his final instructions in the underworld:

> i) *tu regere imperio populos, Romane, memento*
> ii) *(hae tibi erunt artes), pacique imponere morem,*
> iii) *parcere subiectis et*
> iv) *debellare superbos.* (6.851-3)

he actually adds a fourth infinitive, thereby emphasizing the importance of his instruction.

Sources:

Palmer (1954); Smyth (1956, rev.); Lewis and Short (1962); Liddell and Scott (1968); Preminger and Brogan (1993); Allen and Greenough, see Mahoney (2001); Ganiban (2009) 113-18.

Bibliography

Manuscripts:

F = Vaticanus lat. 3225 (4th century)

G = Sangallensis 1394 (5th century)

M = Florentinus Laurentianus xxxix.I, "Mediceus" (5th century)

P = Vaticanus Palatinus lat. 1631, "Palatinus" (4th/5th century)

R = Vaticanus lat. 3867, "Romanus" (5th century)

Adler, E. (2003) *Vergil's Empire: Political Thought in the Aeneid.* Lanham, MD.

Allen, G. (2000) *Intertextuality.* London.

Anderson, W. S. (2005) *The Art of the Aeneid.* Second edition. Wauconda, IL.

Armstrong, D, J. Fish, P. A. Johnston, and M. Skinner (eds.) (2004) *Vergil, Philodemus, and the Augustans.* Austin.

Austin, R. G. (1977) *P. Vergili Maronis Aeneidos Liber Sextus.* Oxford.

Bailey, C. (1935) *Religion in Virgil.* Oxford.

Barchiesi, A. (1979) "Palinura e Caieta: Due 'epigrammi' Virgiliani (*Aen.* 5.870 ff; 7.1-5)," *Maia* 31: 3-11.

----------(1984) *La traccia del modello: effetti omerici nella narrazione virgiliana.* Pisa.

Bleisch, P. (1999) "The empty tomb at Rhoeteum: Deiphobus and the problem of the past in *Aeneid* 6.494-547," *Classical Antiquity* 18: 187-226.

Braund, S. (1997) "Virgil and the cosmos: Religious and philosophical ideas," in *The Cambridge Compantion to Virgil*, ed. C. Martindale. Cambridge: 204-21.

Brenk, F. E. (1986) "*Aurorum spes et purpurei flores*: the Eulogy of Marcellus in Aeneid VI," *American Journal of Philology* 107: 218-28.

----------(1992) "The gates of dreams and an image of life: consolation and allegory at the end of Vergil's *Aeneid* VI," *Collection Latomus: Studies in Latin Literature and History VI*: 277-94.

----------(1999) *Clothed in Purple Light.* Steiner: Stuttgart.

Briggs, W. W., Jr. (1981) "Virgil and the Hellenistic Epic," *Aufsteig und Niedergang der Römischen Welt* 2.31.2: 948-84.

Brooks, R. A. (1953) "*Discolor aura*: reflections on the Golden Bough," *Amerian Journal of Philology* 74: 260-280. Reprinted in Commager (1966) 142-63.

Butler, H. E. (1920) *The Sixth Book of the Aeneid.* Oxford.

Cairns, F. (1989) *Virgil's Augustan Epic.* Cambridge.

Camps, W. A. (1967-68) "The role of the sixth book in the *Aeneid*," *Proceedings of the Virgil Society* 7: 22-30.

Casadio, G. and P. A. Johnston (eds.) (2009) *Mystic Cults of Magna Graecia*. Austin.

Clark, R. J. (1977) "Vergil, *Aeneid* 6.40 ff. and the Cumaean Sibyl's cave," *Latomus* 36: 482-95.

----------(1979) *Catabasis: Vergil and the Wisdom Tradition*. Amsterdam.

----------(1992) "Vergil, *Aeneid* 6: the bough by Hades' gate," in *The Two Worlds of the Poet: New Perspectives on Vergil*, eds. R. M. Wilhelm and H. Jones. Detroit: 167-78.

----------(1996) "The Avernian Sibyl's cave: from military tunnel to Mediaeval spa," *Classica et Mediaevalia* 47: 217-243

----------(2000) "P. OXY. 2078, Vat. Gr. 2228, and Vergil's Charon," *Classical Quarterly* 50: 192-6.

----------(2001) "How Vergil expanded the Underworld in *Aeneid* 6," *Proceedings of the Cambridge Philological Society* 47: 103-16.

----------(2009) "The Eleusinian Mysteries and Vergil's 'appearance-of-a-terrifying-female-apparition-in-the-Underworld," in *Mystic Cults in Magna Graecia*, eds. G. Casadio and P. A. Johnston. Austin: 190-203.

Clausen, W. (1987) *Virgil's Aeneid and the Tradition of Hellenistic Poetry*. Berkeley, CA.

----------(1994) *A Commentary on Virgil, Eclogues*. Oxford.

----------(2002) *Virgil's Aeneid: Decorum, Allusion, and Ideology*. Munich and Leipzig.

Cockburn, G. T. (1992) "Aeneas and the Gates of Sleep: an etymological approach," *Phoenix* 46: 362-4.

Coleman, R. (1977) *Virgil: Eclogues*. Cambridge.

Commager, S. (ed.) (1966) *Virgil: A Collection of Critical Essays*. Englewood Cliffs, NJ.

Conte, G.B. (1986) *The Rhetoric of Imitation: Genre and Poetic Memory in Virgil and Other Latin Poets*, tr. C. Segal. Ithaca, NY.

----------(1999) "The Virgilian paradox: an epic of drama and sentiment," *Proceedings of the Cambridge Philological Society* 45: 17-42.

----------(2007) *The Poetry of Pathos: Studies in Virgilian Epic*. Oxford.

Crook, J. (1996) "Political history: 30 B.C. to A.D. 14," in *The Augustan Empire: 43 B.C. – A.D. 69. The Cambridge Ancient History*, vol. X. Second edition, eds. A. Bowman, E. Champlin, and A. Lintott. Cambridge: 70-112.

Cumont, F. (1969) *Lux Perpetua*. Paris.

Dodds, E. R. (1951) *The Greeks and the Irrational*. Berkeley.

Edgeworth, R. J. (1986) "The ivory gate and the threshold of Apollo," *Classica et Mediaevalia* 37: 145-60.

Edmunds, L. (2001) *Intertextuality and the Reading of Roman Poetry*. Baltimore.

Farrell J. (1991) *Vergil's Georgics and the Traditions of Ancient Epic: The Art of Allusion in Literary History*. Oxford.

----------(1997) "The Virgilian intertext," in *The Cambridge Companion to Virgil*, ed. C. Martindale. Cambridge: 222-38.

----------(2005) "The Augustan Period: 40 BC-AD 14, in *A Companion to Latin Literature*, ed. S. J. Harrison. Oxford: 44-57.

Feeney, D. C. (1986) "History and revelation in Vergil's Underworld," *Proceedings of the Cambridge Philological Society* 32: 1-24.

Fitzgerald, W. (1984) "Aeneas, Daedalus and the Labyrinth," *Arethusa* 17: 51-65.

Fletcher, F. (1941) *Virgil, Aeneid VI.* Oxford.

Fowler, D. (1989) "First thoughts on closure: problems and prospects," *Materiali e discussioni per l'analisi dei testi classici* 22: 75-122.

----------(1990) "Deviant Focalization in Virgil's *Aeneid*," *Proceedings of the Cambridge Philological Society* 216: 42-63.

----------(1997) "Second Thoughts on Closure," in *Classical Closure: Reading the End in Greek and Latin Literature*, eds. D. Fowler, D.H. Roberts, and F. M. Dunn. Princeton: 3-22.

Fratantuono, L. (2007) *Madness Unchained: A Reading of Virgil's Aeneid.* Lanham, MD.

Gale, M. (2000) *Virgil on the Nature of Things: The Georgics, Lucretius and the Didactic Tradition.* Cambridge.

Galinsky, K. (1988) "The anger of Aeneas," *American Journal of Philology* 109: 321-48.

----------(1996) *Augustan Culture: An Interpretive Introduction.* Princeton.

----------(2003) "Greek and Roman drama and the *Aeneid*," in *Myth, History, and Culture in Republican Rome: Studies in Honour of T. P. Wiseman,* eds. D. Braund and C. Gill. Exeter: 275-94.

----------(ed.) (2005) *The Cambridge Companion to the Age of Augustus.* Cambridge.

--------- (2006) "Vergil and *Libertas*," *Vergilius* 52: 5-21.

Ganiban, R. (2009) *Vergil: Aeneid 1.* Newburyport, MA.

George, T. V. (1974) *Aeneid VIII and the Aitia of Callimachus. Mnemosyne* Supplement 27. Leiden.

Goold, G. P. (1992) "The voice of Virgil: the pageant of Rome in *Aeneid* 6," in *Author and Audience in Latin Literature,* eds. A. J. Woodman and J. Powell. Cambridge: 110-23; 241-5.

Gotoff, H. (1985) "The difficulty of the ascent from Avernus," *Classical Philology* 80: 35-40.

Gransden, K. W. (1984) *Virgil's Iliad. An Essay on Epic Narrative.* Cambridge.

Grebe, S. (2004) "Augustus' divine authority and Vergil's *Aeneid*," *Vergilius* 50: 35-62.

Guarducci, M. (1946-48) "Un antichissimo responso dell'oracolo di Cuma," *Bulletino della comissione archeologica communale in Roma* 72: 129-41.

Gurval, R. A. (1995) *Actium und Augustus.* Ann Arbor.

Guthrie, W. K. C. (1952) *Orpheus and Greek Religion.* Second edition. London.

Habinek, T. (1989) "Science and tradition in *Aeneid*," *Harvard Studies in Classical Philology* 92: 223-54.

Hardie, P. R. (1986) *Virgil's Aeneid: Cosmos and Imperium.* Oxford.

----------(1991) "The *Aeneid* and the *Oresteia*," *Proceedings of the Virgil Society* 20: 29-45.

----------(1993) *The Epic Successors of Virgil.* Cambridge.

----------(1997) "Closure in Latin Epic," in *Classical Closure: Reading the End in Greek and Latin Literature,* eds. Fowler, Roberts, and Dunn. Princeton: 139-62.

----------(1998) *Virgil.* New Surveys in the Classics 28. Oxford.

Harrison, S. J. (ed.) (1990) *Oxford Readings in Vergil's Aeneid*. Oxford.

----------(ed.) (2005) *A Companion to Latin Literature*. Oxford.

Heinze, R. (1915) *Virgils epische Technik*. Third edition. Leipzig.

----------(1993) *Virgil's Epic Technique*, tr. H. Harvey, D. Harvey, and F. Robertson. Berkeley.

Henry, E. (1989) *The Vigour of Prophecy: A Study of Virgil's Aeneid*. Carbondale, IL.

Heyworth, S. (2005) "Pastoral," in *A Companion to Latin Literature*, ed. S. J. Harrison. Oxford: 148-58.

Hinds. S. (1998) *Allusion and Intertext: Dynamics of Appropriation in Roman Poetry*. Cambridge.

Horsfall, N. (1995) *A Companion to the Study of the Aeneid*. Leiden.

Hunter, R. L. (2006) *The Shadow of Callimachus: Studies in the Reception of Hellenistic Poetry at Rome*. Cambridge.

Jackson Knight, W. F. (1944) *Roman Vergil*. London.

Jimenez, A. (2009) "The meaning of *bakchos* and *bakcheuein* in Orphism," in *Mystic Cults of Magna Graecia*, eds. G. Casadio and P. A. Johnston. Austin: 46-60.

Johnson, W. R. (1976) *Darkness Visible: A Study of Vergil's Aeneid*. Berkeley.

--------------(2005) "Introduction," in *Vergil: Aeneid*, trans. S. Lombardo, Indianapolis, IN: xv-lxxi.

Johnston, P. A. (1980) *Vergil's Agricultural Golden Age*. Leiden.

----------(1981) "The storm in *Aeneid* VII," *Vergilius* 27: 23-30.

----------(1987) "Dido, Berenice, and Arsinoe," *American Journal of Philology* 108: 649-54.

----------(1998) "Juno and the Sibyl of Cumae," *Vergilius* 44: 13-23.

----------(2002) "The anger of Juno in Vergil's *Aeneid*," in *Approaches to Teaching Vergil's Aeneid*, eds. W. S. Anderson and L. N. Quartarone. New York: 123-130.

----------(2004) "Piety in Vergil and Philodemus," in *Vergil, Philodemus, and the Augustans*, eds. Armstrong, Fish, Johnston and Skinner. Austin: 159-70.

----------(2006) "Horses, Turnus and *Libertas*," *Vergilius* 52: 22-32.

----------(2009) "The mystery cults and Vergil's *Georgics*," in *Mystic Cults of Magna Graecia*, eds. G. Casadio and P. A. Johnston. Austin: 251-76.

Jones, A H. M. (1970) *Augustus*. London.

Jönsson, A. and B.-A. Roos (1996) "A note on *Aeneid* 6.893-98," *Eranos* 94: 21-8.

Kennedy, D. (1992) "'Augustan' and 'Anti-Augustan': reflections on terms of reference," in *Roman Poetry and Propaganda in the Age of Augustus*, ed. A. Powell. Bristol: 26-58.

Knauer, G. N. (1964a) *Die Aeneis und Homer: Studien zur poetischen Technik Vergils mit Listen der Homerzitate in der Aeneis*. Göttingen.

----------(1964b) "Vergil's *Aeneid* and Homer," *Greek, Roman and Byzantine Studies* 5: 61-84. Reprinted in Harrison (1990): 390-412.

Kopff, E.C. and N.M. Kopff (1976) "Aeneas: false dream or messenger of the Manes?" *Philologus* 120: 246-50.

Kraggerud, E. (2002) "Vergiliana (II): What is wrong with the *somni portae*? (*Aen.* 6.893-898)" *Symbolae Osloenses* 77: 128-44.

Leach, E. W. (1988) *The Rhetoric of Space: Literary and Artistic Representations of Landscape in Republican and Augustan Rome.* Princeton.

----------(1999) "Viewing the *spectacula* of Aeneid 6," in *Reading Virgil's Aeneid*, ed. C. Perkell. Norman, OK: 111-27.

Lefevre, E. (1998) "Vergil as a Republican: *Aeneid* 6.815-35." In *Vergil's Aeneid: Augustan Epic and Political Context*, ed. H.-P. Stahl. London: 101-18.

Lewis, C. T. and Short, C. (eds.) (1962) *A Latin Dictionary.* Oxford.

Liddell, H.G. and Scott, R. (eds.) (1968) *A Greek-English Lexicon,* rev. by H. S. Jones and R. McKenzie with supplement. Oxford.

Linforth, I. M. (1941) *The Arts of Orpheus.* Berkeley.

Lyne, R. A. O. M. (1987) *Further Voices in Vergil's Aeneid.* Oxford.

MacKay, L. A. (1955) "Three levels of meaning in *Aeneid* VI," *Transactions of the American Philological Association* 86: 180-9.

MacKay, A. G. (1971) *Vergil's Italy.* Bath.

Maiuri, A. (1969) *The Phlegraean Fields.* Fourth edition. Rome.

Martindale, C. (1993) "Descent into Hell: reading ambiguity, or Virgil and the Critics," *Proceedings of the Virgil Society* 21: 111-50.

----------(ed.) (1997.) *The Cambridge Companion to Virgil.* Cambridge.

Mahoney, A. (ed.) (2001) *Allen and Greenough's New Latin Grammar.* Newburyport, MA.

Mynors, R. A. B. (ed.) (1990) *P. Vergili Maronis Opera.* Oxford.

Nappa, C. (2005) *Reading After Actium: Vergil's Georgics, Octavian, and Rome.* Ann Arbor.

Nelis, D. (2001) *Vergil's Aeneid and the Argonautica of Apollonius Rhodius.* Leeds.

Norden, E. (1957) *P. Vergilius Maro: Aeneis Buch VI.* Fourth edition. Stuttgart.

Norword, G. (1954) "The tripartite eschatology of *Aeneid* 6," *Classical Philology* 49: 15-26.

Nyenhuis, J. E. (2003) *Myth and the Creative Process: Michael Ayrton and the Myth of Daedalus, the Maze Maker.* Detroit.

Ogilvie, R. M. (1965) *A Commentary on Livy, Books 1-5.* Oxford.

O'Hara, J. J. (1990) *Death and the Optimistic Prophecy.* Princeton.

----------(1996) "An unconvincing argument about Aeneas and the Gates of Sleep," *Phoenix* 50: 331-4.

----------(2007) *Inconsistency in Roman Epic: Studies in Catullus, Lucretius, Vergil, Ovid and Lucan.* Cambridge.

Otis, B. (1964) *Virgil: A Study in Civilized Poetry.* Oxford.

Pailler, J.-M. (1995) *Bacchus: Figures et Pouvoirs.* Paris

Palmer, L. R. (1954) *The Latin Language.* London.

Panoussi, V. (2002) "Vergil's Ajax: allusion, tragedy, and heroic identity in the *Aeneid,*" *Classical Antiquity* 21: 95-134.

----------(2009) *Greek Tragedy in Vergil's* Aeneid*: Ritual, Empire, and Intertext.* Cambridge.

Parke, H. W. (1988) *Sibyls and Sibylline Prophecy in Classical Antiquity.* London.

Parker, R. (1995) "Early Orphism," in *The Greek World*, ed. A. Powell. London: 483-510.

Parvulescu, A. (2005) "The Golden Bough, Aeneas' piety, and the suppliant branch," *Latomus* 64.4: 882-909.

Pavlock, B. (1985) "Epic and tragedy in Vergil's Nisus and Euryalus episode," *Transactions of the American Philological Association* 115: 207-24.

Pelling, C. (1996) "The Triumviral period," in *The Augustan Empire: 43 B.C. – A.D. 69. The Cambridge Ancient History*, vol. X. Second edition, eds. A. Bowman, E. Champlin, and A. Lintott. Cambridge: 1-69.

Perkell, C. (1989) *The Poet's Truth: A Study of the Poet in Virgil's Georgics.* Berkeley.

----------(1994) "Ambiguity and irony: the last resort?," *Helios* 21: 63-74.

--------- (ed.) (1999) *Reading Vergil's Aeneid. An Interpretive Guide.* Norman, OK.

Petrini, M. (1997) *The Child and the Hero: Coming of Age in Catullus and Vergil.* Ann Arbor.

Pöschl, V. (1950) *Die Dichtkunst Vergils: Bild und Symbol in der Aeneis.* Innsbruck.

----------(1962) *The Art of Vergil: Image and Symbol in the Aeneid*, tr. G. Seligson. Ann Arbor.

Powell, A. (1992) *Roman Poetry and Propaganda in the Age of Augustus.* Bristol.

----------(1998) "The peopling of the Underworld: *Aeneid* 6.608-27," in *Vergil's Aeneid: Augustan Epic and Political Context*, ed. H.-P. Stahl, London: 85-100.

Preminger, A. and Brogan, T. (eds.) (1993) *The New Princeton Encyclopedia of Poetry and Poetics.* Princeton.

Putnam, M. (1965) *The Poetry of the Aeneid.* Cambridge, MA.

----------(1979) *Virgil's Poem of Earth: Studies in the Georgics.* Princeton.

_____(1993) "The languages of Horace, *Odes* 1.24," *Classical Journal* 88.2: 123-35.

----------(1995) *Virgil's Aeneid: Interpretation and Influence.* Chapel Hill.

----------(1998) *Virgil's Epic Designs: Ekphrasis in the Aeneid.* London.

Reed, J. (2001) "Anchises Reading Aeneas reading Marcellus," *Syllecta Classica* 12: 146-68.

----------(2007) *Virgil's Gaze.* Princeton.

Ross, D. O. (1987) *Virgil's Elements: Physics and Poetry in the Georgics.* Princeton.

----------(2007) *Virgil's Aeneid: A Reader's Guide.* Oxford.

Scullard, H. H. (1982) *From the Gracchi to Nero: A History of Rome from 133 B.C. to A. D. 68.* Fifth edition. London.

Segal, C. P. (1965) "*Aeternum per saecula nomen*: the golden bough and the tragedy of history. Part 1," *Arion* 4: 617-57.

----------(1966) "*Aeternum per saecula nomen*: the golden bough and the tragedy of history. Part 2," *Arion* 5: 34-72.

Shotter, D. (2005) *Augustus Caesar.* Second edition. London.

Skutsch, O. (ed.) (1985) *The Annals of Q. Ennius.* Oxford.

Smith, K. F. (1913) *The Elegies of Albius Tibullus.*

Smith, R. A. (2011) *Virgil.* West Sussex, UK.

Smyth, H.W. (1956) *Greek Grammar*, rev. by G.M. Messing. Cambridge, MA.

Solmsen, F. (1968) "Greek ideas of the hereafter in Virgil's Roman epic," *Proceedings of the American Philosophical Society* 112: 8-14.

----------(1972) "The world of the Dead in Book 6 of the *Aeneid,*" *Classical Philology* 67: 31-41. Reprinted in Harrison (1990) 208-223.

Southern, P. (1998) *Augustus.* New York.

Stahl, H.-P. (ed.) (1998) *Vergil's Aeneid: Augustan Epic and Political Context.* London.

Stansbury-O'Donnell, M.D. (1989) "Polygnotos' *Iliupersis:* a new reconstruction," *American Journal of Archaeology* 93: 203-15.

Syme, R. (1939) *The Roman Revolution.* Oxford.

Tarrant, R.J. (1982) "Aeneas and the Gates of Sleep," *Classical Philology* 77: 51-5.

Thomas, R. (1986) "Virgil's ecphrastic centerpieces," *Harvard Studies in Classical Philology* 87: 175-84.

----------(1988) *Virgil: Georgics.* Two volumes. Cambridge.

----------(1999) *Reading Virgil and His Texts: Studies in Intertextuality.* Ann Arbor.

----------(2001) *Virgil and the Augustan Reception.* Cambridge.

Thornton, A. (1976) *The Living Universe* (*Mnem.* Suppl. 46). Leiden.

Turcan, R. (1986) "Bacchoi ou Bacchants? De la dissidence des vivants à la ségregation des morts," *L'association Dionysiaque dans les sociétés anciennes. Actes de la Table ronde de l'École Française de Rome.* Rome: 227-46.

----------(1992) "L'elaboration des mystères dionysiaques à l'époque hellénistique et romaine: de l'orgiasme à l'initiation", in *L'Initiation: Les rites d'adolescence et les mystères, Actes du Colloque International de Montpellier 11-14 avril 1991,* ed. A. Moreau. Montpellier: 215-33.

Van Sickle, J. (1992) *A Reading of Virgil's Messianic Eclogue.* New York.

Vernant, J. P. and P. Vidal-Naquet. (1988) *Myth and Tragedy in Ancient Greece,* tr. J. Lloyd. New York.

Volk, K. (ed.) (2008a) *Vergil's Eclogues.* Oxford.

----------(ed.) (2008b) *Vergil's Georgics.* Oxford.

Wallace-Hadrill, A. (1993) *Augustan Rome.* London.

Warmington, E.H. (1935-40) *Remains of Old Latin.* Cambridge, MA.

Warwick, H. H. (1975) *A Vergil Concordance.* Minneapolis.

Weber, C. (1995) "The allegory of the golden bough," *Vergilius* 41: 3-34.

Wellesley, K. (1964) "*Facilis descensus Averno,*" *Classical Review* n.s. xiv: 235-38.

West, D. A. (1987) "The bough and the gate," 17th Jackson Knight Memorial Lecture, Exeter University Publications. Reprinted in Harrison (1990) 224-38.

White, P. (1993) *Promised Verse: Poets in the Society of Augustan Rome.* Cambridge, MA.

----------(2005) "Poets in the new milieu: realigning," in *The Cambridge Companion to the Age of Augustus,* ed. K. Galinsky. Cambridge: 321-39.

Wigodsky, M. (1972) *Vergil and Early Latin Poetry.* Wiesbaden.

Wilkinson, L. P. (1969) *Golden Latin Artistry.* Cambridge.

Williams, G. W. (1968) *Tradition and Originality in Roman Poetry.* Oxford.

Williams, R. D. (1964) "The sixth book of the *Aeneid.*" *Greece and Rome* 11: 48-63. Reprinted In Harrison (1990): 191-207.

--------(1972) *The Aeneid of Virgil: Books 1-6.* London.

Wlosok, A. (1976) "Vergils Didotragödie: ein Beitrag zum problem des Tragischen in der Aeneid," in *Studien zum antiken Epos*, eds. H. Görgemanns and E. A. Schmidt. Meisenheim: 228-50.

-------- (1999) "The Dido tragedy in Virgil: a contribution to the question of the Tragic in the *Aeneid*," transl. of Wlosok (1976), in *Virgil: Critical Assessments of Classical Authors*, vol. 4, ed. P. Hardie. London: 158-81.

Zanker, P. (1988) *The Power of Images in the Age of Augustus*, trans. A. Shapiro. Ann Arbor.

Zetzel, J. E. G. (1989) "*Romane, memento*: justice and judgment in *Aeneid* 6," *Transactions of the American Philological Association* 119: 263-84.

List of Abbreviations

abl.	= ablative
acc	= accusative
adj.	= adjective
adv.	= adverb
cf.	= *confer*, compare
comp.	= comparative
conj.	= conjunction
dat.	= dative
dep.	= deponent
f.	= feminine
fig.	= figurative
gen.	= genitive
i.e.	= *id est*, that is
indecl.	= indeclinable
indef.	= indefinite
interrog.	= interrogative
intr.	= intransitive
m.	= masculine
n.	= neuter
nom.	= nominative
part.	= participle
pass.	= passive
poss.	= possessive
pl.	= plural
prep.	= preposition
pron.	= pronoun
rel.	= relative
sc	= *scilicet*, supply
sing.	= singular
subst.	= substantive
superl.	= superlative
tr.	= transitive
v.	= verb
viz.	= *videlicet*, namely

Vocabulary

The words in brackets either indicate the derivation of a word or are closely akin to it.

A

ā, ab, prep. w. abl., *from, by*

abeō, -ire,-iī, -itūrus, *go away, depart*

absistō, -ere, -stitī, *withdraw from, desist, cease, stop*

abstrūdō, -ere, -ūsī, -ūsus, *push or thrust off or away ; conceal, hide*

ac (atque), conj., *and*

accendō, -ere, -cendī, -census, *light up, kindle ; enrage, excite, inspire*

accingō, -ere, -cinxī, -cinctus, *gird on, arm, equip*

accipiō, -ere, -cēpī, -ceptus, *accept, receive; listen to, hear*

accūbō, see **adcubō**

acerbus, -a, -um, adj., *harsh, bitter*

acervus, -ī, m., *a heap, pile*

Achātes, -ae, m., a comrade of Aeneas

Acheron, -ontis, m., a river of Hades

Achilles, -is and **-ī,** m., bravest of the Greeks at Troy

Achīvus, -a, -um, adj., Achaean, Greek; pl., the Greeks

aciēs, -ēī, f ., *edge, sharp sight, gaze;* pl. *eyes; line of battle*

ad, prep. with acc., *to, toward, at, near*

adamas, -antis, m., *very hard metal; adamant*

adcelerō, -āre, -āvī, -ātus, *hasten*

adcūbō, -āre, -cubuī, -cubitus, *lie down near, recline*

adcumulō, -āre, -cubuī, -cubitus, *heap up; crown*

addō, -ere, -didī, -ditus, *add, attach to;* **addere se,** *join*

adeō, -īre, -īvī or **-iī, -itus,** *go to, approach*

adeō, adv., *to this or that point or degree; so*

adferō, afferre, attulī, allātus, *bear or carry to;* with reflexive, *come, go*

adflō, -āre, -āvī, -ātus, *blow upon*

adfor, -ārī, -ātus sum, *speak to, address*

adgredior, -ī, -gressus, *go to or toward, approach; attack; attempt*

adhibeō, -ere, -uī, -itus, *bring to, lay on; summon, invite*

adhūc, adv., *to this place or time, hitherto, still*

adigō, -ere, -ēgī, -actus, *drive to, drive, hurl, force*

aditus, -ūs, m., *approach, access, entrance*

adlabor, -labī, -lapsus, *glide toward, sail to*

adloquor, -loquī, -locūtus, *speak to, address*

admiror, -ārī, -ātus sum, *wonder at, admire*

admittō, -ere, -mīsī, -missus, *admit*

admoneō. -ēre, -uī, -itus, *remind, admonish, warn*

adorior, -īrī, -ortus sum, *rise against,*
attack, attempt

Adrastus, -ī, m. king of Argos, one
of the seven heroes who fought
against Thebes

adsimilis, -e, adj., *similar, like*

adstō, -āre, -āvī, -ātus, *stand by, stay;*
hang, hover, 17

adsuescō, -ere, -suēvī, -suētus, *make*
accustomed to

adsum, adesse, adfuī, adfutūrus, *be*
present for, support, assist (+ dat.)

adulterium, -iī, n., *adultery*

adventō, -āre, -āvī, -ātus, *come to,*
approach

adventus, -us, m., *approach entrance,*
coming

advertō, -ere, -vertī, -versus, *turn*
toward

advolvō, -ere, -volvī, -volūtus, *roll*
toward, roll down

adytum, -ī, n., *the innermost shrine of*
a temple

Aeacides, -ae, m., son or descendant
of Aeacus, king of Aegina, famed
for his justice, father of Peleus,
grandfather of Achilles; = Achilles,
58, 839

Aenēas, -ae, m., the Trojan hero of the
Aeneid

Aenēas Silvius, king of Alba Longa,
6.769

Aeolides, -ae, m., patronymic, son of
Aeolus, 164, 529

aequō, -āre, -āvī, -ātus, *equalize., make*
equal

aequor, -oris, n., *a level surface; the sea*

aequus, -a, -um, adj. *level; impartial;*
favorable, favoring

āēr, āeris, acc. **āera,** m. *air, mist,* 202

āerius, -a, -um, adj. *rising into the air;*
lofty

aes, aeris, n., *copper, bronze;* also *things*
made of bronze (arms, trumpet; a
ship's prow, money), 847

aestuō, -āre, -āvī, -ātus, *boil, seethe,*
surge, swell, be excited, rage

aeternus, -a, -um, adj., *everlasting,*
eternal. **aeternum** adv.,
unceasingly, 401, 617

aether, -eris, accus. **-era,** m, *the bright*
upper air, ether; heaven

aetherius, -a, -um, adj., *etherial, of the*
upper air or ether

Agamemnonius, -a, -um, adj.,
belonging to Agamemnon, king of
Mycēnae and leader of the Greeks
at Troy, 489, 838

agger, -eris, m. *that which is heaped up,*
mound, rampart

agitō, -āre, -āvī, -ātus, *keep moving,*
move, toss about; **agitātus** 68
storm-tossed

agmen, -inis [agō], n., *that which is led;*
troop, column, band

agna, -ae, f., *lamb*

agō, -ere, -ēgī, -actus, *do, lead, drive,*
spend, make; spend time; send 873;
sese agebat 337 *was working his*
way to, approaching; imperative
age! *come now! come!*

aiō, defective verb, *say;* 3rd person sing.:
ait

āla, -ae, f. *wing*

alacer, -cris, -cre, adj. *quick, eager*

Alba, -ae, f. the mother city of Rome,
built by Ascanius son of Aeneas
in Latium, near the Alban lake,
commonly called Alba Longa, 766,
770

Albānus, -a, -um, adj. Alban,
connected with Alba, 763

Alcides, -ae, m., patronymic, *the*
descendant or grandson of

Alceus, (father of Amphitryon
and grandfather of Hercules); =
Hercules 123, 392, 801

aliquī, aliqua, aliquod, indef. adj., *any,*
some

aliquis, aliquid, indef. pron. *anyone,*
someone

aliter, adv., *otherwise*

alius, alia, aliud, adj., *other, another;*
alius ... alius, *the one ... the other*

almus, -a, -um, adj., *nurturing; kindly,*
gracious

alō, -ere, aluī, altus or **alitus,** *nourish,*
feed, sustain, support; 6.726

Alōīdae, -ārum, m., *stepsons of* Alōeus;
(they were Otus and Ephialtes,
sons of Neptune and Iphimedia,
who tried to storm heaven by
piling up mountains and were
slain by Apollo) 582

Alpīnus, -a, -um, adj., *of the Alps,*
Alpine

altē, adv., *on high, aloft; high, highly;*
deep, deeply

alter, -era, -erum, adj., pron., *the*
other, one of two ; another; **alter ...**
alter, *the one ... the other*

alternus, -a, -um, adj., *alternate, by*
turns

altus, -a, -um, adj., *high, lofty, great;*
deep, profound, (not at ground
level); noble

alumnus, -ī, m., *nursling, foster-child,*
son

alveus, -ī, m., *cavity, hollow; hull of a*
ship, boat, skiff 412

alvus, -ī, f., *belly, womb*

amans, -ntis, m. and f. , *a lover*

ambāges, -is, f., usually plural; gen.
pl. **ambāgum,** f. *a going round;*
oracular sayings; mysteries 29

ambiō, -īre, -iī or **-īvī, -itus,** *go around,*
surround, encircle

ambō, -ae, -o, num. adj., *both, two*

amīcus, -ī, m., *friend*

amnis, -is, m., *stream; river*

amoenus, -a, -um, adj., *lovely, pleasant*
to see

amor, amōris, m.; *love, passionate*
longing, yearning

āmoveō, -ēre, -mōvī, -mōtus, *move*
away, remove

Amphrȳsius, -a, -um, adj. *of the*
Amphrysus, a small river in
Thessaly along which Apollo
tended the flocks of Admetus;
applied to the Sibyl because she
was inspired by Apollo, 398

amplexus, -ūs, m., *embrace*

amplus, -a, -um, adj., *large, spacious*

an, interrogative conj., *or*

Anchīses, -ae, abl. **-ā,** m., father of
Aeneas, carried by his son from
the flames of Troy; died in Sicily,
322

Anchīsiades, -ae, m., patronymic, son
of Anchises, 126, 348

ancora, -ae, f., *anchor*

Ancus, -ī, m., Ancus Marcius, fourth
king of Rome

Androgeōs, gen. **-eō,** m. Androgeos,
son of Minos, 20

anguis, -is, m. and f., *snake, serpent*

anhēlus, -a, -um, adj. *panting*

anima, -ae, f., *breath, breath of life, life;*
spirit, shade, soul

animus, -ī, m., *mind, spirit; courage;*
inspiration, exaltation 11

annōsus, -a, -um, adj., *full of years;*
aged

ante, adv., *before, in front;* prep. w. acc.,
before, in front of, beyond

ante ... quam, adv. *before*

Antēnorides, -ae, m., patronymic, son

of Antenor, a Trojan warrior 484

antrum, -ī, n. , *cave, cavern, grotto*

Aornos, -ī, m. and f. *the birdless lake,* Avernus, 242

aperiō, -īre, aperuī, apertus, *uncover, lay bare; disclose, reveal*

apertus, -a, -um, adj., *open, exposed, clear*

apis, -is, f., *bee*

Apollo, -inis, m., Apollo, the god of divination; identified with Phoebus, the sun-god; twin brother of Diana, 9, 101, 344

aprīcus, -a, -um, adj. *exposed to the sun, sunny*

aptus, -a, -um, adj. *fit; fitted*

aqua, -ae, f., *water*

āra, -ae, f., *altar*

arbor or **arbos, -oris,** f., *tree*

arcānus, -a, -um, adj., *hidden, secret, shut up*

arceō, ēre, -uī, ---, *keep off*

accessō, -ere, -īvi, -itus, *cause to come, summon*

Arctos, -ī, f., *the Bear constellation. pl.* = the constellations of the Great and Little Bear, hence, the North, 16

ardeō, -ēre, -arsī, -arsus, *be on fire; burn*

ardēns, -entis, adj., *burning, glowing, blazing, flashing, glistening*

arduus, -a, -um, adj., *high, lofty, towering*

Argos, n. sing. only in nom. and acc., capital town of Argolis in Peloponnesus, 838

arma, -ōrum, n., *arms, weapons; defense,* 353

armipotens, -entis, adj., *powerful in arms; valiant, brave*

armō, -āre, -āvī, -ātus, *arm, equip with arms*

armus, -ī, m., *flank, side, shoulder*

ars, artis, f., *art*

artus, -ūs, m., *joint, limb*

arvum, -ī, n. *ploughed field; field*

arx, arcis, f., *place of defence, citadel, height*

aspectō, -āre, -āvī, -ātus, *look, gaze upon*

aspectus, -ūs, m., *sight, vision*

asper, -era, -erum, adj., *rough; cruel*

aspiciō, -ere, -spexī, -spectus, *look upon, view, behold*

astrum, -ī, n., *star*

at, ast, conj., *but, yet*

āter, -tra, -trum, adj., *black, murky; gloomy*

Atlas, Atlantis, m. Atlas, king of Mauretania, changed by Perseus with Medusa's head into Mt. Atlas, on which the heavens rested

atque (ac), conj., *and*

attingō, -ere, attigī, attactus, *touch; arrive at, come to*

attollō, -ere, *lift, raise up*

attonitus, -a, -um, *thunderstruck; amazed, astonished*

attulit, see **adferō**

auctor, -ōris, m., *one who causes to increase; author, founder*

audeō, -ēre, ausus sum, semi-dep., *dare, venture*

audiō, -īre, -īvī, -itus, *hear; listen to, heed, obey; hear of*

auferō, auferre, abstulī, ablātus, *carry away, take away, rob of*

Augustus, -ī, m. The name assumed in 27 BCE by C. Julius Caesar Octavianus, 792

aura, -ae, f., *air, breath, breeze; gleam of gold,* 204; pl. *sky,* 733; **popularis aura,** 811, *breath of popular favor*

aurēus, -a, -um, adj., *golden*
aurīcomus, -a, -um, adj., *golden-haired*
auris, -is, f., *ear*
Aurōra, -ae, f., *dawn;* Aurora, goddess
of dawn, and wife of Tithonus,
who precedes the chariot of the
sun-god; *morning*
aurum, -ī, n., *gold; anything made of
gold, money, gold plate*
Ausonius, -a, -um, adj., anything
connected with Ausonia
Ausonia, -ae, f., = Ausonia, the land of
the Ausones, an ancient people of
southern Italy, 346, 807
auspicium, -ī, n., *a watching of birds,
taking the auspices,* because this
was done by the general; (hence)
leadership
Auster, -trī, m., *the south wind*
aut, conj., or; **aut ... aut,** *either ... or*
autem, conj., *but, on the contrary,
however*
Autumnus, -ī, m. *the season of
increase, Autumn*
āvellō, -ere, -vellī, -vulsus, *tear off or
away; pull away; steal, carry off*
Avernus, -ī, m., Avernus, a lake near
Cumae. Birds flying over it were
said to be killed by the exhalations.
Near it was one of the fabled
entrances to the Lower World and
also the grotto of the Cumaean
Sibyl. 126, 201; as adj, 186, 564
āvertō, āvertere, āvertī, āversus, *turn
away;* **āversus,** 224, *with face
turned away*
avis, -is, f., *bird*
avus, -ī, m., *grandfather; ancestor*
axis, -is, m., *axle, axis ; the axis of
heaven, pole or zenith,* 536; *heaven*

B

bacchor, -ārī, -ātus sum, v. dep. *revel,
storm in frenzy,* 78
beātus, -a, -um, adj., *made blessed,
happy*
bellum, -ī, n. *war*
bēlua, -ae, f. *beast, monster*
Berecyntius, -a, -um, adj., *of*
Berecyntus, a mountain in Phrygia
sacred to Cybele
bibulus, -a, -um, adj., *desiring to drink*
bidens, -entis, m., *a sheep in its second
year, when two of the second set of
teeth show prominently; sheep*
biformis, -e, adj., *two-shaped*
bis, num. adv., *twice*
Bōla, -ae, f., an ancient town of the
Aequi tribe, near Rome, 775
bonus, -a, -um, adj., *good;* comp.
melior, *better;* superl. **optimus,**
best
bracchium, -iī, n., *arm*
brattea, -ae, f., *a thin piece of metal;
gold-leaf or foil,* 209
breviter, adv., *briefly, shortly*
Brȳăreus (trisyll.), Briareī, m., a
hundred-armed giant, *287*
brūmālis, -e, adj., *of winter, wintry*
Brutus, -ī, m., Lucius Junius Brutus.
He expelled the Tarquins and was
first consul, 818

C

cacūmen, -inis, n. *summit*
cadō, -ere, cecidī, cāsus, *fall; fail*
cadūcus, -a, -um [cadō], adj., *doomed
or destined to fall or die; fallen,* 481
cadus, -ī, m., *jar; urn*
caecus, -a, -um, *blind; dark, obscure;
mysterious*
caedēs, -is, f., *slaughter; bloodshed;* fig.,
blood, gore

caedō, -ere, cecidī, caesus, *cause to fall; cut; slay*

caelestis, -e, adj., *heavenly, celestial, divine;* subst. pl.: *the gods*

caelicola, -ae, m. or f., *inhabitant of heaven, deity, god*

caelifer, -era, -erum, adj., *heaven-bearing*

caelum, -ī, n., *sky, heaven; upper air*

Caeneus, -eī or **-eos,** m., *a Thessalian girl named Caenis, transformed into a boy by Neptune and later restored to her original sex,* 448

caenum, -ī, n., *dirt, mire, filth, mud*

caeruleus, -a, -um, *dark blue, azure*

Caesar, -aris, m., *a cognomen of the gens Julia; the original name of the emperor Augustus was C. Octavius until his adoption by Julius Caesar when it became Caius Julius Caesar Octanianus,* 789, 792

Caiēta, -ae, f., *a town in Latium (now Gaeta), named after the nurse of Aeneas*

calcar, -āris [calx], n., *spur*

calidus, -a, -um, adj., *warm, hot*

cālīgō, -inis, f. , *mist, fog, darkness, obscurity*

callis, -is, m., *foot-path*

Camillus, -ī, m., *M. Furius Camillus, who took Veii and freed Rome from the Gauls, 390 BCE; see* 825

camīnus, -ī, m., *forge, furnace*

campus, -ī, m., *plain, field.* Lugentes Campi, 441; Campus = Campus Martius, the Field of Mars in Rome, on the left bank of the Tiber, 873

candens, -entis, adj. *white, glistening*

candidus, -a, -um, adj., *pure white, white, beautiful, fair*

canis, -is, m. and f., *dog*

cānitiēs, -ēi, f., *greyness, grey hair;* **plurima cānitiēs,** *a mass of grey hair*

canō, -ere, cecinī, cantus, *sing, chant; narrate; foretell, reveal; declare.*

canōrus, -a, -um, adj., *tuneful, musical, harmonious*

cantus, -ūs, m., *song; music*

capiō, -ere, cēpī, captus, *take, seize, capture;* **capere timorem,** *feel fear,* 352

Capitōlium, -iī, n., *the Capitoline hill or the temple of Jupiter Optimus Maximus on the Capitoline hill at Rome,* 836; *pl. = "the summit,"* including the temple and other buildings

caput, -itis, n., *head; summit, top*

Capys, Capyos, m. 1) Companion of Aeneas and commander of one of his vessels. 2) Eighth king of Alba

carcer, -eris, m. *prison, dungeon*

cardō, -inis, m., *hinge, pivot; turning-point, crisis*

careō, -ēre, -uī, -itūrus, with abl., *be without, be free from ; be deprived of, lack*

carīna, -ae, f., *keel; boat, vessel, ship; hull*

carmen, -inis, n., *song, hymn, poem; prophecy, prediction; incantation*

carpō, -ere, -psī, -ptus, *pluck, seize ;* **viam carpere,** *hasten, pursue one's way*

cārus, -a, -um, adj., *dear, precious, beloved*

Caspius, -a, -um, adj., *Caspian, of the Caspian Sea; Asiatic*

castīgō, -āre, -āvī, -ātus, *chastise, punish*

castra, -ōrum, n., *fort, encampment*

Castrum Inuī, a town on the coast of

Latium, near Ardea, 775. Inuus is the god who gives cattle fertility

castus, -a, -um, adj., *chaste, pure, holy*

cāsus, -ūs, m., *fall; chance, misfortune, disaster*

catēna, -ae, f., *chain, fetter*

Catō, -ōnis, m., M. Porcius Cato, the Censor, noted for his stern and uncompromising morality; he died at the age of 85 in the year 147 BCE

causa, -ae, f., *cause, reason; legal case, lawsuit*

cautēs, -is, f., *sharp or pointed rock; cliff, crag*

cavus, -a, -um, adj. *hollow*

Cecropidēs, -ae, m., patronymic, son of Cecrops, the fabled founder of Athens; pl., the Athenians, 21

cēdō, -ere, cessī, cessus, *withdraw, retire, depart; yield; cease*

celer, -eris, -ere, adj., *swift, rapid, speedy*

cēlō, -āre, -āvī, -ātus, *conceal, hide*

celsus, -a, -um, adj., *high, lofty*

Centaurus, -ī, m., Centaur, a fabled monster having human head and shoulders and the legs and body of a horse

centum, indecl. adj., *hundred*

centumgeminus, -a, -um, *hundred-fold; hundred-armed;* an epithet of Briareus

Cerberus, -ī, m., the three-headed dog of Pluto which guarded the entrance to the underworld, 417

Ceres, -eris, f., goddess of agriculture; she was daughter of Saturn and Ops, sister of Jupiter, and mother of Proserpina; by metonymy *corn, grain, bread*

cernō, -ere, crēvī, crētus, *distinguish (with the eyes); discern, perceive*

certāmen. -inis, n., *strife, struggle, contest, combat, fight; rivalry*

certō, -āre, -āvī, -ātus, *strive; struggle, contend, fight; engage in*

certus, -a, -um, adj., *fixed, sure;* **certum facere,** *inform*

cerva, -ae, f, *hind, deer*

cervus, -ī, m., *stag, deer*

cessō, -āre, -āvī, -ātus, *be slow, loiter, hesitate;* **cessas in vota,** 51 *"are you slow to pray?"*

ceu, adv., *as, just as; as if*

Chalchidicus, -a, -um, adj., of Chalcis, in Euboea. Greek settlers in the area of Cumae came from Chalcis, 17

Chăōs, n., acc. **Chăōs,** abl. **Chăō,** *empty space, the abyss,* 265

Charon, -ontis, m., Charon, ferryman of the river Styx, 299, 326

Chimaera, -ae, f., a fabulous fire-breathing monster of Lycia, with the head of a lion, the body of a goat, and the tail of a dragon, 288; also one of the ships of the Trojans, 5.118

chorea -ae, f. *a dance*

chorus, -ī, m., *choral dance, band of dancers; chorus; a troop, company*

cieō, -ēre, cīvī, cītus, *set in motion, rouse*

cingō, -ere, cinxī, cinctus, *surround*

cinis, -eris, m., *ashes*

circā, adv. *around*

circum, adv. and prep. w. acc, *around*

circumdō, -dare, -dedī, -datus, *put around, surround, embrace, enclose*

circumferō, -ferre, -tulī, -lātus, *carry around, carry around lustral water, sprinkle, purify,* 229

circumfundō, -ere, -fūdī, -fūsus, *pour or scatter around* circumstō, -āre, -stetī, *stand around*

circumveniō, -īre, -vēnī, -ventus, *come around, encircle*

circumvolō, -āre, -āvī, -ātus, *fly around, hover around*

cithara, -ae, f., *lute, lyre, harp*

cīvīlis, -e, adj., *belonging to a citizen, civic*

clādēs, -is, f., *disaster, ruin*

clāmor, -ōris, m., *shout, loud cry, war-cry*

clangor, -ōris, m., *clang, noise*

clārus, -a, -um, adj., *clear, bright, famous*

classis, -is, f., *fleet*

claudō, -ere, clausī, clausus, *shut, shut in*

clīens, -entis, m., *client, one dependent on a patron*

Cocytus, -ī, m., *a river of the underworld*

coepī, -isse, coeptus, *begin*

coerceō, -ēre, -uī, -itus, *keep together, confine*

cognōmen, -inis, n., *a name added to that of the gens to mark the familia, e.g. Caesar, name*

cognōscō, -ere, -gnōvī, -gnitus, *ascertain, learn ; recognize*; perf. tense, *know*

cōgō, -ere, coēgī, coāctus, *drive together, compel*

Collātīnus, -a, -um, adj., *of Collatia, a town of the Sabines near Rome; Collatine*

collum, -ī, n., *neck*

color, -ōris, m., *color, hue*

coluber, -brī, m., *snake, serpent*

columba, -ae, f., *dove*

columna, -ae, f., *column, pillar*

coma, -ae, f., *hair, foliage, 629*

comes, -itis, m. or f., *companion, comrade*

comitor, -ārī, -ātus sum, *accompany*

commisceō, -ēre, -miscuī, -mistus or -mixtus, *mingle together*

committō, -ere, -mīsī, -missus, *bring together; allow to approach; bring on one's self, incur, 569*

cōmō, -ere, compsī, comptus, *put together, arrange; comptus, of hair, bound up, neat, trim*

compellō, -āre, -āvī, -ātus, *address*

complector, -ī, -plexus, *embrace*

compleō, -ēre, -ēvī, -ētus, *fill up*

comprendō, -ere, -ndī, -nsus, *grasp; grasp (with the mind), comprehend*

comprimō, -ere, -pressī, -pressus, *check, restrain*

concha, -ae, *shell, conch-shell*

concilium, -ī, n. *assembly, meeting, council*

conclamō, -āre, -āvī, -ātus, *cry out, shout*

concors, concordis, adj., *of one feeling, agreeing*

concrētus, -a, -um, part. of concrescō, *grow up with, ingrown*

concursus, -ūs, m., *assemblage*

concutiō, -ere, -cussī, -cussus, *shake vigorously or thoroughly*

condō, -ere, -didī, -ditus, *put together, hide; found, establish*

conferō, -ferre, contulī, collātus, *bring together; unite; conferre gradum, 488, to pace beside him*

cōnficiō, -ere, -fēcī, -fectus, *complete; finish; wear away*

cōnfundō, -ere, -fūdī, -fūsus, *pour together, confuse*

congerō, -ere, -gessī, -gestus, *heap together*

coniciō, -ere, -iēcī, -iectus, *throw together, pile up*

coniunx, -iugis, m. and f., *husband or wife*

conlābor, -ī, -lapsus, *fall together, fall in*

conor, -ārī, -ātus sum, *try, endeavor, attempt*

consanguineus, -a, -um, adj., *of the same blood*

consīdō, -ere, -sēdī, -sessus, *settle, sink down*

consistō, -ere, -stitī, -stitus, *stand still, halt, take a firm stand*

conspectus, -ūs, m., *sight, aspect*

conspiciō, -ere, -spexī, -spectus, *behold*

constituō, -ere, -uī, -ūtus, *place, set up*

consul, -ulis, m., the Consul, one of the two chief magistrates appointed each year at Rome

consultum, -ī, n., *decree; decision*

contendō, -ere, -tendī, -tentus, *stretch tight, hurl; strive, contend*

conticescō, -ere, -ticuī, *become still or silent*

contingō, -ere, -tigī, -tactum, *touch, reach; happen, turn out;* **contingat,** 109, *may it be my happy lot to*

continuō, adv., *forthwith*

contorqueō, -ēre, -torsī, -tortus, *hurl vigorously, whirl*

contrā, adv. and prep. with acc., *opposite, to face, facing; in answer to*

contus, -ī, m., *pole, pike*

convallis, -is, f., *secluded valley, glen*

convellō, -ere, -vellī, -volsus, *tear violently away*

conventus, -ūs, m., *meeting, assembly*

convexus, -a, -um, adj., *vaulted, arched;* hence n. plur. **convexa,** *the vault of heaven*

cor, cordis, n., *heart*

Cora, -ae, f., a town of the Volsci in Latium, 775

cōram, adv. and prep. with abl., *before anyone; face to face*

Corinthus, -ī, f., Corinth, an important town in Greece on the Isthmus of Corinth, 836

corneus, -a, -um, adj., *of horn*

cornipes, -edis, adj., *having a hoof of horn, horn-footed*

cornu, -ūs, n. *a horn*

corporeus, -a, -um, adj., *of the body, bodily*

corpus, -oris, n., *body; frame*

corripiō, -ere, -ripuī, *snatch eagerly, seize; speed over,* 634, **corripuit sese,** 472, *she started*

cortīna, -ae, f., *caldron, kettle; tripod of Apollo (on which the priestess sat)*

Corynaeus, -ī, m., a Trojan, 228

Cossus, -ī, m., Servius Cornelius Cossus, consul BCE 428, who won the *spolia opima* by slaying the king of Veii

crater, -eris, m., *mixing bowl*

creātrix, -icis, f., *mother, she who brings forth*

crēdō, -ere, -didī, -ditus, with dat., *trust, believe, entrust*

cremō, -āre, -āvī, -ātus, *burn*

crepitō, -āre, -āvī, -ātus, *rattle, tinkle*

crīmen, -inis, n., *accusation, charge*

crīnis, -is, m., *hair*

crista, -ae, f., *crest, plume*

crōceus, -a, -um, adj., *saffron, yellow*

crūdēlis, -e, adj., *cruel*

crūdēliter, adv., *cruelly*

crūdus, -a, -um, adj., *full of blood, fresh, vigorous*

cruentus, -a, -um, adj., *bloody*

cruor, -ōris, m., *blood from a wound; gore*

cubīle, -is, n., *couch, bed*

culter, -trī, m., *knife*

cum, prep. w. abl., *with*

cum, conj., *when, while; although, though; since*

Cūmae, -ārum, f., Cuma, on the coast of Campania, the most ancient Greek colony in Italy, 2

Cūmaeus, -a, -um, adj. *of* Cumae

cumba, -ae, f., boat

cunctor, -ārī, -ātus sum, *delay; linger,* **cunctantem,** 211, *close clinging*

cuneus, -ī, m., *wedge*

cupīdō, -inis [cupiō], f., *desire*

cupiō, -ere, -īvī or **-iī, -ītus,** *desire, yearn for*

cupressus, -ī, f., *cypress*

cūra, -ae, f., *care; anxiety, grief, sorrow*

Curēs, -ium, m. & f., Cures, town of the Sabines east of Rome

currō, -ere, cucurrī, cursus, *run*

currus, -ūs, m., *chariot*

cursus, -ūs, m., *running, course, voyage;* **transmittere cursum,** *traverse the course*

curvus, -a, -um, adj., *curved, bent*

custōdia, -ae, f., *guardianship; watch,* 574

custos, -ōdis, m., *guardian*

Cyclops, -ōpis, m. a giant race of men with one large eye living in Sicily; the workmen of Vulcan at his forge in Aetna, 630

D

Daedalus, -ī, m., Daedalus, the "cunning workman" of Greek legend; see 14-41 n., 29

damnō, -āre, -āvī, -ātus, *condemn*

Danaī, -ōrum or **-um,** m. pl., *Greeks,* so-called from Danaus, an ancient king of Argos

daps, dapis, f., (not usual in nom. sing.) *a sacrificial feast; a feast or the food served there*

Dardania, -ae, f., adj., *the land of Dardanus; a poetic name for Troy*

Dardanius, -a, -um, adj., *Dardanian, Trojan*

dē, prep. w. abl., *from, down from; concerning, about;* 69 *made of;* **dē nomine,** 70, *in the name of;* **dē more,** *duly*

dea, -ae, f., *goddess*

dēbellō, -āre, -āvī, -ātus, *subdue, vanquish, quell, crush, conquer*

dēbeō, -ēre, -uī, -itus, *owe;* pass., *be due, be destined*

dēcēdō, -ere, -cessī, -cessus, *depart*

decerpō, -ere, -psī, -ptus, *pluck off, pluck*

Decius, -iī, m., a Roman plebeian gens; especially P. Decius Mus, father and son, two consuls, who willingly died for their country

decorō, -āre, -āvī, -ātus, *adorn*

decus, -oris, n., *honor, glory, high esteem*

dēdūcō, -ere, -duxī, -ductus, *lead, carry off*

dēficiō, -ere, -fēcī, -fectus, *be wanting; fail*

dēfīgō, -ere, -fīxī, -fīxus, *fix down; fix;* **defixus lumina,** 156, *with downcast eyes*

dēfleō, -ēre, -ēvī, -ētus, *bewail*

dēfungor, -ī, -functus, v. dep. with abl. *bring something to an end; perform thoroughly; complete; finish*

dehinc, adv., *thereafter, then*

dehiscō, -ere, -hīvī, *split open; yawn; gape open*

dēiiciō or **dēiciō, -ere, -iēcī, -iectus,** *cast down*

deinde (dissyll.), *thereafter, then, next;*
766, *in days to come; afterwards*

Dēiphobē, -es or -ae, f. , the Cumaean
Sibyl, priestess of Apollo

Dēiphobus, -ī, m., a son of Priam,
married Helen after the death of
Paris

Dēlius, -a, -um, adj., *of* Delos, the
central island of the Cyclades and
legendary birthplace of Apollo

dēlūdō, -ere, -sī, -sus, *deceive, mock*

dēmens, -entis, adj., *out of one's mind,
mad, frantic*

dēmittō, -ere, -mīsī, -missus, *lower,
send down; shed tears*

dēmum, adv., *at last;* 154, *intensifying:*
sic dēmum or tum dēmum, *so and
so only*

dens, dentis, m., *tooth*

densus, -a, -um, adj., *thick*

dēpendeō, -ēre, (no perf.), *hang down*

dēscendō, -ere, -scendī, -scensus, *go
down, descend*

dēscensus, -us, m., *descent*

dēscrībō, -ere, -scrīpsī, -scrīptus,
describe; trace, 850

dēsinō, -ere, -sīvī or -siī, -situs, *cease*

dēsuescō, -ere, -suēvī, -suētus,
render unaccustomed; dēsuētus,
unaccustomed

dēsum, -esse, -fuī, *be wanting, be
lacking*

dēsuper, adv., *from above*

dētrūdō, -ere, -trūsī, -trūsus, *thrust
down* or *away*

dēturbō, -āre, -āvī, -ātus, *drive away*

deus, -ī, m., *god, deity,* gen. pl. deum or
deōrum or divum, 125; nom. pl.
dī; abl. and dat. deīs

dēveniō, -īre, -vēnī, -ventus, *come
down to*

dexter, -tra, -trum, adj., *on the right*

dextera or dextra, -ae, f. *right hand;
loyalty* 613

dīcō, -ere, dīxī, dictus, *say, speak, call,
name, tell of, utter, recite*

dictum, -ī, n. *word*

Dīdō, -ōnis, f., queen of Carthage,
committed suicide when deserted
by Aeneas, 450, 456

diēs, diēī, m.; in sing. often f. *day; time*

differō, differre, distulī, dīlātum, *put
off*

digitus, -ī, m., *finger*

dignus, -a, -um, adj., *worthy;* w. abl.,
worthy of

dīnumerō, -āre, -āvī, -ātus, *count;
number carefully*

dīrigō, -ere, -rexī, -rectum, *govern,
direct*

dīrus, -a, -um, adj., *fearful, terrible*

Dīs, Dītis, m., Dis, a name of Pluto, the
god of the underworld

discēdō, -ere, -cessī, -cessus, *depart*

discessus, -ūs, *departure*

discō, -ere, didicī, ---, *learn*

discolor, -ōris, adj., *of different color
or hue*

discordia, -ae, f., *dissension*

discrīmen, -inis, n., *distinction,
difference*

dispiciō, -ere, -spexī, -spectus, *see
through*

distringō, -ere, -strinxī, -strictus,
stretch apart

diū, adv., *for a long time*

dīva, -ae, f., *goddess*

dīverberō, -āre, -āvī, -ātus, *smite
asunder*

dīves, dīvitis, adj., *rich, wealthy*

dīvītiae, -ārum, f., *riches, wealth*

dīvum, gen. pl., see deus

dō, dare, dedī, datus, *give, grant, allot,
appoint, utter words, pay penalty;*

76 *make an end*; **collō dare bracchia circum**, *to fling his arms around his neck*, 700

doceō, -ēre, -cuī, -ctus, *teach, inform, tell*

doctus, -a, -um, adj., *wise, learned, skilled*

doleō, -ēre, -uī, -itus, *grieve, be pained, grieve for*

dolor, -ōris, m., *grief*

dolus, -ī, m., *fraud, guile*

domina, -ae, f., *mistress, queen*

dominor, -ārī, -ātus sum, *hold sway*

dominus, -ī, m., *master of slaves, etc.*

domō, -āre, -uī, -itus, *tame, subdue*

domus, -ūs and **-ī,** f ., *house, home, building*; pl. *halls*

dōnec, conj., *until*

dōnum, -ī, n., *gift*

Dōrīcus, -a, -um, adj., connected with the Dorians, an ancient Greek race; Greek

Drūsus, -ī, m., 824: M. Livius Drusus Salinator

dubītō, -āre, -āvī, -ātus, *be in doubt, hesitate*

dubius, -a, -um, adj., *wavering*

dūcō, -ere, dūxī, ductus, *lead, draw, fashion, shape; consider; spend time*

ductor, -ōris, m., *leader*

dulcis, -e, adj., *sweet, dear*

dum, conj., *while, until*

duō, -ae, -ō, num. adj., *two*

dūrus, -a, -um, adj., *hard, unpitying*; 566 **dūrissima rēgna,** *iron sway*

dux, ducis, m. and f., *leader, guide*

E

eburnus, -a, -um, adj., *of ivory*

ecce, interj., *lo ! behold!*

ēdūcō, -ere, -dūxī, -ductus, *lead out; raise; bring forth*

efferō, -ferre, extulī, ēlātus, *bring forth, raise*; 23: **ēlāta,** *rising from*

effingō, -ere, -finxī, -fictus, *shape by moulding, represent*

effor, -ārī, -ātus sum, *speak out, utter, tell*

effugiō, -ere, -fūgī, -fugitus, *flee from, escape*

effundō, -ere, -fūdī, -fūsus, *pour forth*; 339: **effūsus,** *falling overboard*

egēnus, -a, -um, adj., *needy*; 91: **rēs egēnae,** *poverty*

egestas, -ātis, f., *want, poverty*

egō, pers. pron., *I*

egomet, strengthened form of the pron. **ego,** *I myself*

ēgregius, -a, -um, adj., *out of the common herd; illustrious, precious*

ēlātus, -a, -um, see **efferō**

elephantus, -ī, m. , *elephant; ivory*

Ēlis, -idis, f., a district in the NW part of the Peloponnesus, or its chief city, Elis

ēluō, -ere, -uī, -ūtus, *wash out*

Ēlysium, -ī, n., Elysium, the home of the blessed in the underworld

ēmicō, -āre, -micuī, ---, *flash forth; spring forth*

ēmittō, -ere, -mīsī, -missus, *send forth*

ēmoveō, -ēre, -mōvī, -mōtus, *move away; banish*

en, interj., *lo! behold!*

enim, conj., *for*; **neque enim,** *for indeed ... not,* 368: adding emphasis, *in good truth,* 317

ēnō, -āre, -āvī, -ātus, *swim forth; fly aloft, soar aloft*

ēnsis, -is, m., *sword, knife*

ēnumerō, -āre, -āvī, -ātus, *fully count, count over*

eō, -īre, -īvī or **-iī, -itus,** *go, pass*

Eōus, -a, -um, adj., *of the dawn, eastern*

epulae, -ārum, f., pl. *feast*

eques, -itis, m., *horseman*

equidem, adv., *truly, indeed*

equus -ī, m., *horse, steed*

Erebus, -ī, m., *the lower world or place of darkness*, 247, 404, 671

ergō, adv., *therefore, then*; with gen. *for the sake of*

Ēridanus, -ī, m., the river Po in N. Italy

errō, -āre, -āvī, -ātus, *wander*

error, -ōris, m., *wandering; deceit, maze*

ēructō, -āre, -āvī, -ātus, *belch forth*

ēruō, -ere, -uī, -utus, *cause to fall utterly; overthrow*

Erymanthus, -ī, a mountain-range in Arcadia, 802

et, conj., *and; also; even, too;* **et ... et,** *both ... and*

etiam, conj. *also; still*

Evadnē, -es or -ae, f. wife of Capaneus, 447

euhans, -ntis, pres. part. of **euhō:** *crying "Euhan" or ho, Bacchus!; celebrating with Bacchic cries*, 517

Euboicus, -a, -um, adj., *of* Euboea, a large Aegean island stretching along the coast of Boeotia and Attica 2

Eumenides, -um, the Furies, 250, 280, 375 (*"the kindly ladies"*)

ēvādō, -ere, -vāsī, -vāsus, *go up, ascend; go out, pass beyond*

ēvehō, -ere, -vexī, -vectus, *carry out; carry aloft*

ēventus, -ūs, *issue; outcome; event*

ēvocō, -āre, -āvī, -ātus, *call out, forth*

ex, -ē, prep. w. abl., *out of, from*

exanimis, -e, *lifeless*

exaudiō, -īre, -īvī or -iī, -ītus, *hear*

excedō, -ere, -cessī, -cessus, *go out, go forth, quit*

excīdō, -ere, -cidī, -cīsum, *cut, hew out*

excipiō, -ere, -cēpī, -ceptus, *take out, take, lie in wait for, catch*

excolō, -ere, -coluī, -cultus, *make elegant, ennoble*, 663

excudō, -ere, -cūdī, -cūsus, *shape by striking; beat out, fashion, forge*

excutiō, -ere, -cussī, -cussus, *shake off*; **excussa**, 353, *bereft of*

exerceō, -ēre, -uī, -itus, *keep busy, exercise; exact punishment* 543, *ply with* 739; *harass*

exigō, -ere, -ēgī, -actus, *drive out; claim; exact; finish*

exiguus, -a, -um, adj., *small, thin; feeble, ghostly*

eximō, -ere, -ēmī, -emptus, *take away, remove*

exin, or exinde, adv. *thereafter*

exitiālis, -e, adj., *destructive, fatal, deadly*

exitus, -ūs, m., *egress, exit; end, death, result*

exoptō, -āre, -āvī, -ātus, *eagerly long for*

expediō, -īre, -īvī or -iī, -ītus, *disentangle; make ready* 219; *explain, set forth*

expendō, -ere, -pendī, -pensus, *weigh out; pay*

expleō, -ēre, -ēvī, -ētus, *fill up*

exponō, -ere, -posuī, -positus, *put forth or out; disembark*

exsanguis, -e, adj., *bloodless; pale*

exscindō. -ere, -scidī, -scissus, *cut out, extirpate; break down*, 553

exsequor, -sequī, -secūtus sum, *follow, perform*

exsomnis, -e, adj., *sleepless*

exsors, -sortis, adj. w. gen., *without a share in*

exspectō, -āre, -āvi, -ātus, *look for*

eagerly, expect, await

exstō, -stāre (no perf. act. or pass.)[ex + sto], *stand out, tower above*

exsurgō, -ere, -surrexi, -surrectus, *rise up*

exta, -ōrum, n. pl., *entrails*

extemplo, adv. *immediately*

extendō, -ere, -tendī, -tentus, *stretch out, make widely known*

externus, -a, -um, adj., *outer, foreign, alien*

exterreō, -ēre, -terrui, -territus, *alarm greatly*

extrā, prep., *outside, beyond*

extrēmus, -a, -um, superlative adj; *outmost; utmost, last;* **extrēma secūtam,** 457, "*had sought your doom.*"

exurō, -ere, -ussī, *burn out*

F

Fabius, -iī, m., *the name of a famous Roman family,* 845

Fabricius, -iī, m., *a Roman general in the war with Pyrrhus,* 844

faciēs, -ēī, i., *face*

facilis, -e, adj., *easy.*

faciō, -ere, fēcī, factus, *do, make;* Passive **fiō, fierī, factus,** *am made, becomes, happens*

factum, -ī, n., *deed*

fallax, -ācis, adj., *deceitful, treacherous*

fallō, -ere, fefellī, falsus, *deceive, cheat; violate (an oath)*

falsus, -a, -um, adj., *false, treacherous*

fama, -ae, f., *rumor, report; fame, story*

famēs, -is, f., *hunger*

fas, indecl., n., *divine law* 63; *fate* 438; **fas est,** *it is lawful, right; one may*

fascis, -is, m., *bundle;* pl., **fasces,** *the bundle of rods with axe carried by lictors* 818

fātālis, -e, adj., *fated, of destiny; fateful*

fateor, -ērī, fassus, *confess*

fatigō, -āre, -āvī, -ātus, *weary, wear out; dog* 533

fatum, -ī, n., *that which is spoken; oracle, fate;* pl. *sure decrees* 376

fātur, 3rd s. pres. ind. of defective verb **fārī;** *it is spoken*

fauces, -ium, f., *throat, narrow entrance*

favilla, -ae, f., *ashes*

fax, facis, f., *torch*

fēcundus, -a, -um, adj., *fruitful*

fēlīx, -īcis, adj., *happy, fruitful*

fēmina, -ae, f., *woman*

fera, -ae, f., *wild beast*

fērālis, -e, adj., *belonging to the dead*

fēretrum, -ī, n., *bier*

feriō, -īre, (no perf. act. or pass.) *strike*

ferō, ferre, tulī, lātus, *bear, carry; lead; endure, suffer; pay rites* 213; **ferre gressum,** *step onwards* 677; *make known, report, say, relate;* **fert** (absolutely) *tends* 675

ferreus, -a, -um, adj., *of iron*

ferrūgineus -a, -um, adj., *rust-colored*

ferrum, -ī, n., *iron; sword*

ferus, -a, -um, adj., *undomesticated; not tame; uncivilized; fierce*

fessus, -a, -um, adj., *weary*

festinō, -āre, -āvī, -ātus, *hasten, quickly perform*

festus, -a, -um, adj., *festal*

fētus, -ūs, m. *offspring; produce; growth*

fībra, -ae, f., *filament, thread; part of the entrails*

Fidēnae, -ārum, f. pl. (usually pl.), *a town of Latium on the Tiber,* 773

fidēs, -eī, f. *faith, honor, pledge*

fidēs, -is, f. (usually pl.), *string of a musical instrument*

fīdō, -ere. fisus, semi-dep., *trust,*

confide in, have confidence or faith
in; dare, venture

fīdus, -a, -um, adj., *faithful, trusty*

fīgō, -ere, fīxī, fīxus, *fix; transfix,*
pierce; fasten; plant footsteps; set up
laws 622

figūra, -ae, f., *figure, form, shape*

fīlius, ī, m. *son*

fīlum, -ī, n., *thread*

findō, -ere, fīdī, fissus, *cleave, divide*

fingō, -ere, finxī, fictum, *shape,*
mould; train 80

fīnis, -is, m., and f., *end*

fīnitimus, -a, -um, adj., *neighboring;*
subst. *neighbor*

fīō, fierī: deponent verb, = passive form
of **faciō**

firmus, -a, -um, adj., *firm, strong*

fissilis, -e, adj., *easily split*

flagellum, -ī, n., *scourge, whip*

flamma, -ae, f. , *flame; torch*

flectō, -ere, flexī, flexus, *bend, turn,*
turn aside; guide a chariot 804

fleō, -ēre, -ēvī, -ētus, *weep, weep for*

flētus, -ūs, m., *weeping*

flōs, -ōris, m., *flower, blossom*

fluctus, -ūs, m., *wave*

fluentum, ī, n., *stream, current*

flūmen, -inis, n. *river*

flūvius, -ī, m. *river*

fodiō, -ere, fōdī, fossus, *dig; dig in a*
spur, 281

folium, -iī, n., *leaf*

for, fārī, fatus sum, dep. v.: *speak, say,*
utter

foris, -is, f., *gate;* pl. *two leaves of a*
door; door

forma, -ae, f., *shape, beauty*

formīdo, -inis, f., *fear*

fornix, -icis, m., *arch, vault*

fors, f., *chance;* only used in nom. s.
and abl. s. **forte;** as adv., **fors,** 537

perhaps; adv. **forte,** *by chance*

fortis, -e, adj., *brave; strong*

fortūna, -ae, f., *fortune, luck*

fortūnātus, -a, -um, adj., *fortunate,*
blessed

forus, -ī, m. *gangway in a ship*

frāter, -tris, m., *brother*

fraus, fraudis, f., *guile, deceit*

fraxineus, -a, -um, adj., *made of ash*
wood

fremō, -ere, -uī, -itus, *roar, murmur;*
lament

frēnum, -ī, n. *bridle, reins*

frequens, -entis, adj., *crowded,*
numerous

frequentō, -āre, -āvī, -ātus, *crowd,*
haunt

frētus, -a, -um, adj. w. abl., *relying on*

frīgidus, -a, -um, adj., *cold, frigid, chill;*
frosty, wintry, chilling

frīgus, -oris, n., *cold*

frondeō, -ēre, *be in leaf;* **frondens,**
-entis, *leafy*

frondescō, -ere, *put forth leaves,*
burgeon forth

frons, frondis, f., *foliage*

frons, frontis, f., *forehead*

frustrā, adv. *in vain*

frustror, -ārī, -ātus sum, *mock, deceive*

[frux], frūgis, f., (defect. noun, mostly
in pl., **frūgēs**), *fruit of the earth;*
grain; meal, 420

fugiō, -ere, fūgī, fugitus, trans. and
intrans., *flee, flee from, escape*

fugō, -āre, -āvī, -ātus, *put to flight,*
drive

fulcrum, -ī, n., *support, prop*

fulgeō, -ēre, fulsī, and **fulgō, -ere,**
gleam, shine

fulmen, -inis, n., *thunderbolt*

fulvus, -a, -um, adj., *yellow, tawny*

fūmeus, -a, -um, adj., *smoky*

funditus, adv., *from the bottom, utterly*

fundō, -āre, -āvī, -ātus, *found, establish; moor a ship*

fundō, -ere, fūdī, fūsus, *pour, spread out;* pass. *stream;* 423 **fūsus,** *sprawling*

fundus, -ī, m., *bottom;* 581 **fundō in īmō,** *at the bottom of a pit*

fungor, fungī, functus sum, dep. v. w. abl., *perform*

fūnus, -eris, n., *funeral; dead body, corpse; death;* 510 *the dead;* 429 *the grave*

Furiae, -ārum, f. pl., *the Furies (goddesses of vengeance) Allecto, Megaera, and Tisiphone,* 605

furō, -ere, -uī, ---, *rave, rage*

furor, -ōris, m. *rage, madness*

furtum, -ī, n., *theft, fraud, deceit;* **furtō** as adv. *by stealth, secretly*

futūrus, -a, -um, fut. part. of **sum;** as adj. *future;* n., pl. **futūra,** *the future*

G

Gabiī, -ōrum, m., *an ancient town of Latium near the Alban Hills, twelve miles from Rome,* 773

Gallus, -ī, m. *a Gaul, inhabitant of Gallia (France)*

Garamantes, -um, m., *a tribe in the interior of northern Africa*

gaudeō, -ēre, gāvīsus sum, semi-dep., *rejoice, be pleased*

gaudium, -iī, n., *joy*

gelidus, -a, -um [gelu], adj., *cold*

geminus, -a, -um, adj., *twin, double, twofold, two*

gemitus, -ūs, m., *groaning, groan, wail*

gemō, -ere, -uī, -itus, *groan*

gēna, -ae, f., *cheek*

gener, -erī, m., *son-in-law*

generō, -āre, -āvī, -ātus, *beget*

genialis, -e, adj., *belonging to the genius or tutelar spirit of a man which promotes his happiness; festal*

genitor, -ōris, *father*

gens, gentis, f., *family, race, tribe*

genus, -eris, n., *race, birth, descent, offspring, son*

gerō, -ere, gessī, gestus, *bear, carry;* **bellum gerere,** *wage war*

gignō, -ere, genuī, genitus, *bring forth, give birth to;* **dīs genitī,** *sprung from the gods*

Glaucus, -ī, m, (1) *The father of Deiphobe, the Cumaean Sibyl,* 36; (2) *A Trojan hero,* 483

glaucus, -a, -um, adj., *bluish-gray, gray*

globus, -ī, m., *globe, ball*

glomerō, -āre, -āvī, -ātus, *form into a ball; gather together;* in pass. *flock together.* **gloria, -ae,** f., *glory*

Gnosius, -a, -um, adj., *belonging to Gnosus, an ancient name of Crete; Cretan*

Gorgō, -ōnis, f., *female creatures with serpent locks and the power of turning beholders into stone,* 289

Gracchus, -ī, *surname of the Sempronian gens,* 842

gradior, -ī, gressus sum, *take steps; walk*

gradus, -ūs, m., *step;* **conferre gradum,** 488, *to pace beside him*

Grāïius or **Grāius, -a, -um,** adj., *Greek;* as subst., **Graiī,** *Greeks,* 242, etc.

grāmen, -inis, n., *grass*

grāmineus, -a, -um, adj., *grassy*

grātia, -ae, f., *grace, beauty; delight,* 653

gravis, -e, adj., *heavy; pregnant,* 516; *of smell noisome;* **grave olentis,** 201, *foul smelling*

gravō, -āre, -āvī, -ātus, *make heavy,*

burden, weight down

gressus. -ūs, m., *step*

grex, gregis, m., *flock*

gubernaculum, -ī, n., *rudder*

gubernator, -ōris, m., *steersman, helmsman*

gurges, -itis, m., *whirlpool, eddy, flood*

guttur, -uris, n., *throat*

H

habēna, -ae, f., *rein*

habeō, -ēre, -uī, -itus, *have, hold*

habitō, -āre, -āvī, -ātus, *dwell*

haereō, -ēre, haesī, haesus, *cling; roost,* 284

hālitus, -ūs, m., *breath, exhalation*

harēna, -ae, f., *sand*

Harpȳiae, -ārum (trisyll. *har-pwī-ae*), f. pl., ravenous and foul birds with the face of a woman and claws of a vulture, 289

hasta, -ae, f., *spear*

haud, adv., *not at all; not*

hauriō, -īre, hausī, haustus, *drain, drink in; of sound drink in with the ears (hear),* 559

hebetō, -āre, -āvī, -ātus, *make dull*

Hecatē, -ēs, f., a name of Diana as a goddess of the underworld, 118, 247, 564

Hector, -oris, acc. **–ora,** m., son of Priam, bravest of the Trojans, slain by Achilles, 166

Hectoreus, -a, -um, adj., *belonging to* Hector

herba, -ae, f., *grass*

hērōs, -ōis, m., *hero*

Hesperius, -a, -um, adj., *western,* and so *Italian* (when contrasted with Greece or Asia), 6

heu, interj., *alas!*

hiātus, -ūs, m., *the act of yawning; a* *opening; hiatus* 237, 567

hībernus, -a, -um, adj., *wintry, stormy*

hīc, adv. *here, in this place; on this occasion*

hic, haec, hoc, dem. pron. *this*

hinc, adv. *hence, from here; after this*

hiō, -āre, -āvī, -ātus, *gape, open the mouth, yawn, gape*

homō, -inis, m., *man, human being*

honor, -ōris, m., *honor; badge of dignity,* 780

hōra, -ae, f., *hour*

horrendus, -a, -um, adj., *dreadful, awful;* **horrendum strīdens,** 288, *hissing horribly* (**horrendum** = cognate acc.)

horreō, -ēre, horruī, ---, *to be stiffly erect; bristle, shudder*

horrescō, -ere, horruī, ---, *begin to shudder; become agitated*

horridus, -a, -um, adj., *have a rough surface; rough or unkempt; harsh*

horrisonus, -a, -um, adj. *making a dreadful sound*

hortātor, -ōris, m., *instigator, one who rouses to action*

hortor, -ārī, -ātus sum, *encourage, exhort, cheer on*

hospitus, -a, -um, adj. *foreign, stranger; hospitable*

hostis, -is, m., *stranger, enemy*

hūc, adv., *to this place, hither*

humō, -āre, -āvī, -ātus, *cover with earth, bury*

humus, -ī, f., *ground,* **humi,** locative case used adverbially, *on the ground*

Hȳdra, -ae, f. (the -y- is a long vowel, = ū), *water serpent;* the Lernaean Hydra, a monster slain by Hercules, 576

hymenaeus, -ī, m, *song in honor of Hymen, the god of marriage;*

marriage-song; marriage

I

iaceō, -ēre, -uī, -itum, *lie, be prostrate*

iaciō, -ere, iēcī, iactus, *fling, cast*

iactans, -ntis, adj., *boastful*

iactō, -āre, -āvī, -ātus, *keep flinging, toss; throw at random; of words, utter boastfully;* reflexive: *boast, take pride in,* 877

iam, adv. *already, by now, now*

iampridem, adv., *now for a long time*

iānitor, -ōris, m., *doorkeeper*

iānua, -ae, f. *gate, portal*

ibi, adv., *there, then*

Īcarus, -ī, son of Daedalus, 31 n.

īcō, -ere, īcī, ictus, *strike*

Īdaeus, -ī, m., Priam's charioteer, 485

īdem, eadem, idem, dem. pron., *the same; he too,* 116

iecur, -oris, or **–inoris,** n. *liver*

ignārus, -a, -um, adj., *not knowing, ignorant*

igneus, -a, -um, adj., *fiery*

ignis, -is, m., *fire*

ilex, -icis, f., *ilex, holm oak*

Īlia, -ae, f., another name of Rhea Silvia, daughter of Numitor, mother of Romulus, 778

Īliacus, -a, -um, adj., *belonging to Ilium*

ille, illa, illud, dem. pron. or adj., *that; that famous; that man, that yonder, he, she, it*

Īlus, -ī, m. grandfather of Priam, founder of Ilium or Troy, 650

imāgō, -inis, f., *phantom, spectre, form; semblance,* 293; *vision,* 405

imitābilis, -e, adj. *that may be imitated;* **nōn imitābilis,** 590, *not to be imitated*

imitor, -ārī, -ātus sum, *imitate*

immānis, -e, adj., *huge, vast, awful*

immemor, -oris, adj., *unmindful, forgetting*

immensus, -a, -um, adj., *immeasurable, boundless*

immergō, -ere, -mersī, -mersus, *plunge, cause to sink*

immineō, -ēre, ---, + dat., *overhang, threaten*

immittō, -ere, -mīsī, -missus, *send on, send to; fling into,* 262; *let loose*

immortālis, -e, adj., *undying*

imperium, -iī, n. *military command; rule, behest; empire.* [**imperō**]

impius, -a, -um, adj., *showing no regard for the divinely imposed deities governing mortal relationships with the gods and between themselves; impious, unholy*

impōnō, -ere, -posuī, -positus, v.a. + dat., *place on, set over, impose, build up over*

impūne, adv., *without punishment, unharmed, with impunity*

īmus, -a, -um, adj., used as superl. of **inferus,** *lowest depth of*

in, prep. w. acc. *towards, into, on to, against;* **in certāmina,** 172, *to rivalry; for,* 798; w. abl. *in, on; at,* 547

inamābilis, -e, adj., *that cannot be loved; disagreeable*

inānis, -e, adj., *empty, unreal, ghostly, vain*

incānus, -a, -um, adj., *hoary, gray*

incendō, -ere, -cendī, -census, *set fire to, kindle*

incertus, -a, -um, adj., *uncertain, doubtful, not sure*

incestō, -āre, ---, *defile, pollute, make impure*

inclūdō, -ere, -clūsī, -clūsus [**in** + **claudō**], *shut up, shut in, confine*

inclutus, -a, -um, adj., *famous, renowned, celebrated*

incohō, -āre, -āvī, -ātus, *begin, lay
the foundations of; inaugurate,
consecrate,* 252

incolō, -ere, -coluī [in + colō], *inhabit,
dwell in; haunt*

incolumis, -e, adj., *unharmed, safe*

increpō, -āre, -uī, -itus, *rebuke,
upbraid, chide*

incubō, -āre, -uī, -itus, *brood over*

incultus, -a, -um, adj., *untrimmed,
unkempt*

inde, adv., *from that place or time,
thence, thereafter, then*

indēbitus, -a, -um, adj., *not owed*

indignus, -a, -um, adj., *unworthy,
undeserved*

indulgeō, -ēre, -dulsī, -dultus, + dat.
*be indulgent or lenient to; look
favorably on; accede to (a request,
etc.); take pleasure in*

Īndus, -a, -um, adj. Indian; as subst.,
an Indian, 794

inextricābilis, -e, adj., *not to be
unravelled*

infans, -antis, m. and f., *infant* [in +
fārī]

infectus, -a, -um, see **inficiō**

infēlix, -icis, adj., *unhappy, unlucky,
ill-fated*

infernus, -a, -um, adj., *having to do
with the lower world, infernal*

inferus, -a, -um, adj., comp. *inferior,*
superl. **infimus,** and **īmus,** *low;*
nōn inferiōra secūtus, 170,
following no meaner fortunes

inficiō, -ere, -fēcī, -fectus, *make or
put in;* infectum scelus, *inwrought
guilt; guilty stain,* 742

informis, -e, adj., *shapeless*

infundō, -ere, -fūdī, -fūsus, *pour in;*
infūsus 726, *permeating*

ingemō, -ere, -gemuī, -itus, *utter a cry*
of pain; groan at or over

ingens, -tis, adj., *huge, mighty*

ingrātus, -a, -um, adj., *thankless,
ungrateful*

ingredior, -ī, -gressus sum, *walk into;
begin, walk onwards*

inhonestus, -a, -um, adj., *shameful*

inhumātus, -a, -um, adj., *unburied*

inimīcus, -a, -um, adj., *unfriendly*

inīquus, -a, -um, adj., *unfair, hard*

iniciō, or iniiciō, ere, -iēcī, -iectus,
fling on

iniussus, -a, -um, adj., *unbidden*

inlustris, -e, adj., *renowned*

innectō, -ere, -nexuī, -nexus, v. a. *weave
in, entwine; devise against,* 609

innō, -āre, -āvī, -ātus, v. + dat., *swim
in; sail on*

innumerus, -a, -um, adj., *countless*

innuptus, -a, -um, adj., *unmarried*

inolescō, -ere, -olēvī, -olitus, *grow up
in; become ingrained in*

inopīnus, -a, -um, adj., *unexpected*

inops, -opis, adj., *without means, poor*

inremeābilis, -e, adj., *irretraceable;
along or across which one cannot
return,* 425

inrumpō, -ere, -rūpī, -ruptus, *burst in*

inruō, -ere, -uī, ---, *rush in or on,* 294

insānus, -a, -um, adj., *mad; inspired*

inscius, -a, -um, adj., *ignorant; in his
ignorance or wonder,* 711

insidō, -ere, -sēdī, -sessus, *sink down,
settle*

insignis, -e, adj., *distinguished, famous*

insistō, -ere -stitī, ---, *stand on, enter
on, tread on*

insomnium, -ī, n., *dream*

insons, -sontis, adj., *guiltless*

inspirō, -āre, -āvī, -ātus, *breathe into,
inspire*

instar, n. indecl., *image, model; dignity,*

865

instaurō, -āre, -āvī, -ātus, *repeat; start anew; renew*, 530

instituō, -ere, -uī, -ūtus, *set up, establish, ordain*

instruō, -ere, -struxī, -structus, *arrange, draw up, array against*

insuētus, -a, -um, adj., *unaccustomed*

insultō, -āre, -āvī, -ātus, *leap upon; taunt*

insum, -esse, *be in*

intactus, -a, -um, adj., *untouched*

intentō, -āre, -āvī, -ātus, *stretch towards* or *against*

inter, prep. w. acc, *among, between*

intereā, adv., *meanwhile*

interfundō, -ere, -fūdī, -fūsus, *pour between.*

intexō, -ere, -texuī, -textus, *interlace*

intonō, -āre, -uī, ---, *thunder*

intra, prep. w. acc., *within*

intrō, -āre, -āvī, -ātus, *enter*

intus, adv., *from within, within*

Inuī, see Castrum Inuī

Inuus, -ī, m., *the god who gave fertility to cattle*

invādō, -ere, -vāsī, -vāsus, *enter on, attack*

invalidus, -a, -um, adj., *lacking strength, weak*

invehō, -ere, -vexī, -vectus, *carry upon;* equis invectus, 587, *borne in a chariot*

inveniō, -īre, -vēnī, -ventus, *come upon, find, discover*

invergō, -ere, ---, *to incline, turn to; to pour upon*

invictus, -a, -um, adj., *unconquered, invincible*

invīsus, -a, -um, adj, *hated, hateful*

invītus, -a, -um, adj., *unwilling*

invius, -a, -um, adj. *pathless*

involvō, -ere, -volvī, -volūtus, *envelope, veil in* 100; *engulf* 336

ipse, -a, -um, pron., *self, himself, herself, itself, very*

īra, -ae, f., *anger*

is, ea, id, demonst. pron., *that, this ; he, she, it;* ea frēna, 100, *such reins*

iste, -a, -ud, demonstr. pron., *that (or this) of yours; often contemptuous,* 37

istinc, adv., *from there*

ita, adv., *so, in this way, thus*

Ītalia, -ae, f., *Italy*

Ītalus, -a, -um, adj., *Italian*, 757; subst., Ītalī, -ōrum, m., *the Italians*

iter, itineris, n., *road, journey, path*

iterum, adv., *again, a second time*

iubeō, -ēre, iussī, iussus, *bid, command*

iūcundus, -a, -um, *pleasant*

iūdex, -icis, m., *judge*

iūgerum, -ī, n., *acre*

iugum, -ī, n., *yoke, animals under the yoke;* iuga flectit, 804, *guides his car; cross bench*, 411; *ridge* [iungō]

iungō, -ere, iunxī, iunctus, v.a. *join;* iūngere dextram, 697, *grasp hand in hand*

Iūlus, -ī, m., *son of Aeneas*, 364, 789

Iūno, ōnis, f. *queen of heaven, wife of Jupiter, the bitter enemy of Troy,* 90; Iūno inferna = Hecate, 138

Iuppiter, Iovis, m. *Jupiter, the greatest of the gods;* 123 etc. *the god of the clear sky, heaven, the sky* (= Diupater, gen. = Diovis)

iūrō, -āre, -āvī, -ātus, v. a. *swear; swear by* (w. acc.) 324

iussum, -ī, n., *command*

iustitia, -ae, f., *justice*

iuvencus, -ī, m. *bullock, steer*

iuvenis, -is, m. and f. originally adj.,

young, then used as subst. *youth*

iuvō, -āre, -āvī, -ātus, *assist;* **iuvat,** impersonally, *it delights*

iuxtā, adv. and prep. w. acc. *next, close to, near at hand*

Īxīon, -onis, m., king of the Lapiths, bound to a revolving wheel for his attempted seduction of Juno, 601

L

lābes, -is, f., *spot, stain, corruption*

lābor, -ī, lapsus sum, *glide; drop down,* 202; *slip,* 602

labor (labōs), -ōris, m., *labor, toil*

Lacaena, -ae, f., Spartan woman, 511

lacer, -era, -erum, adj., *torn, mangled*

lacrima, -ae, f., *tear*

lacus, -ūs, m., *lake*

laetor, -ārī, -ātus sum, *rejoice*

laetus, -a, -um, adj., *glad, happy joyful*

laevus, -a, -um, adj., *left, on the left;* **laeva** (sc. **manus**), *left hand*

lampas, -adis, f., *torch*

laniō, -āre, -āvī, -ātus, *rend, mangle*

Lāodamia, -ae, f., wife of Prōtesilāüs, 447

Lapithae, -ārum, m. pl., The Lapiths, a people of Thessaly famous for their contest with the Centaurs at the marriage of Pirithoüs, 601

largus, -a, -um, adj., *plentiful, abundant, ample*

latē, adv., *widely, far and wide*

lateō, -ēre, -uī, ---, *lie hid*

latex, -icis, m., *water*

Latīnus, -ī, m., Latinus, the king of Latium and father of Lavinia, 891

Latīnus, -a, -um, connected with Latium, *Latin,* 875

Latium, -iī, n., a district around Rome, 67, 89

lātrātus, -ūs, m. *barking*

lātrō, -āre, -āvī, -ātus, *bark, howl*

latus, -eris, n. *side*

lātus, -a, -um, adj., *broad*

Laurens, -entis, adj., *of* Laurentum, a town on the coast of Latium, 891

laurus, -ūs, f., *laurel, bay-tree*

laus, laudis, f., *praise, fame, renown*

Lavīnia, -ae, f., daughter of Latinus, wife of Aeneas, 764

Lavīnium, -iī, n., a town that will be founded in Latium, after the events of the *Aeneid,* 84

lavō, -āre, lavāvī, lautus or **lōtus** or **lavātus,** *wash; drench,* 277

laxō, -āre, -āvī, -ātus, *loosen; clear,* 412

legō, -ere, lēgī, lectus, *pick out, choose; gather up,* 228; *survey; scan;* **lectus,** *chosen*

leniō, -īre, -īvī or **-iī, -itus,** *soften, soothe*

lēnis, -e, adj., *gentle*

lentus, -a, -um, adj., *pliant*

Lerna, -ae, f., a forest and marsh, near Argos, 287, 803

Lēthaeus, -a -um, adj., *of Lethe,* the river of oblivion, 705

lētum, -ī, n., *death*

Leucaspis, -is, m., a Trojan, companion of Aeneas, 334

levis, -e, adj., *light; lightly poised,* 17

lex, lēgis, f., *law, statute*

libāmen, -inis, n., *libation, offering;* **libāmina prīma,** 246, *first fruits*

Līber, -erī, m., the god who gives freedom from care, etc.; Bacchus

lībertas, -ātis, f., *freedom*

Libya, -ae, f., Africa, 694, 843

Libycus, -a, -um, adj., African

licet, -ēre, licuit or **licitum est,** v. impers. *it is lawful, one may;* **cui tantum dē tē licuit,** 502, *who has had his will of you so far.* With subj.

often, *although*

lilium, -ī, n., *lily*

līmen, -inis, n., *threshold;* pl. *door*

līmes, -itis, m., *boundary; path*

līmus, -ī, m., *mud*

lingua, -ae, f., *tongue*

linquō, -ere, līquī, ---, *leave*

liqueo, -ēre, liquī, ---, *be liquid, clear*

liquidus, -a, -um, adj., *liquid, fluid; yielding,* 202

lītus, -oris, n., *shore, coast*

lituus, -ī, m., *augur's staff; a straight trumpet bent at the end,* 167

līvidus, -a, -um, adj., *yellow; lead-colored*

locus, -ī, m. (pl. **locī,** m. and **loca,** n.) *place, region*

longaevus, -a, -um, adj., *of great age, aged*

longē, adv., *afar, at a distance*

longus, -a, -um, adj., *of long duration* 715; **longa diēs,** *lapse of time* 745

loquor, -ī, locūtus sum, *speak, utter*

lūceō, -ēre, luxī, ---, *shine, gleam*

luctor, -ārī, -ātus sum, *wrestle*

luctus, -ūs, m. *grief*

lūcus, -ī, m., *grove*

lūdibrium, -iī, n. *object of jest; the sport of,* 75

lūdus, -ī, m. *game*

lūgeō, -ēre, luxī, luctus, *bewail, mourn;* **Lūgentēs Campī,** *fields of mourning,* 441

lūmen, -inis, n. *light, eye, day*

lūna, -ae, f. *moon*

lustrō, -āre, -āvī, -ātus, *purify; pass round* or *over; pass in review, regard*

lux, lūcis, f., *light*

luxus, -ūs, m., *luxury*

Lycius, -a, -um, adj., *belonging to Lycia in Asia Minor*

M

mactō, -āre, -āvī, -ātus, *sacrifice*

madīdus, -a, -um, adj., *dripping*

Maeōtius, -a, -um, adj., *having to do with Lake Maotis, the Sea of Azoff,* 799

maestus, -a, -um, adj., *sad*

magis, adv., *more*

magister, -tri, m., *master, guide,* 353

magnanimus, -a, -um, adj., *great-souled*

magnus, -a, -um, adj., *great, mighty, noble; loud;* comp. **māior;** superl. **maximus**

malesuādus, -a, -um, adj., *evil-counseling*

malignus, -a, -um, adj., *grudging, niggardly*

malum, -ī, n., *evil, misfortune*

malus, -a, -um, adj., *bad, evil;* comp. **pēior;** superl. **pessimus; malī,** 542, *evil doers*

mālus, -i, m., *mast*

mandātum, -i, n., *trust, command* [= **manu datum**]

mandō, -āre, -āvī, -ātus, *commit to, entrust to*

maneō, -ēre, mansī, mansus, *remain; wait for, await*

Mānes, -ium, m. pl., *the souls* or *ghosts of the dead,* 119, 506, 743; **suōs Mānes,** 896, *his own ghost(s)*

manus, -ūs, f., *hand,; handful, band;* plur. 683, *exploits;* **manū,** 395, *with personal violence*

Marcellus, -ī, m., *(1)* M. Claudius Marcellus, famous general, 855 *(2)* M. Claudius Marcellus, nephew and adopted son of Augustus, 43-23 BCE; 883

mare, -is, n., *sea*

marmor, -oris, n., *the gleaming thing,*

marble; sea

marmorēus, -a, -um, adj., *like marble*

Marpēsius, -a, -um, adj., belonging to Marpesus, a mountain in Paros famous for its marble, 471

Mars, Martis, m., god of war

Massȳlī, -ōrum or **-um**, m. pl., a Numidian tribe

māter, -tris, f., *mother*

māternus. –a, -um, adj., *belonging to a mother, mother's*

Māvors, -ortis, m. archaic form of the name "Mars"

Māvortius, -a, -um, adj., belonging to Mars; used of Romulus, the son of Mars, 872

maximus, -a, -um, superl. of **magnus**, q.v.

Maximus, -ī, m., Quintus Fabius Maximus (Cunctator), 845

meātus, -ūs, m., *wandering, movement*

mēcum, or **cum mē**, *with me*

medicātus, -a, -um, adj., *drugged*

medius, -a, -um, adj., *middle, in the middle, in the midst of, central, intervening*; **media omnia**, 131, *all the intervening space*

Medon, -ontis, m., a Trojan hero

mel, mellis, n., *honey*

melior, comp. of *bonus, better*

melius, adv., comp. of **bene**, *well*

membrum, -ī, n., *limb*

meminī, -isse, v. def. (fut. imperative, **memento**, 851), *remember*

memor, -oris, adj., *mindful*; w. gen., *mindful of*

memorō, -āre, -āvī, -ātus, *relate, speak of, mention, say*

Menelāus, -ī, m., king of Sparta, brother of Agamemnon, husband of Helen, 525

mens, mentis, f., *mind, intelligence;*

insight, 11

mensa, -ae, f., *table*

mensis, -is, m., *month*

mentum, -ī, n., *chin*

mereō, -ērī, meritus sum, *deserve, merit*

mergō, -ere, mersī, mersum, *to cause to sink, immerse, plunge in, bury*

metallum, -ī, n., *mine, metal*

metuō, -ere, metuī, metūtus, v. *fear*

metus, -ūs, m., *fear*

meus, -a, -um, possessive adj., *my*; **meī**, 717, *my children*

mī, contr. of **mihi**, from **ego**, 123

mille, indecl. adj., *thousand*; subst., pl., **milia, milium**, n., *thousands*

minae, -ārum, f., *threats*

Minerva, -ae, f., goddess of wisdom; often represents Greek Pallas Athena, 840

minimē, adv., *least, very little, not at all*

ministerium, -ī, n., *service*

ministrō, -āre, -āvī, -ātus, v. w. dat., *attend to*

Mīnōius, -a, -um, adj., *of* Minos, the king of Crete

minor, minus, comp. of **parvus**; *smaller, less*; **minōrēs**, *younger people, posterity*, 822

Mīnos, -ōis, m., (1) a famous king of Crete who became a judge in the underworld, 432; (2) his grandson, for whom see 14 n

Mīnōtaurus, -ī, m., the Minotaur, 26

minus, comp. adv. of **parvus**, *in a less degree, less*

miror, -ārī, -ātus sum, *wonder, wonder at*

mirus, -a, -um, adj., *wonderful*

misceō, -ēre, miscuī, mistus and **mixtus**, *mingle*

Mīsēnus, -ī, m., trumpeter of Aeneas,

162; Mount Misenus, now Capo Miseno, near Naples, 234 n.

miser, -era, -erum, adj., *wretched*

misereor, -ērī, -itus sum, *pity*

miseror, -ārī, -ātus sum, *pity;* **miserandus,** *pitiable, unhappy*

mittō, -ere, mīsī, missus, *send, let go; banish from,* 85

modus, -ī, m., *measure, method, way*

moenia, -ium, n. pl., *walls, a fortress*

mōles, -is, f., *mass, bulk*

molior, -īrī, -ītus sum, *perform with toil, undertake; toil along path,* 477

molliter, adv., comp. **mollius,** *gently, smoothly*

moneō, -ēre, -uī, -itus, *warn, advise*

monimentum, -ī, n. *memorial, token*

monitus, -ūs, m. *warning*

Monoecus, -ī, m., *a name of Hercules;* **arx Monoecī,** *a promontory in Liguria sacred to him, Monaco,* 830

mons, montis, m., *mountain, rock, boulder*

monstrō, -āre, -āvī, -ātus, v., *show*

monstrum, -ī, n., *monster;* pl. *monstrous forms,* 285. [**monstrō**]

mora, -ae, f., *delay;* **haud mora,** 177, *there is no delay,* i.e., *quickly*

morbus, -ī, m., *disease*

moribundus, -a, -um, adj., *subject to death, dying* [**mors**]

moror, -ārī, -ātus sum, *delay, linger*

mors, mortis, f., *death*

mortālis, -e, adj., *mortal, human;* **mortale sonans,** 50, *making mortal/human utterance* (**mortale** = cognate accus.)

mortifer, -era, -erum, adj., *death-bearing*

mōs, mōris, m., *custom, manner, habit; civilization;* pl. *character;* **dē mōre,**

39, *duly*

moveō, -ēre, mōvī, mōtus, *move, trouble; stir up war*

mūgiō, -īre, -īvī or **-iī, -ītus,** *bellow*

multum, adv., *much*

multus, -a, -um, adj., *much, many a; deep shade;* in pl. *many*

mūnus, -eris, n., *gift, duty, task*

murmur, -uris, n., *murmur; humming of bees,* 709

mūrus, -ī, m., *wall*

Mūsaeus, -ī, m., *a legendary Greek poet*

Mycēnae, -ārum, f. pl., *the royal city of Agamemnon in Argolis,* 838

myrteus, -a, -um, adj., *of myrtle*

N

nam, namque, conj., *for*

nāris, -is, f, *nostril;* pl. *nose*

nascor, nascī, nātus sum, *be born*

nāta, -ae, f. , *daughter*

nātus, -ī, m., *son, child*

nāvis, -is, f., *ship*

nāvita, -ae, m., *sailor, boatman* [**nauta**]

-ne, interrog. enclitic particle, introducing a question

nē, adv. with imperative, *not, do not;* conj. with subj. *in order that ... not;* **neve** or **neu ... neve** or **neu,** *neither ... nor*

nec, see **neque**

necesse, neut. adj. only in the nom. and acc. sing., *needful;* **necesse est,** *it is necessary, must be*

nec nōn, [double negative = **litotes**] *nor not; = and also, moreover*

nefandus, -a, -um, adj., *unutterable; impious; monstrous*

nefas, n., indecl. n., *that which divine law forbids; guilt, crime;* **est nefas,** *it is forbidden* nemus, -oris, n., *grove, forest*

nepos, -ōtis, m., *grandson, descendant*

neque or nec, adv. and conj. *neither;*
neque ... neque, *neither ... nor;* nec
non, *moreover*

nequeō, -īre, -īvī or -iī, nequitus, *be
unable*

nēquīquam, adv., *in vain, to no purpose*

nesciō, -īre, -īvī or -iī, -ītus, *not to
know*

neu, see nē

neve, see nē

nī or nisi, conj., *unless, if not*

niger, -gra, -grum, adj., *black*

nigrō, -āre, -āvi, -ātus, v. *be black*

nihil or nīl, n., indecl., *nothing;* as adv.,
in no way [ne + hilum, *not a bit*]

Nīlus, -ī, m., the river Nile, 800

nimbus, -ī, m., *rain-cloud*

nimium, adv., *too much*

Nīsa, -ae, m., mountain in India,
birthplace of Bacchus, 805

nisi, see nī

niteō, -ēre, -uī, ---, *shine, am bright;*
nitens, *shining, glossy*

nītor, -ī, nīsus or nixus sum, with abl.
rest on; strive

niveus, -a, -um [nix], adj., *snow-white*

noceō, -ēre, -uī, -itus, with dat. *am
harmful to, hurt, injure*

nocturnus, -a, -um [nox], adj., *of the
night*

nōdus, -ī, m., *knot*

nōmen, -inis, n. *name*

Nomentum, -ī, n., a town of the
Sabines, 773

nōn, adv., *not*

nōndum, adv., *not yet*

nōrunt, or nōvērunt, see noscō

noscō, -ere, nōvī, nōtus, *learn,* in perf.,
know

noster, -tra, -trum, *our*

nōtus, -a, -um, adj., *well-known; usual*

Notus, -ī, m., *the south wind*

novem, numerical adj., *nine*

noviens, adv., *nine times*

novus, -a, -um, adj., *new, strange, fresh;*
novissima verba, 231, *the last
words*

nox, noctis, f., *night, darkness*

noxius, -a, -um, adj., *harmful,
dangerous*

nūbila, -ōrum, n. pl., *clouds*

nūllus, -a, -um, adj., *not any, no, none;*
nūlla movet, 405, *moves you not
at all*

nūmen, -inis, n., *nod, divine will,
pleasure;* 266; *divine power; deity*
[nuō, *nod*]

nūmerus, -ī, m., *number;* pl. often
musical, *measures,* 646

Nūmitor, -ōris, m., king of Alba
Longa; father of Rhea Silvia,
grandfather of Romulus and
Remus, 768

nunc, adv., *now*

nuntius, -iī, m., *messenger*

nūper, adv., *lately*

O

O, interjection, *O!*

ob, prep. w. acc., *on account of*

obeō, -īre, -īvī or -iī, -itum, *go to, enter
on; pass over; of sea, wash,* 58

obiciō, -ere, -iēcī, -iectus, *fling to*

oblivium, -iī, n., *forgetfulness*

oblōquor, -ī, -locutus sum, *utter* or
play as an accompaniment, 646

obmūtescō, -ere, -mutuī, ---, *become
speechless, silent*

oborior, -īrī, -ortus sum, *spring up*

obruō, -ere, -ruī, -rutus, *overwhelm*

obscūrus, -a, -um, adj., *dim, dark;*
neut. pl. *darkness,* 100

observō, -āre, -āvī, -ātus, *watch*

obstō -āre, -stitī, -stātus, v. with dat., *stand in the way, withstand*

obuncus, -a, -um, adj., *bent inwards; hooked beak,* 597

obvertō, -ere, -vertī, -versus, v., *turn towards*

obvius, -a, -um, adj., *in the path, opposite, to meet*

occurrō, -ere, -currī or -cucurrī, -cursus, *run up to, meet, come before*

oculus, -ī, m., *eye*

odōrātus, -a, -um, adj., *scented*

offa, -ae, f. *lump, cake*

offerō, -ferre, obtulī, oblātus, *put before, present*

oleum, -ī, n., *oil*

olīva, -ae, f., *olive tree*

olīvum, ī, *oil*

olle, archaic form of **ille**

Olympus, -ī, m., a mountain in Thessaly, the seat of the gods; *heaven,* 579 etc.

omniparens, -entis, adj., *all-producing, all-bearing*

omnipotens -entis, adj., *almighty, all-powerful*

omnis, -e, adj., *all, whole, every; wholly,* 736

opācō, -āre, -āvī, -ātus, *make shady, shade*

opācus, -a, -um, adj., *shady*

operiō, -īre, -uī, -pertus, *cover*

opīmus, -a, -um, adj., *rich;* **spolia opīma**, *rich spoils,* 855 n

optimus, -a, -um, superl. adj. of **bonus**, *best*

optō, -āre, -āvī, -ātus, *desire, choose*

opus, -eris, n., *work, labor; toil;* **opus est** + abl. *there is need of*

ora, -ae, f. *shore, coast*

orbis, -is, m., *round, circuit, cycle*

Orcus, -ī, m., *the lower world, the grave*

ordior, ordīrī, orsus sum, *begin*

ordō, -inis, m., *order, row, array*

orgia, -ōrum, n. pl., *revels; feasts in honor of Bacchus,* 517

orīgō, -inis, f., *origin, source*

ornus, -ī, f., *mountain-ash tree*

ōrō, -āre, -āvī, -ātus, *ask, pray for, pray, plead*

Orontēs, -is, a Lycian companion of Aeneas; the chief river of Syria

Orpheus (two syll.), -eos or –eī, m., an ancient bard of Thrace, 119

ortus, -ūs, m., *rising*

ōs, ōris, n., *mouth; face; lips; portals of a door,* 53

os, ossis, n., *bone*

ostendō, -ere, -endī, -entus, *to show, reveal*

ostentō, -āre, -āvī, -ātus, *show often; display*

ostium, -iī, n., *mouth, entrance*

otium, -iī, n., *rest, repose*

ovō, -āre, -āvī, -ātus, *exult, triumph*

P

pacō, -āre, -āvī, -ātus, *appease, tame*

paean, -ānis, m., *paean, song of praise in honor of Apollo the Healer,* 657

palaestra, -ae, f., *wrestling*

Palinūrus, -ī, m., helmsman of Aeneas

palla, -ae, f., *a woman's robe*

palleō -ēre, -uī, ---, *be pale;* **pallens**, *pale*

palma, -ae, f., *palm of the hand*

palus, -ūdis, f., *marsh, marshy ooze*

pampineus, -a, -um, *having tendrils or vine leaves*

pandō, -ere, pandī, pansus or passus, *open, unfold, spread wide*

par, paris, adj., *equal, matched, like*

parcō, -ere, pepercī, parcitum or

parsum, v. w. dat., *spare; cease, refrain*

parens, -entis, m. and f., *parent*

pariō, -ere, peperī, partus, *produce; procure, gain*

Paris, -idos, m., son of Priam who carried off Helen; distinguished as an archer, 57

pariter, adv., *equally, side by side*

parō, -āre, -āvī, -ātus, *prepare, make ready*

pars, partis, f., *part, portion;* often *some;* pars ... pars, *some ... others*

Parthenopaeus, -ī, m., one of the seven heroes who fought against Thebes, 480

partus, -ūs, m., *bringing forth, birth, offspring* [pariō]

parum, adv., *too little*

parumper, *for a little while*

parvus, -a, -um, adj., *small; humble;* comp. minor superl., minimus

pascō, -ere, pāvī, pastus, *feed;* in pass. and pres. part. in middle sense, *feed upon, graze upon*

Pāsiphaē, -ēs, f., wife of Minos. 25, 447

passim, adv., *everywhere*

passus, -ūs, m. *pace*

pateō, -ēre, -uī,, ---, *be open, lie open, fly open; yawn open*

pater, patris, m., *father*

patera, -ae, f., *open saucer-shaped cup, bowl*

patior, -ī, passus sum, v. dep. act. *suffer, endure, bear;* patiens, -tis, as adj. with gen., *enduring; brooking the control of,* 77

patria, -ae, f., *fatherland*

patrius, -a, -um, adj., *belonging to a father or fatherland; father's, country's*

patruus, -ī, m., *uncle*

paucus, -a, -um, adj. , *small;* in pl. *few;* paucīs, *in few words*

paulātim, adv., *little by little*

pauper, -eris, adj., *poor,* i.e., *in humble circumstances, but not destitute*

pauperiēs, -ēi, f., *poverty*

pavitō, -āre, -āvī, -tus, *be in great fear, cower with fear*

pax, pācis, f., *peace*

pecten, -inis, m., *comb; an instrument with which to strike the strings of the lyre*

pectus, -oris, n., *breast, heart*

pecus, -udis, f., *single beast;* pl., *flock, cattle*

pedes, -itis, m., *foot-soldier,* (collectively) *infantry*

pelagus, -ī, n., *sea*

Pelasgī, -ōrum, m. pl., Pelasgians, the oldest inhabitants of Greece, 503

pellō, -ere, pepulī, pulsus, *drive away*

pendeō, -ēre, pependī, ---, *hang; hang about, linger,* 151

pendō, -ere, pependī, pensus, *suspend, weigh; pay,* 20

penetrāle, -is, n. *inmost place, shrine*

penitus, adv., *from within; deep in, deeply; far distant; utterly*

penna, -ae, f. *wing*

per, prep. w. acc., *through, over along;* in appeals *by,* 364, etc.; per tālia, 537, *in such ways*

peragō, -ere, -ēgī, -actus, *go through; ponder; carry out, accomplish; proceed on,* 384

percurrō, -ere, -(cu)currī, -cursus, *go rapidly through; hastily recount,* 627

percutiō, -ere, -cussī, -cussus, *strike, smite*

peredō, -ere, -ēdī, -ēsus, *consume*

perferō, -ferre, -tulī, -lātus, *bear to the*

end, endure

perficiō, -ere, -fēcī, -fectus, *finish, complete;* **perfecta,** 895, *cunningly wrought*

Pergama, -ōrum, n. pl. *Pergamum,* the citadel of Troy, 516

Pergameus, -a, -um, adj., *Trojan,* 63

pergō, -ere, perrexī, perrectus, *proceed*

perīculum, -ī, n. *danger*

perimō, -ere, -ēmī, -ēmptus, *destroy, cut off*

perlegō, -ere, -lēgī, -lectus, *review, scan*

perōdī, -ōdisse, -ōsus sum, semi-dep. v. a., *hate thoroughly*

personō, -āre, -uī, -itus, *to make to resound* or *re-echo, resound*

pes, pedis, m. *foot*

pestis, -is, f., *plague*

petō, -ere, -īvī or **-iī, -ītum,** *seek, ask*

Phaedra, -ae, f., wife of Theseus, 445

phalanx, -angis, f. *phalanx; dense mass of troops*

Phlegethon, -ontis, m. one of the rivers of the underworld

Phlegyās, -ae, m., father of Ixion, 618

Phoebus,- ī, m., poetic name of Apollo, lit., "the radiant one"

Phoenissa, -ae, f. Phoenician; Dido, 450

Phrygius, -a, -um, adj., of Phrygia in Asia Minor, 785; **Phrygiae,** *Phrygian women,* 518

piāculum, -ī, n., *atoning sacrifice, atonement, sin offering, expiation, crime,* 569

picea, -ae, f., *pine-tree*

piētas, -ātis, f., *dutiful affection, piety*

pinguis, -e, adj., *fat, rich, resinous,* 214

piō, -āre, -āvī, -ātus, *appease*

Pīrithous, -ī, m., king of the Lapiths,

friend of Theseus, whom he aided in an attempt to carry off Proserpina, 393, 601

pius, -a, -um, adj., *showing due regard* or *reverence, pious, righteous*

plangor, -ōris, m., *beating of the breast, mourning, wailing*

plaudō, -ere, plausī, plausus, *beat, strike; clap the hands, applaud*

plēnus, -a, -um, adj., *full*

plūrimus, -a, -um, adj., superl. of **multus,** *very much; very great, vast crowd,* 667; **plūrimus amnis,** 659, *the full flood*

plūs, plūris, comp. adj. of **multus,** in plural **plūres, plūra,** *more;* in sing. mostly used as neut. subst.

poena, -ae, f., *punishment, penalty, penance, vengeance*

Poenī, -ōrum, m. pl., Carthaginians

Pollux, -ūcis, m., son of Jupiter and Leda, brother of Castor, 121

Polyboētēs, -ae, m., a Trojan priest of Ceres, 484

Pōmetiī, -ōrum, m. pl., Pometii or Suessa Pometia, (town of the Volsci), 775

pondus, -eris, n., *weight*

pōnō, -ere, posuī, positus, *place, set up; build, rear; set aside,* 611

pontus, -ī, m., *sea*

populāris, -e, adj., *of the people, popular;* **populāris aura,** 816, *breath of popular favor*

populō, -āre -āvī, -ātus or **populor, -ārī, populātus sum,** *lay waste; mutilate*

populus, -ī, m., *people, nation*

porrigō, -ere, -rexī -rectus, *stretch out*

porro, adv., *further; in the distance, yonder*

porta, -ae, f., *gate*

portitor, -ōris, m. *ferryman*

portō, -āre, -āvī, -ātus, *carry*

portus, -ūs, m., *harbor*

poscō, -ere, poposcī, ---, *demand, claim*

possum, posse, potuī, ---, *be able, have the power, can*

post, prep. w. acc., *after*; adv. *afterwards*

postquam, conj., *after*

postumus, -a, -um, superl. adj. of posterus, *latest, last, latest born*

potens, -entis, adj., *powerful*; **parvō potentem**, 843, *great with little*

potior, -īrī, -ītus sum, v. dep with abl. *gain possession of, attain*

potō, -āre, -āvī, -ātus, *drink*

praeceps, -cipitis, adj., *head-foremost; precipitous*; **in praeceps**, 578, *sheer downward*

praeceptum, -ī, n., *precept, bidding, order*

praecipiō, -ere, -cēpī, -ceptus, *grasp beforehand; teach*

praecipitō, -āre, -āvī, -ātus, *fall headlong*

praecipuē, adv., *especially*

praeda, -ae, f., *booty; a prize,* 361

praemittō, -ere, -mīsī, -missus, *send forward*

praenatō, -āre, -āvi, ---, *flow past*

praepes, -etis, adj., *swift*

praescius, -a, -um, adj. w. gen., *foreknowing*

praesideō, -ēre, -sēdī, ---, v. w. dat., *preside over*

praestans, -antis, adj., *excellent*

praestō, -āre, -stitī, -stitus, *stand in front of, excel*; **praestat**, impers., *it is better,* 39

praetendō, -ere, -tendī, -tentus, *stretch in front*

praetereā, adv., *moreover*

praeterlabor, -ī, -lapsus sum, *glide by*

praetexō, -ere -texuī, -textus, *edge, border, fringe*

prātum, -ī, n., *meadow*

preces, -um, f. pl., *prayer;* (sing. rare: dat. **precī**; acc. **precem**; abl. **prece**)

premō, -ere, pressī, pressus, *press; weigh down; control; close lips; imprison; check* footsteps; **premendō**, 80, *by strong control*

prendō, -ere, prendī, prensus, *grasp*

prensō, -āre, -āvī -ātus, *grasp strongly*

pretium, -iī, n., *price, bribe*

Prīamides, -ae, m. patronymic, son of Priam, 494, 509

prīmum, adv. *first, firstly;* **ut primum,** *as soon as*

prīmus, -a, -um, adj., superl. of **prior,** *first;* **prīmam urbem,** 810, *infant city;* **prīmō mense,** 453, *at the beginning of the month*

principium, -ī, n. *beginning;* **principiō,** used as adv. *in the first place, firstly*

prior, -us, comp. adj., *before, earlier, first*

priscus, -a, -um, adj., *ancient*

pristīnus, -a, -um, adj., *ancient, former*

prius, adv. comp. *before, first, sooner;* **prius quam,** *sooner than, before that*

prō, prep. w. abl., *for, on behalf of*

Procas, -ae, m., legendary King of Alba Longa, 767

proceres, -erum, m. pl., *chieftains, the leading men of a community*

Procris, -is (and **idis**), f., Procris, wife of Cephalus, who killed her when he was out hunting, 445

procul, adv., *at a distance, from afar, far off; vaguely, hard by,* 9

prōcumbō, -ere, -cubuī, -cubitus, *sink forwards* or *down*

prōdeō, -īre, -īvī or **-iī, -ītus,** *go forward, advance*

prōdigium, -iī, n., *portent, omen*

profānus, -a, -um, adj., *outside the shrine, unhallowed*

proferō, -ere, -tulī, -lātus, *advance, bring forward*

profundus, -a, -um, adj., *deep, abysmal*

prōgeniēs, -ēī, f., *offspring*

prohibeō, -ēre, -uī, -itus, *hinder, prevent*

proiciō, -ere, -iēcī, -iectus, *fling away*

prōlēs, -is, f., *offspring, race*

prōmittō, -ere, -mīsī, -missus, *hold out, promise*

propāgō, -inis, f., *offshoot, offspring*

properē, adv., *hurriedly, quickly*

propinquō, -āre, -āvī, -ātus, v. w. dat., *approach*

propior, -us, comp. adj., *nearer*

proprius, -a, -um, adj., *one's own,* 871

prōra, -ae, f., *prow of a ship*

prōsequor, -ī, -secūtus sum, *follow up, escort, attend,* 476

Prōserpina, -ae, f., *wife of Pluto and queen of the underworld,* 142, 251, 402

prospiciō, -ere, -spexī, -spectus, *discern, see in front*

prōtinus, adv., *forthwith; successively,* 33

proximus, -a, -um, superl. adj. of **prope,** *nearest, next*

pūbes, -is, f., *youth; body of youths*

puella, -ae, f., *girl, maiden*

puer, -erī, m., *boy, youth*

pugna, -ae, f., *fight*

pugnō, -āre, -āvī, -ātus, *fight*

pulcher, -chra, -chrum, adj., *fair, beautiful*

pulsō, -āre, -āvī, -ātus, *strike*

pulsus, -ūs, m., *trampling, beating*

purpureus, -a, -um, adj., *purple; with the sheen of purple, bright, dazzling,* 641

pūrus, -a, -um, adj. *pure, unsullied;* **pūra hasta,** 760, *headless spear*

putō, -āre, -āvī, -ātus, *think*

pyra, -ae, f., *funeral pyre*

Q

quā, adv. *by what way, where;* indef. *by any means,* 882

quadrīgae, -ārum, f. pl., *four-horse chariot*

quaerō, -ere, quaesīvī or **-iī, quaesītus,** *seek, search, enquire about*

quaesītor, -ōris, m., *examiner, inquisitor,* 432

quālis, -e, adj., *of what sort, as, what sort of*

quam, adv., *how,* conj., *than*

quamquam, conj, *although*

quandō, adv., *when,* conj., *because, since*

quantus, -a, -um, adj., *of what size;* **tantus ... quantus,** *so great ... as;* **quantum** used as adv., *as far as*

quartus, -a, -um, adj., *fourth*

quassō, -āre, -āvī, -ātus, *shake, brandish*

quatiō, -ere, ----, *shake,; keep in restless motion, hound on,* 571

quattuor, num. adj., *four*

-que, conj. enclit., *and;* **-que ... -que,** *both ... and*

queō, quīre, quīvī or **-iī, quitus,** *be able, can*

quercus, -ūs, f., *oak*

qui, quae, quod, rel. pron., *who, which;* interrog. adj., *what? which?*

quid, adv., *why?*

quiēs, -ētis, f., *rest, repose*

quiescō, -ere, -ēvī, -ētus, *rest, grow*

calm

quīn, conj., *but that; to corroborate, nay more; moreover*

quinquagīnta, num. adj., *fifty*

Quirīnus, -ī, m., name of Romulus after he was deified; **Quirīs, Quirītis**, m., Roman citizen

quis, quae, quid, interr. pron., *who? what?*; **quis, qua, quid**, as an indef. pron. (= **aliquis, aliqua, aliquid**), *anyone, anything*

quisquam, quidquam or **quicquam**, indef. pron. (after a negative expression), *anyone, anything*

quisque, quaeque, quodque or, as substantive, **quidque** or **quicque**, indef. pron., *each*

quisquis, quicquid or **quidquid**, indef. pron., *whoever, whatever*

quō, or **ut eō** (purpose), *that thereby*

quō, adv. *whither, to where*

quod, used as adv., *because, as to the fact that*, 363; **quod si**, *but if*

quondam, adv., *once, formerly; at any time, ever*, 876

quoque, adv, *also, too*

quotannīs, adv., *every year, yearly*

R

rabidus, -a, -um, adj., *raging, frenzied, foaming*

rabiēs, (no gen. or dat.), **rabiem, rabiē**, f., *rage, frenzy*

radius, -ī, m., *staff; rod for drawing diagrams*, 850; *spoke*

rāmus, -ī, m., *branch, bough*

rapidus, -a, -um, adj., *swift*

rapiō, -ere, rapuī, raptus, *seize, snatch, tear away; hurry over, scour*, 8

ratis, -is, f., *raft, ship, boat, bark*

raucus, -a, -um, adj., *hoarse*

rebellis, -e, adj., *renewing war,*

rebellious

recens, -entis, adj., *fresh*

recenseō, -ere, -uī, -us, *reckon up, review*

recipiō, -ere, -cēpī, -ceptus, *take back, recover*

recolō, -ere, -coluī, -cultus, *think over again, reflect on*; **studiō recolens**, 681, *in eager meditation*

rectus, -a, -um, adj., *right, straight*; **rectō lītore**, 900, *straight along the coast*

recubō, -āre, ---, *recline, lie*

reddō, -ere, -didī, -ditus, *give back, restore; recall*, 768; *give answer*, 672; *reply to*, 689; in middle sense **reddar**, 545, *I will get me back*

redeō, -īre, -īvī or **-iī, -ītus**, *return*

redimō, -ere, -ēmī, -emptus, *buy back, redeem*

redūcō, -ere, duxī, ductus, *lead back*; **in reductā valle**, 703, *in a remote or secluded valley*

referō, -ferre, rettulī, relātus, *bring back; duly place in*, 152; *restore*

refīgō, -ere, -fixī, -fixus, *unfasten, pull down*, 622

refringō, -ere, -frēgī, -fractus, *break, break back*, 204

refulgeō, -ēre, -fulsī, v. intr., *radiate light; shine brightly*, 204

refundō, -ere, -fūdī, -fūsus, *pour back*; in pass. *overflow*, 107

rēgificus, -a, -um, *royal*

rēgīna, -ae, f., *queen*

regiō, -ōnis, f., *district, region*

regnō, -āre, -āvī, -ātus, *hold rule*; **regnatus**, 793, *governed*

regnum, -ī, n., *kingdom, realm, sway*

regō, -ere, rexī, rectus, *rule, direct, guide*

relinquō, -ere, -līquī, -lictus, *leave*

reliquiae, -ārum, f., *remains*

rēmigium, -ī, n., *the oars of a vessel, orage*

remūgiō, -īre, īvī or **-iī, -ītus,** *bellow back* or *again; echo*

rēmus, -ī, m., *oar*

Remus, -ī, m., twin brother of Romulus, by whom he was killed

renascor, -ī, -nātus sum, *be born again*

reor, rērī, ratus, *think*

reperiō, -īre, -pperī, -pertus, *find*

repōnō, -ere, -posuī, -positus, *replace, place duly*

reposcō, -ere, ---, *demand in return, claim as due*

repostus (= repositus), -a, -um, adj., *placed far back, distant*

requiēs, -ētis or **-ēī,** f. *rest*

requīrō, -ere, -sīvī or **-siī, -situs,** *seek again, inquire*

rēs, reī, f., *thing; affair;* pl. *fortunes;* **rēs egēnae,** 91, *poverty;* **dubiīs rēbus,** 196, *this crisis of my fate;* **rem Rōmānam,** 857, *the fortune of Rome;* **rem,** 846, *our fortunes*

rescindō, -ere, -scidī , -scissus, *tear off, tear down*

reses, -īdis, adj., *inactive.* [**resideō**]

resīdō, -ere, -sēdī, ---, *settle down*

resolvō, -ere, -solvī, -solūtus, *unloose, disentangle, unravel, unstiffen*

respiciō, -ere, -spexī, -spectus, *look back, regard, look at*

respondeō, -ēre, -spondī, -sponsus, *answer, answer to; match,* 23

restituō, -ere, -uī, -ūtus, *restore*

revellō, -ere, -vellī, -vulsus, *tear off*

revertor, -vertī, -versus sum, *return*

revīsō, -ere, -vīsī, -vīsus, *revisit*

revocō, -āre, -āvī, -ātus, *recall*

revolvō, -ere, -volvī, -volūtus, *roll back, change*

rex, rēgis, m., *king*

Rhadamanthus, -ī, m., brother of Minos and a judge in the underworld, 566

Rhoetēus, -a, -um, *belonging to Rhoetēum,* a promontory in the Troad, 505

rigō, -āre, -āvī, -ātus, *moisten, bedew*

rīmor, -ārī, -ātus sum, *make clefts, explore, grope,* 599

rīmōsus, -a, -um, adj., *full of cracks or crevices, leaky*

rīpa, -ae, f., *bank*

rīte, adv., *duly*

rīvus, -ī, m., *stream, brook, rivulet*

rōbur, -oris, n., *oak-wood, oak; strength*

rogus, -ī, m., *funeral pyre*

Rōma, -ae, f., Rome, 781

Rōmānus, -a, -um, adj., *Roman; as* noun, **Rōmānī,** *Romans*

Rōmulus, -ī, m., brother of Remus and founder of Rome, 778; *as adj., of Romulus,* 876

rōs, rōris, m., *dew*

roseus, -a, -um, adj., *rosy*

rostrum, -ī, n., *beak*

rōta, -ae, f., *wheel; wheel of time,* 748

rumpō, -ere, rūpī, ruptus, *break; break the barrier of,* 882

ruō, -ere, ruī, rutus, *rush;* **nox ruit,** 539, *night hastens on, rises*

rūpēs, -is [**rumpo**], f., *a steep, rocky cliff; a crag*

rursus, adv., *again, once more; backwards*

S

sacer, sacra, sacrum, adj., *holy, sacred;* **sacra,** n. pl. *sacred rites, sacred vessels*

sacerdos, -ōtis, m. or f., *priest, priestess, seer*

sacrō, -āre, -āvī, -ātus, *make sacred, dedicate*

saeculum, -ī, n., *generation, age*

saepe, adv., *often*

saeta, -ae, f., *bristle, hair*

saeviō, -īre, -iī, -ītus [saevus], *act ferociously, rage*

saevus, -a, -um, adj., *fierce, cruel*

sāl, sālis, m., *salt; sea*

Salmōneus, (three syll.) -eos, m., a son of Aeolus, who pretended to be Jupiter and was struck by Jupiter with a real thunderbolt, 585

saltem, adv., *at least*

saltus, -ūs, m., *leap, bound*

saltus, -ūs, m., *glade, woodland*

salūs, -ūtis, f., *safety*

sanctus, -a, -um, adj., *holy, reverend*

sanguis, -inis, m., *blood; descendant, offspring; lineage*, 500

satis, indecl. adj., and adv., *enough*

Sāturnus, -ī, m., deified king of Latium, identified by the Romans with the Greek Cronos, who came to Italy where he created the agriculture-based "Golden Age"

satus, -a, -um, p.p. of serō, *sown; sprung from*

saxum, -ī, n., *rock, stone*

scelerātus, -a, -um, adj., *guilty*

scelus, -eris, n., *guilt, wickenness;* infectum scelus, 742, *the guilty stain*

scīlicet, adv., *certainly, doubtless*

scindō, -ere, scidī, scissus, *tear, cleave*

Scīpiades, -ae, m., patronymic, a son of Scipio, a member of the family of the Scipios, 843

scrūpeus, -a, -um, adj., *of sharp stone, rugged*

Scylla, -ae, f., *a sea-monster, the upper half like a maiden, the lower like a*

fish; pl. Scyllae, 286

sē or sēsē, suī, sibi, reflex. pron., *himself, herself, itself, themselves*

seclūdō, -ere, -clūsī, -clūsus, *shut off;* seclūsus, 704, *secluded*

secō, -āre, secuī, sectus, *cut, cleave; trace his way*, 899

sēcrētus, -a, -um, adj., *set apart, separated;* as subst. sēcrētum, ī, n., *secret*, 10

sēcum, or cum sē, *with himself,* etc.

secūris, -is, f., *axe*

sēcūrus, -a, -um, adj., *without care; care-banishing* [= sine cūrā]

sed, conj., *but;* sed enim, *but indeed*

sedeō, -ēre, sēdī, sessus, *sit*

sēdes, -is, f., *seat, resting place, home*

semel, adv., *once, only once*

sēmen, -inis, n., *seed, spark*

sēminō, -āre, -āvī, -ātus, *sow*

semper, *always*

senecta, -ae, f., and senectus, -ūtis, f., *old age*

senex, senis, adj., *old;* comp. *senior*

sensus, -ūs, m. *feeling, sense*

sentus, -a, -um, adj., *thorny, rough, ragged*

sepeliō, -īre, -īvī, or -iī, sepultum, *bury; bury in sleep*, 424

septem, num. adj., *seven*

septemgeminus, -a, -um, adj. *consisting of seven more or less identical elements*

septēnī, -ae, -a, distrib. adj., *seven each; repeated seven times; septuple*

sepulcrum, -ī, n., *tomb;* āra sepulchrī, 177, *the funeral altar*

sequor, -ī, secūtus sum, *follow; attend, seek*, 457

serēnus, -a, -um, adj., *clear, bright, sunny*

sermō, -ōnis, m., *conversation, words,*

speech, talk

serō, -ere, sēvī, satum, sow; remark, say, 160; **satus,** w. abl., born of, descendant of

Serrānus, -ī, m., Caius Atilius Regulus Serrānus, consul 257 BCE, 844

sērus, -a, -um, adj., late, too late

servō, -āre, -āvī, -ātus, keep; keep in view; watch, guard; keep within, 402; keep in memory, 537

sēsē, see **sē**

seu, see **sī**

sevērus, -a, -um, adj. stern, cruel

sī, conj., if; in prayers, if only, would that, 187, 882; **sīve** or **seu ... sīve** or **seu,** whether ... or

Sibylla, -ae, f., the name given to several prophetic women, the most famous of whom was the Sibyl of Cumae, 10, 44, etc

sīc, adv., in this way, so, thus

sīdō, -ere, sīdī (sēdī), ---, settle

sīdus, -eris, n., star, constellation

signō, -āre, -āvī, -ātus, mark, distinguish

signum, -ī, n., sign, standard

sileō, -ēre, -uī, ---, be (or remain) silent; **silens,** silent; **silentes,** 432, the (silent) dead

silex, -icis, m. and f,. flint, rock

silva, -ae, f., wood, forest

Silvius, -ī, m., (1) Silvius, first king of Alba Longa, 763; (2) Aeneas Silvius, a later king of Alba Longa, 769

similis, -e, adj., like

Simoīs, Simoentis, m., Simois, a tributary of the river Scamander in the Troad, 88

simplex, -plicis, adj., one-fold, simple; elemental, 747 [**semel, plico**]

simul, adv., at the same time

simulō, -āre, -āvī, -ātus, imitate, feign

sine, prep. w. abl., without

singulī, -ae, -a, distrib. adj., one to each; n. pl. **singula,** each thing separately

sinister, -tra, -trum, adj., on the left; ill-omened; **sinistra, -ae,** f., the left hand

sinō, -ere, sīvī, sītus, let be; permit, allow

sinus, -ūs, m., fold

sistō, -ere, stitī, status, place; support, establish; stay, check

situs, -ūs, m., position; neglect; decay, 462

socer, -erī, m., father-in-law

socius, -iī, m., companion, comrade

sōl, sōlis, m., the sun

sōlācium, -iī, n., solace, consolation

soleō, -ēre, solitus sum, semi-dep., be accustomed (to), make it a practice (to)

solidus, -a, -um, adj., solid, whole

solium, -iī, n., throne

sollemnis, -e, adj., religious, solemn; **sollemne,** n., as subst., sacrifice, 380

solum, -ī, n., ground

sōlus, -a, -um, adj., alone, only, solitary

solvō, -ere, solvī, solūtus, loosen or untie; loosen from a debt, pay

somnium, -ī, n., dream

somnus, -ī, m., sleep; vision of the night, 701

sonitus, -ūs, m., sound

sonō, -āre, -uī, -itus, sound, echo, rustle; **mortale sonans,** 50, making a human sound or utterance

sons, sontis, adj., guilty

sopor, -ōris, m., sleep

soporō, -āre, (no perf. act.), **-ātus,** make drowsy

sopōrus, -a, -um, adj., *sleepy, drowsy; that induces sleep*

sordidus, -a, -um, adj., *filthy, squalid*

soror, -ōris, f., *sister*

sors, sortis, f., *lot, portion; condition*

spargō, -ere, sparsī, sparsus, *scatter, sprinkle*

spatium, -ī, n., *space*

speciēs, -ēī, f., *appearance*

spectaculum, -ī, n, *spectacle, show*

spēlunca, -ae, f., *cave*

spērō, -āre, -āvī, -ātus, *hope, hope for*

spēs, -ēī, f., *hope, expectation*

spīritus, -ūs, m., *breath, spirit*

spīrō, -āre, -āvī, -ātus, *breathe*

spoliō, -āre, -āvī, -ātus, *strip, spoil, rob of*

spolium, -ī, n., *spoil;* **spolia opīma,** 855, *rich spoils*

sponte, subst. f. only in abl. sing. (from obsolete noun, **spons**); **sponte suā,** *of one's own accord, voluntarily*

spūmō, -āre, -āvī, -ātus, *foam*

spūmōsus, -a, -um, adj., *foaming*

squalor, -ōris, m., *filth, dirt*

stabulō, -āre, -āvī, -ātus, *house;* intr.: *have a stall*

stabulum, -ī, n., *stall, stable, lair; a building for housing domestic (stable) or wild (lair) animals,* 179

stagnum, -ī, n., *pool, marsh*

statuō, -ere, statuī, -ūtus, *set up*

stella, -ae, f., *star*

sterilis, -e, adj , *barren*

sternō, -ere, strāvī, strātus, *stretch out, lay low*

stimulus, -ī, m., *goad, spur*

stirps, stirpis, f ., *stock, stem*

stō, -āre, stetī, status, *stand, stand firm*

strages, -is, f., *overthrow, destruction, carnage*

strepitus, -ūs, m., *noise, din*

strepō, -ere, -uī, -itus, *make a noise, sound*

strīdeō, -ēre, strīdī, ---, *make a harsh, grating sound; hiss,* 288

strīdor, -ōris, m., *grating*

stringō, -ere, strinxī, strictus, (of a sword) *unsheath, draw*

struō, -ere, struxī, structus, *build*

studium, -iī, n., *zeal, eagerness*

Stygius, -a, -um, adj., *Stygian, of the Styx*

Styx, Stygis, f., *the river in the underworld that surrounds the final abode of the dead*

sub, prep. w. acc., *beneath, towards;* w. abl. *under, deep in, beneath*

subdūcō, -ere, -duxī, -ductus, *draw from under, withdraw*

subeō, -īre, -iī, -ītus, *go under; follow; come up to, approach, enter;* **subiēre ferētrō,** 222, *shoulder the bier*

subigō, -ere, -ēgī, -actus, *drive up, compel; push from below, push along,* 302

subitō, adv., *suddenly*

subitus, -a, -um, adj., *sudden*

subiciō, -ere, -iēcī, -iectus, *place beneath, subdue*

subiectus, -a, -um, adj., *subject*

sublīmis, -e, adj., *lofty, aloft*

submoveō, -ēre, -mōvī, -mōtūs, *move away*

subtrahō, -ere, -traxī, -tractus, *withdraw*

subvectō, -āre, -āvī, -ātus, *carry upstream*

succingō, -ere, -cinxī, -cinctus, *gird up;* **succinctus,** *with girded loins,* 555

sulcus, -ī, m., *furrow*

sum, esse, fuī, futūrus, *to be;* impersonal **est** w. infin., *it is possible to;* fut. part. **futūrus,**

-a, -um, as adj., *future;* neut. pl. **futura,** *the future,* 12

summus, -a, -um, adj., superl. of **superus;** *highest, very high, topmost, top of, crest of.* See **superus**

sumō, -ere, sumpsī, sumptus, *take*

super, adv., *above;* prep. w. acc., *on to, above; beyond;* w. abl., *on, above*

superbus, -a, -um, adj., *haughty, proud*

superēmineō, -ēre, ---, *rise above, tower over*

superne, adv., *from above*

superō, -āre, -āvī, -ātus, *traverse, pass over*

supplex, -icis, adj., *bending the knee, suppliant*

supplicium, -iī, n., *punishment, vengeance*

suppōnō, -ere, -posuī, -positus, *place beneath*

suprēmus, -a, -um, adj., *highest.* See **superus**

surgō, -ere, surrexī, surrectus, *rise*

suscipiō, -ere, -cēpī, -ceptus, *undertake,; take up conversation, catch from below,* 249

suspectus, -ūs, m., *view upwards*

suspendō, -ere, -dī, -pensus, *hang, suspend; hang up*

suspensus, -a, -um, adj., *uncertain, in suspense*

suspiciō, -ere, -spexī, -spectus, *look up at*

sūtilis, -e, adj., *stitched*

suus, -a, -um, possess. reflex. pron., *his own, her own, its own, their own; own special,* 142; **sua arbor,** 206, *parent tree;* **suī,** 611, *their kinsfolk*

Sychaeus, -ī, m., the husband of Dido

Syrtis, -is, f. , name of two quicksands in North Africa, 60

T

tābēs, -is, f. *decay, wasting*

taceō, -ēre, -uī, -itus, *be silent, be silent about*

tacitus, -a, -um, adj., *silent; not spoken of*

taeda, -ae, f., *pine-torch*

tālis, -e, adj., *of such kind, such*

tam, adv., *so*

tamen, adv., *notwithstanding, nevertheless*

tandem, adv., *at length, at last*

tantum, adv., *thus much, so much, as far; only*

tantus, -a, -um, adj., *so great, so much;* **in tantum,** 876, *so high;* **tanto magis,** 79, *so much the more*

tardō, -āre, -āvī, -ātus, *cause to slow down, delay; restrain*

tardus, -a, -um, adj., *slow, dull*

Tarquinius, -ī, m., Tarquinius Priscus, the fifth, or Tarquinius Superbus, the seventh king of Rome, both of whom were overthrown, 817

Tartareus, -a, -um, adj., *connected with* Tartarus, 295, etc.

Tartarus, -ī, m., and **Tartara, -ōrum,** n. pl., the infernal regions; the deepest part of the underworld, 135, etc.

taurus, -ī, m., *bull*

tectum, -ī, n., *roof, building, palace; lair, den of wild animals,* 8

tēcum, for **cum tē,** *with you*

tegō, -ere, texī, tectus, *cover, hide*

tellūs, -ūris, f., *the earth, land*

telum, -ī, n., *weapon, dart*

temerō, -āre, -āvī, -ātus, *violate*

temnō, -ere, tempsī, ---, *despise*

templum, -ī, n., *temple*

tempus, -oris, n . 1) *time, season;* 2) (usually pl.) *the sides or temples of* *the forehead*

tenax, -ācis, adj., *clinging, biting,* 3

tendō, -ere, tetendī, tentus or **tensus,**
stretch; direct one's course

tenēbrae, -ārum, f., *darkness, gloom*

tenēbrōsus, -a, -um, adj., *gloomy*

teneō, -ēre, -uī, tentus, *hold, possess;
clasp, grasp, keep, reach;* **vulgō
tenēre,** *throng,* 284

tenuis, -e, adj., *thin*

tenus, post-positive prep. w. abl., *as far
as;* **hāc tenus,** *thus far,* 62

tepidus, -a, -um, adj., *warm*

ter, num. adv., *three times, thrice*

teres, -etis, adj., *smooth, shapely,
rounded*

tergum, -ī, n., *back*

terra, -ae, f., *earth, dry land, land*

terreō, -ēre, -uī, -itus, *terrify, scare*

terribilis, -e, adj., *dreadful*

tertius, -a, -um, num. adj., *third*

testor, -ārī, -ātus sum, *call to witness,
testify*

Teucer, -crī, m., the ancestor of the
Trojan kings, father-in-law of
Dardanus, 500, 648

Teucrī, -ōrum, m. pl., *Trojans,
descendants of* Teucer

thalamus, -ī, m., *marriage chamber;
marriage,* 94; *chamber,* 280

Thersilochus, -ī, m., a Trojan hero, 483

Thēseus, -eī, or **-eos,** m., king of
Athens, 122, 393, 618

Thrēicius, -a, -um, adj., *Thracian,* 120,
645

Thybris, -idis, acc. **Thybrim,** m., the
river Tiber

Tiberīnus, ī, m., the god of the river
Tiber

tīgris, -is, or **-idis,** m. and f. *tiger,
tigress*

timeō, -ēre, -uī, ---, *fear*

timidus, -a, -um, adj., *fearful*

timor, -ōris, m. *fear*

Tīsiphone, -ēs, f., one of the Furies and
the avenger of murder, 555, 571

Titanius, -a, -um, adj., *Titanic:* (1)
*having to do with the Titans, a
giant race who endeavoured to
storm heaven,* 580; (2) *having to do
with* Titan, *the Sun-god,* 725

Tityos, -ī, m., acc. **Tityon,** a giant slain
by Apollo for offering violence to
Latona, 595

tollō, -ere, sustulī, sublātus, *pick up;
raise, take;* **sē tollunt,** 203, *of birds,
they tower*

tondeō, -ēre, totondī, tonsus, *cut or
clip the hair or beard; shear (sheep),
graze, feed on,* 598

Torquātus, -ī, m., Titus Manlius
Torquatus, who wore the necklace
(*torques*) of a Gaul whom he had
slain in single combat

torqueō, -ēre, torsī, tortus, *twist; turn;
roll along*

torreō, -ēre, -uī, tostus, *scorch, bake;*
torrens, *boiling, surging*

torus, -ī, m., *couch,* **rīpārum torōs,**
674, *the soft, cushioned riverbanks*

torvus, -a, -um, adj., *fierce; stern-looking*

tot, num. adj., *so many*

totidem, num. adj., *just as many*

totiens, adv., *so many times*

tōtus, -a, -um, adj., *whole*

trabs, trabis, f., *beam*

trahō, -ere; traxī, tractus, *drag, trail,
draw out, protract; spend (time)*

trāiciō, -ere, -iēcī, -iectus, *throw
across; pass,* 536

trāmes, -itis, m , *cross-path*

tranō, -āre, -āvī, -ātus, *swim across*

trans, prep. w. acc., *across*

transmittō, -ere, -mīsī, -missus, *send*

across

tremefaciō, -ere, -fēcī, -factus, *make to tremble*

tremō, -ere, -uī, ---, *tremble*

tremor, -ōris, m., *a trembling*

trepidō, -āre, -āvī, -ātus, *tremble much*

tres, tria, num. adj., *three*

tricorpor, -oris, adj., *with three bodies*

trifaux, -faucis, adj., *with three throats*

triplex, -icis, adj., *threefold, triple*

tristis, -e, adj., *sad; stern, gloomy*

Triton, -ōnis, m., *the sea-god with whom Misenus dared to compete in playing on a sea-shell,* 173

triumphō, -āre, -āvī, -ātus, *triumph;* **triumphatus,** *triumphed over,* 836

triumphus, -ī, m., *triumph*

Trivia, -ae, f., *epithet of Diana and Hecate, who were worshipped where three roads meet,* 13, 35, 69

Trōia, -ae, f., *Troy, the city of the Trojans until it was destroyed by the siege of the Greeks, the subject of the* Iliad, *56, etc.*

Trōiānus, -a, -um, adj., *Trojan*

Trōius, -a, -um, adj., *Trojan*

Trōs, Trōis, adj., *Trojan*

truncus, -ī, m., *the body of a man, the torso; trunk of a tree*

truncus, -a, -um, adj., *mutilated, mangled* [**truncō**]

tū, tuī, tibi, tē, tē, 2nd pers. sing. pron., *you*

tuba, -ae, f., *trumpet*

tueor, -ērī, tuitus sum, *scan, view; catch sight of, look at*

Tullus, -ī, m., *Tullius Hostilius, third king of Rome,* 814

tum, adv., *at that time, then, next, then too*

tumeō, -ēre, -uī, ---, *swell*

tumidus, -a, -um, *swollen, distended*

tumultus, -ūs, m., *uprising, tumult,*

upheaving

tumulus, -ī, m., *mound, tomb*

tunc, adv., *then*

turba, -ae, f., *crowd, throng*

turbidus, -a, -um, adj., *violently agitated (sea, storms); wild, stormy (weather); wild, dishevelled (hair); in a state of turmoil; confused, muddy, thick;* **loca turbida,** 534, *the dwelling of disorder*

turbō, -āre, -āvī, -atus, *throw into confusion, shake;* rarely, intrans., *be in confusion,* 800

turbō, -inis, m., *whirlwind, whirl*

tūreus, -a, -um, adj., *of frankincense*

turpis, -e, adj., *foul, disfiguring, sordid,* 276

turris, -is, f. , *tower*

turritus, -a, -um, adj., *crowned with towers*

tūtus, -a, -um, adj., *safe;* neut. pl. **tūta,** 358, *safety*

tuus, -a, -um, 2nd sing. poss. adj., *your* (s.); subst. **tuī,** *your* (s.) *descendants,* 868

Tydeus, -eī, or **-eos,** m., *king of Calydon, father of Diomedes, one of the seven heroes who fought against Thebes,* 479

Tyrrhēnus, -a, -um, adj., Tyrrhenian/ Etruscan, 698

U

ūber, -eris, n., *mother's breast; udder*

ubi, adv., *where, when*

ulciscor, -ī, ultus sum, *avenge*

ūllus, -a, -um, adj., *any*

ulmus, -ī, f., *elm tree, elm*

ulterior, -ius, comp. adj., *further;* superl., **ultimus, -a, -um,** *farthest*

ultor, -ōris, m., *avenger*

ultrā, adv. or prep. w. acc., *beyond*

ultrix, -icis, adj., *avenging*

ultrō, adv., *beyond what is needed* or *asked; voluntarily; unprovoked*, 387, 499

ululō, -āre, -āvī, -ātus, *howl*

ulva, -ae, f., *sedge, grass-like plants found in swamps*

umbra, -ae, f., *shade; spirit, ghost*

umbrifer, -era, -erum, adj., *shade-bearing, shady*

umbrō, -āre, -āvī, -ātus, *overshadow*

umerus, -ī, m., *shoulder*

umquam, adv., *at any time, ever*

ūnā, adv., *together, at one (or the same) time with, together; along with them*, 528

uncus, -a, -um, adj., *hooked*

unda, -ae, f., *wave, water*

unde, adv., *whence; from whom, from which*

undō, -āre, -āvī, -ātus, *rise in waves, bubble*

unguō, -ere, unxī, unctus, *anoint*

ūnus, -a, -um, adj., *one, alone; the same as before*, 47

urbs, urbis, f., *city*; in sing. often of Rome: *the City*

urna, -ae, f., *urn, jar*

usquam, adv., *anywhere*

usque, adv., *all the way (to or from), continually*

ut or utī, adv. and conj.; *as; when; how*; ut primum, *as soon as*; w. subj. (purpose) *so that, in order that*; (result) *that*; w. indic. *as, when*

utcumque, adv., *however; whenever*

uterque, utraue, utrumque, pron. or adj., *each of two*

ūtor, -ī, ūsus sum, dep. v. w. abl., *use; experience; enjoy*, 546

V

vacca, -ae, f. , *cow*

vacuus, -a, -um, adj., *empty*

vādō, -ere, ---, *go*

vadum, -ī, n., *shallow water*; pl. *shallows, pool*, 320

vāgīna, -ae, f., *scabbard, sheath*

vāgītus, -ūs, m., *wailing of young children*

vagor, -ārī, -ātus sum, *wander*

valeō, -ēre, -uī, -itus, *be strong*; w. infin. *be strong enough to, be able to*

validus, -a, -um, adj., *strong*

vallis, -is, f., *valley*

vānus, -a, -um, adj., *empty, vain*

varius, -a, -um, adj., *different, changing, many-colored*

vastus, -a, -um, adj., *huge, desolate*

vātes, -is, m. or f., *bard, seer; prophet, prophetess*

-ve, enclitic conj., *or*

vectō, -āre, -āvī, -ātus, *carry* [freq. of veho]

vehō, -ere, vexī, vectus, *carry*; pass. *be carried, go, voyage*; vectōs, 335, *while voyaging*

vel, conj., *or*; vel ... vel, *either ... or*

vēlāmen, -inis, n., *covering*

Velīnus, -a, -um, adj., *of Velia (ancient Elis), a town on the coast of Lucania*, 366

vellus, -eris, n., *fleece*

velum, -ī, n., *sail*

velut, adv., *just as*

vēna, -ae, f. , *vein*

vendō, -ere, -didī, -ditus, *sell*

venerābilis, -e, adj., *worthy of veneration, to be revered*

veniō, -īre, vēnī, ventus, *come*

ventōsus, -a, -um, adj., *windy, full of wind*

Venus, -eris, f., *goddess of love, mother*

of Aeneas; hence *love,* 26

verber, -eris, n. *stroke, lash*

verbum, -ī, n. *word*

vērē, adv., *in truth*

vereor, -ērī, -itus sum, *fear; be afraid*

vērō, adv., *in truth*

verrō, -ere, verrī, versus, *sweep, sweep over*

versō, -āre, -āvī, -ātus, *keep turning, tossing*

vertex, icis, m., *top, summit; head*

vertō, -ere, vertī, versus, *turn; ply, goad,* 101

vērum, -ī, n., *the truth*

vērus, -a, -um, adj., *true*

vescor, -ī, ---, *feed; feed on* w. abl.

vester, -tra, -trum, possess. adj., *your* (pl.)

vestibulum, -ī, n., *porch, entrance*

vestīgium, -iī, n. *footprint, trail,* 273

vestīgō, -āre, -āvī, -ātus, *track*

vestiō, -īre, -īvī or **-iī, -ītum,** *clothe*

vestis, -is, f., *dress, robe, garments*

vetō, -āre, -uī, -itum, *forbid*

vetus, -eris, adj., *old*

via, -ae, f., *road, way*

[vic-], vicis, vicem, vice, f. defect. n., *change, interchange*

vicissim, adv., *in turn*

victor, -ōris, m., *conqueror*

videō, -ēre, vīdī, vīsus, *see*; pass. *seem;* **viden,** 779 = **vidēsne,** *do you see?*

vigor, -ōris, m., *vigor, force*

vīmen, -inis, n. *twig*

vincō, -ere, vīcī, victus, *conquer, overcome*

vinculum or **vinclum, -ī,** n., *chain*

vīnum, -ī, n. *wine*

violentus, -a, -um, adj., *violent*

vīpereus, -a, -um, adj., *of vipers*

vir, virī, m., *man, hero, husband*

virectum, -ī, n. *green spot,* 638

vireō, -ēre, ---, *be fresh, green, blooming;* **virens,** *green*

vīres, see **vīs**

virga, -ae, f., *twig, rod*

virgō, -inis, f., *maiden*

virgultum, -ī, n. *thicket, brake,* 704

viridis, -e, adj., *green*

virtūs, -ūtis, f., *manliness, virtue, worth*

vīs, f., no gen., acc. s. **vim,** abl. s. **vi,** *force, violence;* pl. **vīres, vīrium,** f. *strength*

viscum, -ī, n., *mistletoe*

vīsus, -ūs, m., *sight*

vīta, -ae, f., *life*

vitta, -ae, f., *fillet, garland*

vīvus, -a, -um, adj., *alive, living*

vix, adv., *scarcely*

vocō, -āre, -āvī, -ātus, *call, summon, invoke, challenge*

volens, -entis, adj., *willing, willingly*

volitō, -āre, -āvī, -ātus, *keep flying, flit about* [freq. of **volō**]

volō, -āre, -āvī, -ātus, *fly;* **volantēs,** 239 etc., *flying creatures, birds*

volō, velle, voluī, ---, *be willing (to), wish, want*

volucer, -cris, -cre, adj., *winged, swift*

voluntas, -ātis, f., *wish, will, purpose*

volūtō, -āre, -āvī, -ātus, *keep turning over; ponder*

volvō, -ere, volvī, volūtus, *roll,* pass. *roll; writhe,* 581

vorāgō, -inis, f., *abyss*

vōs, plur. pers. pron. of **tū,** *you* (s.)

vōtum, -ī, n., *vow*

vox, vōcis, f., *voice, shout;* plur. *words, sounds, notes*

vulgō, adv., *in a way common to all, commonly; en masse*

vulnus, -eris, n. *wound*

vultur, -uris, m., *vulture*

vultus, -ūs, m., *countenance, face*

Xanthus, -ī, m., *a river near Troy,* 88

Index

This index lists grammatical, metrical, and stylistic items mentioned in the commentary; numbers refer to lines in the Latin text and the corresponding commentary notes. Terms with an asterisk are defined in the glossary.

Ablative
  Absolute: 59, 98 258, 836
  Degree of difference: 79
  With special verbs: 83
Accent*: See Appendix A [pp. 111 ff.]
Achates: 14-41, 240
Accusative: 114, 551, 618, 743, 754, 818
  cognate accusative*: 50, 117, 223-24, 324, 466, 644, 646
  of duration: 355
  Greek accusative: 122, 202, 657, 670
  Internal: 313
  With verbs of swearing: 351
Actium: 67-70, 800
Adjectives:
  participial: 243
  archaic *inclutus*: 479, 496-7
  pius, of Aeneas: 9, 176, 232
  ollis: 730
Aemilius Paullus: 838-9
Aeneas: 1, 9, 40, 52, 103, 156, 169, 176, 183, 210, 219, 232, 250, 261, 291, 317, 403, 413, 424, 467, 475, 539, 548, 559, 635, 685, 703, 711, 769, 860
Aeolus: 164-65, 529
Ajax, son of Oileus: 840
Alba Longa: 766, 770
Alcides: 123, 392, 801 (see Hercules)
Alliteration*: 46-49, 62, 100-1, 160, 165-67, 168, 225-36, 370, 506, 570-71, 644, 683, 833
Allusion*: 104, 309, 800, 842
Amphrysia: 398
Anachronism*: 2, 356-66
Anaphora*: 9, 32-3, 47-8, 110-12, 133-34

Anchises: 126, 321, 322, 348, 670, 679, 713, 723, 752, 784, 854, 867, 888, 897
Ancus Martius: 815
Androgeos: 20
Antithesis*: 512, 776, 858
Anio (river): 775
Apodosis: 870-71
Apollo (Phoebus): 18, 35, 56, 69-70, 77, 347, 628, 662
  (Amphrysia): 398
  Apollo: 1-263; 9, 71, 101, 104, 172, 237-38, 344, 431-33, 595-96, 618
Apostrophe*: 18-19, 30-31, 251, 841, 873
Archaic*:
  Forms: 249, 277, 316, 321, 479, 544, 614, 730
  Genitive (*aurai*): 747
  Imperative: 74, 614
  Names: *Mavortius:* 777
  Prepositions (*ergo*): 670
Arctos: 16
Ardea: 773-76
Ariadne: 27-30; 28, 30-31
Aristotle, *Nicomachean Ethics*: 806
Arvae Beatae: 639
Ascanius: 784 (see Iulius)
Assaracus: 650, 778
Assonance: 164-65, 204, 237, 426, 493, 858
Asyndeton: 32-3, 47-8, 128-29, 133-34
Atlas, Mt.: 796
Augustus: 792
  Augustus' *Res Gestae*: 825
Aurora: 535
Ausonia: 346, 807

175